CONTEMPORARY CHINA

CONTEMPORARY

CHINA

edited by **Ruth Adams**

Pantheon Books

A Division of Random House ‖ New York

‖ CONTENTS

‖ INTRODUCTION

*I*t has become fashionable recently to say of the course of
events in eastern Asia during the forties and fifties that it
is now ancient history and no longer a fitting subject for political debate. In a certain sense the most important of those
events were never recognized as history at all by the American
people. How many among us remember, or ever were aware
that according to official American estimates at the time when
the Nationalist government turned its full weight against the
Chinese Communists after the Japanese surrender, it "possessed
an estimated five to one superiority in combat troops and in
rifles, a practical monopoly of heavy equipment and transport,
and an unopposed air arm"? (China White Paper, p. 311)

In spite of massive and continuing US assistance, including
the airlifting of whole Nationalist armies northward into zones
of contention with Communist partisans, the dissolution and
expulsion of this formerly overwhelming Nationalist force took
only the short space of three and one-half years. There has
also been very little American awareness of the agonizing
crescendo of violence and destruction accompanying this single, most cataclysmic example of revolutionary warfare that
swept across the north Chinese landscape in those years. The

vii

battles were always all but nameless to the American public. Yet at Hwai-hai, alone, for example, Nationalist losses in late 1948 numbered more than a half a million men—comparable only to such historic turning points as Stalingrad and Verdun.

The United States reacted to the outcome of this titanic struggle with a policy of nonrecognition ramifying into many fields. Trade was completely cut off; American scholars, reporters, businessmen retired to Formosa and Hong Kong; the People's Republic of China, representing one-fourth of the world's population, was denied membership in the United Nations. At the diplomatic level, the same policy of nonrecognition continues today. Not surprisingly, a recent study of the American public's view of US policy toward China (prepared for the Council on Foreign Relations by the Survey Research Center at the University of Michigan) reports that one out of every four Americans still does not know that the Chinese people have a communist government. In truth, the communist revolution in China for years remained almost a nonevent for the American people.

Undoubtedly a major agent in this scission was the atmosphere of McCarthyism in the late forties and fifties. Open inquiry and public discussion on China became virtually impossible, and in the State Department, following the Senate investigation of employee loyalty, most of the old China hands, on whose knowledge and experience an understanding of the new China would have had to be based, were discharged or removed from positions of influence. Scholars found themselves accused of communist sympathies, driving many into silence and others into specialized, noncontroversial studies. The House investigation of the Institute of Pacific Relations is still recommended reading for those interested in the suffocating effect of the atmosphere of those years upon American research and upon public discussion of policy alternatives.

Official postures change more slowly, but in the late fifties scholars, editors, and members of public affairs organizations began to renew their interest in China, not initially advocating radical shifts in policy but generally expressing concern that

Introduction

it was dangerous to ignore what gave evidence of being an increasingly viable society composed of 700 million people. This was a time when sardonic phrases like "Great Leap Forward" and "Hundred Flowers" were directly incorporated into the language, generally with little thought or awareness of the anguish of revolution and slow reconstruction from which they originally emerged. Since then publications on China have appeared—and been read—in increasing numbers, and reports from foreign correspondents who could visit China have become standard fare in the American press. However, American writers and scholars still are confined to secondary information —Chinese government releases, newspapers, interviews with refugees, discussions with foreign visitors, and plain rumor.

The objective then of these papers is to contribute to the renewed discussion of China that is now much in evidence. One of the purposes for which they have been assembled is the presentation of a more generous sample than heretofore has been available of the variety of differing viewpoints, experiences, and bodies of specialized knowledge from which an informed appraisal of the course of the Chinese revolution and our attitudes toward it must stem. A common thread that is drawn through all the papers is the link between the civil war, the characteristics of the Communist government, and the appraisals of China's future prospects.

Another, equally important basis upon which the papers were invited is their quality of immediate, personal experience. All of the foreign panelists at the conference where these papers first were presented are acquainted at first hand with postrevolutionary China, whether as scholars, businessmen, or correspondents.

The thirty-two panelists were invited to come to Chicago for the week of February 7–12, 1966, to talk and think about China. There were a Czech Orientalist, British and Australian scholars and writers, Canadian journalists, a businessman and physician; the Indian statistician Dr. Mahalanobis; the physician and novelist from Hong Kong, Han Suyin; the Swedish writer Jan Myrdal; and many American and Chinese-American scholars affiliated with institutions ranging from universities and research institutes to the State Department. These people were the experts of the conference whose background papers were circulated in advance. The invited audience of 125 who participated spiritedly after the formal panel presentations brought together representatives from US government agencies, business, journalism, universities, and civic organizations.

The conference was sponsored and organized by five established Chicago institutions—the Chicago Council on Foreign Relations, Northwestern University, the University of Chicago, the American Friends Service Committee, and the Bulletin of the Atomic Scientists. Initial response to the proposed conference was so encouraging and the acceptances so exciting that the committee decided to share the event with a much larger number of people than had been originally anticipated. The conference design became an expanding one and arrangements were made for the experts, following the private three-day discussions at the University of Chicago's Center for Continuing Education, to participate in public sessions in Chicago and in five other midwestern cities—St. Louis, Madison, Minneapolis, Cleveland, and Detroit. The conception of a radiating conference was perhaps unique; it certainly proved a success. The concluding public sessions in Chicago, for example, were attended by 2,500 people and the four panel discussions were televised by National Education Television. Local newspaper and television coverage was detailed and accurately reflected the broad spectrum of ideas and experiences of the panelists.

"Off-the-record" meetings at the University of Chicago occupied the first three days, and the panelists and participants engaged in intensive discussion and at times sharp debate. In brief, the experts agreed that there seems no doubt that the present regime has succeeded in unifying China under a central government for the first time in living memory; that it has successfully coped with inflation, famine, and disease to a degree unprecedented in Chinese history; and that it possesses the substantial allegiance of the Chinese people. There was little doubt that China's leaders seek big power status, that

*they want to make China industrially and militarily strong,
and that they presently feel threatened and encircled by American
military bases and military power.*

*Matters of sharp debate were: How far and in what way
does China want to export revolution? Is she fostering or supporting revolution for ideological or purely national interests?
What would be the posture of a China less threatened and less
defensive? How will China's continued economic development
modify ideology and internal policies? How does the US involvement in Vietnam affect possibilities of change within
China and within the United States?*

*The Chicago China Conference was an expensive undertaking, and even without reference to the contributed time of
experienced individuals from the sponsoring institutions, the
budget was a large one. The Johnson Foundation of Racine,
Wisconsin, made the initial substantial grant which not only
enabled planning to go forward but provided the base from
which the committee could seek additional funds. The Christopher Reynolds Foundation, the William and Mary Swartz
Fund, and the Institute for International Order were among
the other contributors to the conference.*

*There is of course still a minimum of mutual knowledge
and a maximum of ideological misconception between China
and the United States. Yet it is now recognized that Americans
need to know the intentions and aspirations of the Chinese
people and their government; Americans need to know and
understand the successes and failures in the campaign to reorganize and improve the Chinese society and economy. Americans especially need to know, as Senator Fulbright said in
Chicago (March 14, 1966), ". . . because China and America
may be heading toward war with each other and it is essential
that we do all that can be done to prevent that calamity, starting with a concerted effort to understand the Chinese people
and their leaders."*

*The sponsors of the Chicago China Conference hope and
believe that the papers in this volume are a useful contribution
toward that effort.*

Foreign Policy and Internal Politics

*W*hen a revolutionary government becomes firmly established in a country—as the Soviet government in Russia had become after the determination of the civil war and the Chinese after the expulsion of the Nationalist army—its policies tend to be increasingly responsive to deeply rooted geographic, economic, and cultural factors. Two motivations meet and mingle, the traditional perception of national interest and the new one of revolutionary goals. As time goes on, the identification of the revolutionary government with national symbols and problems is perhaps inevitably strengthened and its subordination to original ideological aims correspondingly weakened. Yet in the short run these processes are often sharply irregular, and even in the aggregate can hardly be said to unfold smoothly and irreversibly. Hence the problem for an analyst of a revolutionary state is to evaluate continuously the changing importance and mutual interaction of the two ingredients.

Unfortunately, little first-hand information is available about the interaction of these powerful forces in New China. Even the most penetrating outside observers must depend for many of their conclusions on hazardous extrapolations from past

3

trends in Chinese history or on secondary sources of doubtful representativeness or even accuracy. Hence it is not surprising that there were sharp cleavages among the Conference panelists over the dominant considerations which have determined Chinese foreign policy. Some argued that the threat of US intervention has been the decisive factor; others insisted that since 1949 Chinese foreign policy has been little more than the external reflection of powerful internal trends, and that the American policy of nonrecognition and the exclusion of China from the United Nations has made little difference.

Nevertheless, there was consensus at the conference that the Chinese leadership wants to eliminate the power of the United States in Asia and feels herself threatened by the possibility of a US-USSR détente. The panelists also shared the view that China was completely aware of the devastation that would result from a nuclear confrontation with the United States. The Chinese remain confident, it was generally agreed, that the long-term historical trends are in her favor in spite of the overwhelming power currently arrayed against her. Hence her short-term policies need to be flexible, based upon an avoidance of direct confrontations while patiently seeking to exploit favorable combinations of circumstances elsewhere in the underdeveloped world through the proven tactics of locally based wars of liberation.

A related question on which there was great interest but equally widespread controversy involved the nature of the internal political process. One view was that Party leadership in all sectors of the society is firm and centralized. Others maintained that the public emphasis on developing a Maoist political doctrine only conceals an atrophy affecting both the Party structure and its sphere of influence. It was even suggested that China may conceivably be moving toward a situation where its Communist Party, in defiance of all formal theory, could wither away while the managerial organs of the state remained intact. Unfortunately, the question of whether there is in fact a growing differentiation of function and distribution of power along these lines requires better and more diversified

4

geographic and institutional data than are currently available.

The following three articles deal with some aspects of these questions. C. P. Fitzgerald, Professor of Far Eastern History at the Australian National University, discusses the importance of national interests in the determination of Chinese foreign policy which, he believes, makes the policy limited in aim and cautious in method. A. M. Halpern, of the Center for International Affairs, Harvard, analyzes the role of power in the foreign policy. Josef Kolmas, of the Oriental Institute, Prague, deals with a problem little considered in the West—relationships between the dominant Han and the national minorities in China.

5

CHINESE FOREIGN POLICY
C. P. Fitzgerald

THIS ASSESSMENT of Chinese foreign policy starts from the postulate that the foreign policy of any sovereign state is conditioned by two unchanging factors: the geographical location of the country, and its size and potential strength. The third factor, ideological motivation, can and does vary with changing times and circumstances. China can be no exception to these rules: the foreign policies of all states are conditioned by them and take the double form of national interests and ideological aspirations. Thus each of the Western powers frames its policy first on the basis of its national interest, and second in accordance with the ideology which it supports at home and would wish to see triumph abroad. The foreign policy of a liberal democratic state will strike a balance between national interests and the hope that these will not conflict with the spread of liberal democratic institutions in other parts of the world. The foreign policy of a communist state, such as China, will similarly be based upon a calculation of national interests and ideological aspirations, and it will also be found that these cannot always be harmonized.

Changes in foreign policy are mainly due to shifts in ideo-

7

logical emphasis rather than to reassessment of the national interests, which by their nature are not susceptible to major changes. All states will give national safety and security first priority, but at different times they will either stress or play down the degree to which policy should promote the prevailing ideology, or counter an opposed one. In the years before World War II, American foreign policy sought to safeguard the country against alien dangers by withdrawing as far as possible from the ideological conflict then brewing between the European democracies and the fascist states. In the postwar years the United States has considered that the national security was better assured by participating in the new ideological conflict between communist and noncommunist countries. But the safety of the state has at all times been the first consideration.

Chinese foreign policy is conditioned in the same way, and has three general objectives: the security of the state, the promotion of national interests, and the advancement of ideological aspirations. Since policy is made by Chinese leaders for China, the interpretation of these objectives can only be understood by recognizing that foreigners will not always agree with Chinese views, but that Chinese foreign policy cannot be appreciated correctly by stating what others think it ought to be, rather than by considering what in fact it is. Chinese views of what constitutes the security of the state and what circumstances menace that security, are the product of Chinese understanding of the history of their country, and stem from the outlook of men born and educated in China during the past three-quarters of a century. To Chinese of every political opinion, China's security has been menaced throughout this period by interventions and at times invasions of foreign powers: the British and French, the Russians and Japanese, and now, and not least, the Americans. Views may vary on the importance of these dangers, some stressing the former imperialism of the European powers and Japan, others more concerned with what they believe to be the present threat from the United States. But all will agree

8

that China has lived and still lives in peril. Saving the state from partition and destruction or from outright foreign conquest has been the main preoccupation of Chinese statesmen from the time of the late Empire to the present. All other national interests have been subordinate, for unless this objective were attained, no other national interests could survive.

Under these conditions, for a long time the Chinese paid little attention to ideological motives: no one seriously contended that foreign policy could promote among neighbors near or far "the Chinese way of life." Such ideas had once been upheld by the Emperors and Confucian statesmen of earlier times, when China did indeed exert such influence upon the countries around her. But it was recognized from at least the end of the last century that Confucian principles no longer attracted foreign rulers or peoples; that new, Western ideologies had won support in the former arena of Chinese influence; and that China herself could only regain any standing by adopting a new ideology of this type. The only ideological question at issue was which of the Western systems would suit China best, and thus contribute to the first essential, the salvation of the Chinese nation. In general terms China experimented with three systems, all of Western origin. Parliamentary democracy was the ideal of the early revolutionaries who dethroned the Manchu dynasty in 1912. It did not work in China, collapsed in chaos, and introduced the vicious rule of self-seeking military officers. The Nationalist Party, or Kuomintang, abandoned parliamentary democracy in favor of the party state, conforming in some degree to the model of fascist Italy. This experiment also failed. Then the Chinese Communist Party emerged victor after a long civil war and established the People's Republic, a socialist state aiming to achieve the still distant goal of communism.

Whatever the new regime may have accomplished in China itself, the essential change in foreign policy was the reintroduction of the ideological motive, and the high importance given to it in framing that policy. The new Chinese way of life, communism, was accepted not only as the sole road to

9

national security, but also as the best hope for neighboring countries, and indeed for the whole world. Such ideas are not unique to China. The Western powers themselves, particularly in the nineteenth and early twentieth centuries, believed that democracy was not only the surest safeguard for the state's future security and prosperity, but also the most, indeed the only, desirable form of government to be adopted by nations who wished to be counted among the civilized peoples of the world. The psychological shock of the Russian Revolution was due as much to the overt repudiation of this dogma as to the violence and brutalities of the Revolution itself. Revolution had been a glorious word; whether it applied to the fall of the Stuarts in the late seventeenth century, the expulsion of the English from America in the late eighteenth century, the overthrow of the absolute monarchy in France and the liberal movement of 1848, revolution had always meant a step toward liberty, away from authoritarian rule, an abolition, or at least a diminution of, class privilege.

No one can any longer cherish these illusions. Since the end of World War I, major revolutions have occurred which have not set up free governments, but subverted them and established in their place authoritarian regimes of varying ideology. Fascism won massive popular support both in Italy and Germany; nor can it be doubted that in some of the present communist countries, of which China is the most conspicuous example, the government now in power is supported by a vast majority of the nation. Chinese foreign policy must be expected to reflect this fact, to be framed in accordance with an ideology which its supporters believe —as the nineteenth century liberals also believed about their ideology—will be the hope of the world, the inevitable victor in the conflict of systems. The content of Chinese foreign policy will therefore be a blend of national interests and ideology, with rather more stress on the latter than is normal in states which have not recently experienced revolution.

The general objectives of Chinese foreign policy will continue to be the security of the state, the promotion of national

10

interests, and the advancement of ideological aspirations, which means the propagation of communism. It is the way in which these objectives are sought, and the immediate steps taken to implement them, which concern the rest of the world. We will not impose our ideas of what constitutes the security or national interests of China upon the Chinese; we may, or may not, successfully oppose the propagation of communism; but here, too, the conflict occurs in the minds of men rather than on any battlefield. We can best understand Chinese policy by looking at the three objectives through Chinese eyes, even if we continue to think such vision distorted.

The security of the Chinese state is held to be threatened by US military power established in eastern Asia. America now holds in effect all the power points formerly controlled by Japan, and when so controlled, used against Chinese interests. Japan herself, South Korea, the Ryukyu Islands, Taiwan, the Philippines, and South Vietnam, constitute a ring of US bases around China's eastern coast and southern border. US air and sea power ensure a control of the seas more effective than that which Japan, or Britain in earlier periods, ever exercised. The Chinese remember that such sea power in the hands of her enemies was the first cause of her frequent and severe defeats at their hands, preliminary to invasions. Therefore the first and overruling objective must be to diminish and eventually to eliminate US military power in the Far East and exclude US naval power from the adjoining seas. A tall order, and a long task. China's leaders know that China is not strong enough to achieve this aim by direct confrontation in war. But there are other ways than war, and here the uses of ideology and the blending of ideological motive and national interest point the way. If conversion of the main enemy to the Chinese way of thinking is in itself an unlikely and remote prospect, the erosion of support for the American cause in the countries now under US military protection is a different matter.

Chinese policy is therefore largely directed, not to converting Japan and other Far Eastern countries to communism by way of revolution (unless the prospects for this are exceedingly favorable), but to promoting neutralism, anti-Western feeling, "anti-neocolonialism," and anti-imperialism. Imperialism is understood as the presence of a Western military power in the region under any pretext, but does not apply to the extension of Asian military power beyond the frontiers of an Asian state. Indonesian confrontation of Malaysia is not imperialism; British protection of Malaysia against such confrontation is. This definition applies with even more force to Vietnam or Laos. Chinese national interests here partly coincide—and partly basically conflict—with the propagation of communism. It is a Chinese national interest to support a neutralist government which excludes US bases from its territory. Consequently Cambodia, ruled in effect by a monarch (even if he does not occupy the ceremonial position on the throne) is supported and favored. Yet it is impossible to view Prince Sihanouk as an appropriate ruler for Cambodia from the standpoint of communist ideology.

President Sukarno has many of the characteristics of a nationalist or even a fascist dictator, rather than those of a democratic leader or a communist chairman. But he is anti-Western, he permits extremist demonstrations against American and British representatives, he excludes US bases, and openly supports movements hostile to the presence of Western forces in southeast Asia. Even before September 30, Sukarno was not clearly aligned on the side of the Indonesian Communist Party; he continued to balance, precariously as it proved, one foot upon the army, the other on the PKI. From the communist point of view he was at best a passing phase, a last example of unregenerate nationalism, not the man of the future. But his policy suited Chinese national interests. In the immediate situation it is these interests which clearly dominate Chinese foreign policy in southeast and eastern Asia. There is a large and growing body of opinion in Japan critical of US policy in Vietnam. It is not pro-communist, but it is anti-Western, neutralist in aspiration. It is therefore a Chinese national interest to further these views and strive

12

to make them prevail in Japanese politics. It is not in itself a movement favorable to communism and might prove a strong barrier against communism in Japan, but this consideration is not at the moment so important. The list could be continued: in all the countries which are at present subject to strong American political influence, or military protection, the aim of Chinese policy is to foster those trends of opinion—nationalist, racist, or political—which will weaken American control, cause trouble for the United States, and if possible, convert a base country into a scene of involvement and intervention. The mainspring of these activities is not primarily communist aspirations, but Chinese national interests which require the elimination of US power in the Far East to protect the security of China.

There is a third specific objective of present policy, this time fought upon the purely ideological plane—the defeat of what the Chinese call Russian Revisionism, or Khrushchevism. It may seem at first sight that this aim is not connected either with the security of the nation or with the promotion of Chinese national interests, however defined; yet it is probable that the Chinese see a close relationship between these objectives. Russian Revisionism, by which is meant the policies followed by Khrushchev and his successors, has two aspects which are equally abhorrent to China's leaders. On the one hand, they accuse the USSR of having, in effect, abandoned the aims of communist revolution, acquiesced to the survival of the capitalist world, and betrayed the revolutionary cause in the underdeveloped countries of Asia, Africa, and South America. This is "heresy," backsliding from the doctrines of Marx and Lenin, and Chinese polemics are filled with citations and quotations to prove their point. On the other hand, they suspect, or now openly accuse, the Russians of what amounts to treachery: breaking the alliance, first, by the sudden, unilateral withdrawal of Soviet experts, technicians, and blueprints at a moment calculated to do the Chinese economy the most possible harm; and second, by working for "coexistence" with the United States, which the Chinese see as

13

betraying the communist cause, and in particular, sacrificing Chinese national interests without exacting any compensation beneficial to China. From the Chinese point of view, these accusations cannot easily be refuted.

The evil consequences of Russian policy are thus twofold: first, the cause of communism is weakened and forsaken by its former champion; second, China is weakened in her confrontation with the United States, and the American enemy is encouraged to adopt harsher policies. The purpose of the sustained ideological war with the USSR is therefore to undermine these policies, to appeal to the communist parties of the world, and to make it increasingly difficult for the Kremlin to follow through with policies which are held to be anticommunist and treacherous. The objective is to reverse the trend of Russian policy by mobilizing against it the opinion of the communist world: if this involves a change of leadership in the USSR, the sooner the better. The ideological struggle to keep communism Left has in this way a direct bearing upon Chinese national interests; ideology and national policy blend inextricably.

If these are the main guidelines of Chinese foreign policy, their interpretation and followthrough in various areas can nonetheless exhibit a number of variations, both in manner and in emphasis. A general objective is to assert China's right to the status of a world power; on the grounds of size, population, and rapidly expanding industrialization, this is both inevitable and natural. Any other Chinese government would demand as much under similar conditions. In this view, China has as much right to a policy toward the African states as any other major power; as much right to play a part in international conferences for the limitation of armaments, or any other purpose, as other nations exercise; and the sole right to represent China in the UN. There is the further advantage that in keeping these claims active and well publicized, China wins a measure of support outside the communist world or the underdeveloped nations. A growing number of capitalist, anticommunist governments and their citizens support Peking's

14

claim to China's seat at the UN. In pursuing this general aim
of attaining equality with and acceptance by other and noncommunist powers, Chinese policy has met with considerable
success and seems likely to make further steady gains. Insofar
as this isolates American policy from that of her allies and
other nations, it is from the Chinese point of view well worth it.

China's blending of ideological and national interests is
most complete and conspicuous in southeast Asia. Farther west,
the separation of these two strands is clearer. The Indian
frontier dispute is an example of national interest—or pre-
judice—prevailing over ideology. The history of this dispute,
the legal rights and wrongs, are complex and far from clear-
cut. The facts—that the dispute flared into a major clash of
arms in 1962 and has since clouded formerly good relations
between China and India—are well known. Obviously these
events were grave for the Indian Communist Party. The Party
split: the Indian government arrested and interned the majority
of the leadership, and the Party's formerly important role in
Indian politics has been much reduced. China's interests may
have been served; those of world communism were damaged.
Those who still believe in a "world communist conspiracy"
are hard put to explain a situation where one communist
state takes action ruinous to a promising communist party
and at the same time quarrels on this issue with the other
major communist government.

But in the light of Chinese national interests, the whole
picture comes into focus. The Chinese reassertion of the former
Empire's control over Tibet—in Chinese eyes, "a national
right"—was followed by unrest in Tibet, revolt, and the flight
of the defeated rebels to India. In the Chinese view, India
protected and encouraged these dissidents. The Chinese then
decided to patrol and occupy the frontier in strength to prevent subversion from the exiles. The frontier was in dispute.
The Chinese government insisted on the line which their
predecessors had claimed, the Indians rejected these claims,
and fighting followed. The Chinese won the clash of arms,
prudently decided not to follow up their victory, but retained

the fruits of victory in the form of the frontier they claimed. Imperial powers have in the past frequently engaged in similar disputes, as the USSR did with Japan in the Manchurian-Mongolian border zone in the years immediately before World War II. All this has little or nothing to do with communism, except to do it harm in India. But Chinese national interests were involved. A successful Tibetan revolt would place that country in a position to appeal to the West for protection and give it the power to grant air bases, which could take China in the rear. Tibet is strategic to China and could not be left at stake. The Tibetan government before Chinese occupation was extremely backward—medieval in fact—and could not be expected to be left in this condition. If China had not taken over Tibet, someone else, in Chinese eyes someone worse, would have. While the harm to the Indian Communist Party cannot be denied, the situation is countered by the claim that at least the Tibetan people have been liberated from their feudal masters and jerked into the modern world.

Another consequence, representing a success for China and stemming from the Indian frontier dispute, has been the building of a close relationship with Pakistan. That country is ruled by a military dictator, its democracy in abeyance; but this situation, so unpalatable to communist doctrinaires, has not prevented friendly relations, even collaboration, approaching an alliance directed against India. Here, too, there is clear Chinese national interest. Pakistan has been virtually detached from the American sphere and brought close to China; her position at the rear of India gives China a useful weapon to brandish and outflanks the "containment of communism" which India in her resentment might be inclined to support. Chinese support for Pakistan also wins approval in the Moslem nations of Asia, where Arab suspicions of British policy are deep and continuing. Yet most of these countries are anticommunist and imprison, or kill, their own communists.

A year or so ago, Chou En-lai is said to have described Africa as "ripe for revolution"—an expression having more

16

significance than mere rhetoric. This is communist language for a condition in which the discontents within a country have reached boiling point, and violence is probable or certain. At this point, and not before, the local communist party should come forth and assume the leadership, direction and control of the revolutionary ferment. Any earlier is too soon, for an abortive revolt may be crushed and the whole movement set back for many years; to wait longer runs the risk of effective foreign ("imperialist") intervention or the emergence of a revolutionary leadership of noncommunist complexion, which will ultimately "betray the revolution." Numerous examples of both mistakes have occurred. But, in fact, it does not appear that Africa is yet ripe for revolution. Ripe, and overripe, for liberation from colonial rule or white settler domination: for these causes no communist leadership was needed, for they had a political, more than a social purpose. It is already plain that their triumph in many parts of Africa has installed in power an elite group of aristocrats, descendants of tribal chiefs and kings, lawyers trained in London or Paris, and other educated people—few of whom have any sympathy with the economic ideals of communism, and many of whom are frankly opposed to its social goals.

Chou En-lai was misinformed—Africa is not a region with which China had hitherto had much contact, and the number of Chinese with a real knowledge of the continent must have been small. It would appear that the mistake was tacitly acknowledged. Chinese policy in Africa has become less ambitious, if not necessarily abandoning long-term objectives. The mobilization of African opinion against the West—in the Congo, over Rhodesia, or any other place where an opportunity offers—is a policy similar in design and intent to that followed in southeast Asia. It seeks to secure for China a large measure of influence in Africa, but probably does not, at this stage, any longer envisage open communist revolutions, if only because the local communist parties are weak and inexperienced, and China herself could give them no real material aid if active steps were taken to prevent such aid

17

from reaching them. Chinese national interests are comparatively minor in Africa; the general interests of enhancing China's world status and winning a majority of votes in the UN Assembly are the most important, and would not be furthered by open support of weak communist parties regarded as subversive by governments now in power. Ideological interest in one of the greatest of the underdeveloped regions is likely to continue, but its manifestations may well be restrained by the weight given to national interests. If mishandled, the Rhodesian crisis could offer China an opportunity of supporting an anti-imperialist movement without running the wider risk of promoting a communist revolution.

There remains a wide field for Chinese foreign policy in which there can be no question of forceful methods or direct support of revolution: Europe, and with Europe, the "Old Dominions" of the British Commonwealth—Australia, New Zealand, and Canada. Although these three countries are far from Europe within the strategic zones of North America or the western Pacific, in the sphere of diplomacy and foreign policy they are, from the Chinese point of view, closer to the European situation than to that of the United States or any country of Asia. Europe itself divides naturally. With the countries of eastern Europe, apart from Greece, China has normal diplomatic relations, even though those maintained with "revisionist" Russia and Yugoslavia are chilly. Albania, on the other hand, is China's improbable client state in the West, a useful mouthpiece at the UN, and a handy base to conduct the ideological war against the USSR in the capitals of the eastern European communist countries. For China, the main importance of eastern Europe outside of the Soviet Union is as an ideological battleground and also as a source for technical experts and industrial products, and as a market for some Chinese exports.

Western Europe, from the Chinese point of view, is itself divided by a line which does not follow either the economic division between the European Common Market and states outside it, or the division between former allies and former

18

enemies of World War II. The Scandinavian states (including Finland), Switzerland, Holland, Britain, and more recently, France recognize the People's Republic and exchange diplomatic missions with Peking, albeit some of these—Britain for one—are not established at ambassadorial level. Italy, West Germany, Spain, Belgium, Portugal, and Ireland do not recognize Peking—but all of these whose international trade is important trade freely with China. Thus the Common Market group is split on this issue, Holland and France recognizing, the others not; and so are the neutrals and the nations outside the Common Market. This lack of a common European policy toward China gives Chinese foreign policy a field of maneuver in which it is increasingly active. The most important achievement has been the "conversion" of France, formerly a non-recognizer on account of the Chinese support for North Vietnam in the earlier phase of the Vietnamese War. Now, having rid herself of the Vietnamese incubus and ready to move in Asia on new lines, France is congenial to China. Since the views of France count for much in the ex-French states of north and west Africa, Chinese winning of French recognition was a major diplomatic triumph.

The aim of Chinese policy in western Europe is therefore to expand the number of states which recognize China and must therefore vote for Peking's representation at the UN. The second objective is to cultivate trade relations with these countries to offset previous dependence on Soviet and eastern European technical aid and scientific technology. China has purchased Viscount aircraft from Britain for her internal air services, and freely admitted the necessary technicians to instruct the Chinese pilots, ground staff, and engineers in the flying and servicing of these aircraft. France and Holland have built, or are building, advanced chemical plants in China; West Germany, although a strongly anticommunist state, trades with the People's Republic, but will not recognize a government which has diplomatic relations with East Germany. Until the adherence of France to the group who recognize Peking, the division in western Europe was, curiously enough, strictly on the ancient religious frontier, between the Catholic south and the Protestant northwest. Italy, Spain, Portugal, Belgium, and Ireland, the countries where Vatican influence was strongest, would not recognize Communist China. There are several signs suggesting that this attitude is changing, at least in Belgium and Italy, although not in Spain and Portugal. Italy and Belgium do an increasingly important trade with China; Spain and Portugal do not.

Most of the west European states have little fear of China as a military menace, and have long been accustomed to dealing with communist countries on a trade basis. Britain, still committed to Far Eastern responsibilities which none of the other European states now are, tends to move rather unhappily in the wake of American policy, clearly torn between a desire to keep on good terms with her principal ally and at the same time to avoid violent courses which would embroil her with China and jeopardize the safety of such remaining commitments as Hong Kong, Malaysia, or Singapore. Insofar as the European states follow the American line of nonrecognition, China treats them as "satellites of the USA." Insofar as they pursue independent diplomatic and trade policies which acknowledge China and assist her policy, they are encouraged to continue and go further. France, under de Gaulle, as an open critic of US policy in Vietnam and elsewhere, is treated virtually as a friend, if not yet as an ally.

In this policy, once again, the national interest aspect weighs as much as the ideological. Britain for thirteen years was under Conservative governments, extended trade relations with China year by year, and never at any time proposed to reverse the previous Labour government's decision to recognize Peking. But Britain can and does supply many things needed by China in her industrial expansion. There is also Hong Kong, useful earner of foreign exchange, which lives daily on food bought and grown in China and provides a port which cannot be blockaded by the Nationalist forces from Taiwan. The Chinese press and public comment may deride Hong Kong as a sink of bourgeois vices, a dustbin of

20

greedy capitalists, but this tribute to ideology does not interfere in any way with smooth day-to-day relations, the supply
of food and water, and a large investment by the Peking
government in the real estate market of the capitalist "sink."
France is under a form of government which is certainly not
"left" and which has placed great obstacles in the way of the
French Communist Party, one of the most powerful in Europe,
but China, for national interests, ignores these awkward aspects
of the Gaullist regime. On the other hand, China actively
seeks to convert the Communist Parties of France, Belgium,
and Italy to the Chinese view in the ideological struggle with
the USSR.

Trade matters more than the ideological character of the
governments of west European states. Having cleared her
debt to the Soviet Union, which bound the Chinese economy
in the days of Soviet aid and assistance, China has now large
funds for financing her overseas trade with countries which
can supply her needs just as well as the USSR could. Not all
of these are in Europe; China buys such large quantities of
wheat and wool from Australia as to place her in a central
position in Australia's overseas trade. Wheat purchases from
Canada are also considerable. It is true that neither Canada,
Australia, nor New Zealand (whose trade with China is very
slight) have moved toward recognition of Peking, but their
attitudes are far from uniform. Canada refrains simply to
avoid an unpleasant issue with the United States. Canadian
statesmen continue to talk as if they intended to recognize
and advocate the seating of the Peking delegates at the UN,
but no action follows. Australia, under the government of
Sir Robert Menzies, follows American policy in words, but
less closely in deeds. Recognition is denounced by a strongly
anticommunist government. Australia votes against Peking at
the UN, but trade increases, travel between the two countries
is free, and the Chinese market for wheat has saved Australia's
balance of payments and become a major factor in her agricultural export program.

In former times there was probably no part of the world

with which China was so little concerned as Latin America. Some Chinese migration to Brazil and Peru provided a reason for diplomatic relations with those countries, as well as with Mexico and some of the small Caribbean states. All of Latin America refused recognition to the People's Republic, and even these relations ceased. Cuba, after Castro, resumed relations, and for a time Chinese influence in the sole communist state of Latin America appeared to be increasing; but the development of the ideological quarrel with Russia seems to have checked this. Castro decided that Codlin was the friend, not Short. Under the government of President Goulart in Brazil, Chinese trade missions were welcomed, but were closed down, and for a time their members detained, by his successor. Although many South American countries are critical of American policies, none has gone so far as to open diplomatic relations with Peking, and most continue to vote against Peking at the UN. With little trade, no diplomatic relations, and no possibility of direct involvement in any revolution which may break out, China's sphere of activity in Latin America is confined to the ideological field, where no doubt she seeks to promote communism, and to ensure that communist parties shall be sympathetic to the Chinese side in the ideological war with the USSR.

The fears that China is planning some huge subversive movement on this continent are certainly greatly exaggerated. Words and deeds remain far apart; there is very little that China can do which the local communists cannot do better, and possibly sooner. Chinese policy will be watchful to seize any opportunity such as another Castro-type revolution, and give it all the support that is possible, but as relations with Castro's Cuba have proved, China is not sufficiently credible in Latin America as the ally against "US imperialism" to be preferred to the Soviets. If Chinese policy has immediate objectives in this region, it is to win friends who will switch their vote at the UN and open trading relations. The expectation of Chinese influence upon communist regimes not yet in existence is a hope rather than a policy.

22

Chinese foreign policies—ideological commitment to the advance of communism on a world-wide basis, and the more restricted aspect of promoting Chinese national interests—are found in all sovereign states, their emphasis varying with the importance of the country concerned and with the nature of the ideology it upholds. To small and medium states national interests will be most important because they must survive by seeking the protection of great powers. They do not have the influence to modify prevailing ideologies, or to promote their own. Great states may believe that their own power guarantees their national interests and assures their survival, but they too must watch the policy of their powerful rivals lest they become involved in a catastrophic war. They will use ideology to muster followers and solidify support from their own citizens. It is improbable that any of the rulers of the great powers seriously expect to convert their rivals to their own way of thinking, whether this be one form of democracy rather than another, or one view of communism rather than another. It is just possible, however, that the Chinese believe they can convert the USSR through the activity or discontent of the Soviet Communist Party and the communist parties of other countries. It is more probable that they seek to restrain the USSR from following national interests which are prejudicial to Chinese interests. It is certain that they have no expectation of converting the American people to communism, and improbable that they entertain any such hopes concerning western Europe—with the possible exception of Italy. States like the People's Republic which have risen as a result of recent revolution will be inclined to stress ideological motives and mask the operation of national interests with ideological smokescreens, but they are bound to frame their policy with these interests, primarily the security of the state, constantly in mind.

Chinese foreign policy is no exception to these considerations. The present seemingly intransigent disposition of the Chinese leadership is the product of a long resentment felt by all Chinese against the West for the encroachments and

FOREIGN POLICY AND INTERNAL POLITICS

humiliations of the nineteenth century and later. That these misfortunes were in part, perhaps in the major part, due to China's own mistakes, obscurantism and unwillingness to recognize a new situation, is no doubt historical truth, but will not modify these feelings. Men are more angered by their own mistakes than by the crimes of others. There is in China today a passionate determination to wipe out this past weakness, to recover strength, to reclaim lost territories and win recognition of China's rightful place in the world. These ideas and motives are shared by the vast majority of the Chinese people, and are not likely to change with any change in leadership. Many of them would be expressed by the Nationalists if they had retained power and won new strength, and certainly by the Emperors if the dynasty had been able to survive.

Failure to realize this aspect of China's policy is the weakness of Western current thinking. Obsessed with the belief that communist states are somehow fundamentally different from others—not merely in social and economic organization, but in the mental processes of their leaders—many Western observers and policy makers seem quite unable to see their mirror image in their Chinese rivals. Great powers have at all times followed, more or less ruthlessly, their own interest, which is to sustain their power and outmatch their rivals. Communism in Cuba is by itself no possible menace to the rich and expanding economy of America, but it provides a footing for a rival power to exercise pressure, to challenge American power. Therefore it is intolerable. Anticommunist dictators, corrupt and weak, are no danger to China in southeast Asia, but to sustain themselves they invoke the power which China sees as her enemy and the supporter of her opponents. Consequently, such regimes are intolerable to the pursuit of China's interests.

As all history shows, these "intolerable" situations are in the end tolerated. The menace is seen to be unreal, or is modified by time. National enmities are transitory; they frequently pass away, and then recur, even in one generation. Japan

24

was the ally of Britain, then the enemy, now once more the friend, all in one lifetime. There are other examples of these metamorphoses in the relations of sovereign states and no historical reason for supposing that the present enmity of America and China is likely to be more lasting. No real national interests are at stake. China certainly never dreams of annexing American territory; America has no desire to set up imperial dominion of Chinese territory nor even to overthrow the communist regime of North Vietnam, although the logic of the present struggle may lead to such a result. If the aims of Chinese foreign policy are not likely to change in our time, it is at least possible that the framework in which they operate will change profoundly in the next decade. These changes may be brought about by a realignment of the great powers, or by a reassessment of the true national interests of China and the United States in the light of improved knowledge and overdue adjustment to a new and unfamiliar situation.

THE PLACE OF FORCE IN COMMUNIST CHINA'S FOREIGN POLICY

A. M. Halpern

THE CONCEPT which any country holds of the applicability and usefulness of military force in conducting its relations with the rest of the world is obviously an important topic for anyone who professes to analyze that country's foreign policy. Much has been said about this aspect of Communist China's foreign policy, and a good deal has been said with polemical intent. If I now approach the question again, it is not because it has not been touched on by others, and certainly not because I think this is the only aspect of China's foreign policy worth discussing. But the subject bears repeated examination, and I hope here to bring together some observations on several facets of the problem which have not always been considered in a single overview.

I propose, then, to comment on the following topics:

(1) The legacy of the revolutionary period. Here the question is: How far and in what ways has China's experience of using force to achieve power shaped the views of her leaders on the applicability of military means to international relations?

(2) China's experience of the use of military force since 1949. Here I will not confine myself to cases where Chinese

armed forces have been directly employed, but will also consider cases where there is reason to believe the Chinese contributed to military decisions or actions made by others. The Chinese have evidently believed their interests to be importantly engaged in cases where their forces were not; there is no direct proportion between the importance they have attached to an incident and the military forces they have used in it.

(3) Strategic doctrine. Here I shall consider how the Chinese see their own strategic situation, and what contingencies they apparently think it necessary to plan for.

(4) Chinese atomic capability. When was the decision (or, since the circumstances changed between the time of the first decision and the first detonation, the decisions) made to develop a Chinese capability? What considerations affected it? What can we deduce about Chinese plans for using atomic weapons?

(5) Alternatives to force. What is the Chinese approach to disarmament?

Background

The role of military force in the Chinese revolution cannot of course be entirely neglected as a factor affecting present-day thinking. For twenty years the Chinese Communist movement continued to exist thanks to having an army at its command. Basic concepts of strategy and tactics were developed in the course of two "revolutionary civil wars" and of "anti-Japanese resistance." The victory of the revolution was finally achieved through a large-scale military operation. In Chinese Communist theory, this experience is regarded as valid for other countries as well. They emphasize in this connection that legal or parliamentary methods cannot be relied upon, and that therefore military force is essential for the success of a revolutionary movement.

The importance that the Chinese Communists attach to their own revolutionary history could be ignored, but for

28

two facts. One is that the leadership of the Chinese Communist Party still consists largely of men who fought in the twenty-year revolution and for whom the experience is a living memory. Second, in commenting on the contemporary world situation, these leaders constantly refer to their revolutionary experience to support arguments in favor of a certain strategy in their foreign relations.

For example, Lin Piao still quotes a famous phrase of Mao's: "Political power grows out of the barrel of a gun." One should not make too much of this phrase and other slogans which come from the revolutionary period. They do not necessarily mean that nothing has changed in the military thinking of the Chinese Communists since they came to power. There is a qualitative difference in thinking between the leaders of a state which operates as such on the international scene and those of a revolutionary movement. The leaders of a state must develop a complete foreign policy, containing many elements other than military. This policy is tested pragmatically every day and inevitably re-examined according to whether it succeeds or fails. Further, the kinds of military (or military-political) situations Communist China has been involved in since 1949 presented different problems from those the movement met before 1949. In particular, military policy after 1949 was developed in a world environment where weapons technology was undergoing revolutionary development.

Several basic concepts remain in the Chinese leaders' minds from the early period. First, in ideological terms, they view conflict as an inherent structural feature of world politics, just as of national politics. Westerners do not always hold this belief; rather conflict is thought of as a temporary malfunction in a system which normally should work without it. Yet, I think everyone, regardless of basic philosophy, would say that in the next decade the chances of conflict breaking out here and there in the world are very high. The Chinese Communist belief is to some extent confirmed by reality.

Second, the basic Chinese strategy is one of "active defense." This was reconfirmed in May of 1966 by Lo Jui-ching. The

Chinese believe that initiative is in the hands of their adversaries, and, to defeat this initiative, it is necessary to conduct "protracted war" in two phases. There is a phase of withdrawal, which pulls the enemy in deeper, makes him increase the resources he has to invest and at the same time scatter them; this is followed by a counteroffensive. The Chinese argue that this basic strategic pattern applies to "national liberation" wars, to revolutionary wars generally and to the world revolutionary movement. It is, in their eyes, the method by which weakness can be transformed into strength.

Third, the Chinese continue to think of themselves as "encircled." The Soviets no longer (perhaps since 1955 or 1956) regard encirclement as a salient feature of their or the communist world's strategic situation. This difference of outlook evolved in the Sino-Soviet controversy.

Military Experience Since 1949

In analyzing the effects of Chinese military experience since 1949, one can take several concrete cases. Only a few involved the direct use of force by the Chinese. In others, their military power was held in reserve, but affected the conflict because its possible use had to be calculated by the other side. In some, the Chinese contributed resources to one side in a conflict; in others, they believed their interests were involved, but contributed only moral and political support.

In each case, we can ask similar questions. Who originally had the initiative and how did it shift? What was at stake? What were the costs and risks to the Chinese? Did they use their resources intelligently? How did the outcome affect their policies?

Korean War

As the Chinese saw it, their intervention in Korea was defensive, not initiative. The stakes were very high, no less than China's ambition to be a world power, her ability to affect Asian

30

affairs, and her national security. The costs were heavy, but were partly compensated for by improved military capability as a result of Soviet aid, especially in the creation of a Chinese air force. Potentially the risks were extreme, and very sophisticated calculations had to be made. In these the Chinese showed considerable skill. The possibility of escalation existed until 1952, and what is now thought of as the classic problem of "sanctuary" in limited wars had to be faced as a fresh problem in Korea.

In some operations—her initial intervention in October 1950, the Chongchon River battle of November 1950, the development of a logistic system—the Chinese showed great skill in the use of resources. In others—the fifth-phase offensive, April–May 1951—they showed poor judgment. There is some evidence that they regard some of their moves as errors, and that they now recognize that they were operating under conditions unfavorable to the kind of actions at which they do best.

A recent *People's Daily* article (reprinted in *Peking Review*, 32, 1965) is of particular interest in this connection. It recognizes that in Korea the Communists fought in a constricted area, which cut down their ability to maneuver, and without the support of a "powerful people's guerrilla movement," whose normal functions would presumably include logistic and intelligence support. The same article indicates that the Chinese, then and now, regarded America's long supply lines and defective morale as her chief weakness. The importance of equipment and the level of troop training, either in Korea or in other incidents, has rarely been objectively evaluated in Chinese public statements; but, judging by their efforts since 1955, they are well aware of these factors. Finally, there are a variety of ancillary political conditions and devices, of whose importance the Chinese have never lost sight, which affect the military outcome. The Korean war was exceptional because it was a coalition effort. In later Chinese operations, this feature has been lacking.

It is very important to evaluate the outcome of Korea from

the Chinese point of view. Clearly in their minds the consciousness of victory dominates all other conclusions. They gained their major goals—security, influence on Asian affairs, increased prestige especially in Asia, a foothold toward great-power status—but they lost something in their ability to deal with Taiwan, in their chances for entering the UN, and they stimulated US military commitments in Asia. In purely military terms, the Korean war demonstrated the need for reorganizing and modernizing the Chinese armed forces, and perhaps it can be seen as the source of later disputes on military affairs with the Soviet Union. Probably this war determined a policy of avoiding direct clashes with American military power. At the same time it showed that status and influence could be achieved through military operations and confirmed their belief in force as indispensable to foreign policy. A specifically Chinese foreign outlook and policy emerged during the Korean war and the years immediately following. The PRC first established its position in the world by meeting obstacles, struggling against them, and succeeding.

Taiwan

Why didn't the Chinese Communists undertake military liberation of Taiwan in 1949? Nobody knows the answer, but circumstances were never again as favorable.

The threats of force against Taiwan in 1954–55 and in 1958 were clear cases of initiative taken by the Chinese Communists. The stakes were potentially high. They were higher in 1958 than in 1954–55, partly because of the passage of time, partly because in 1958 Chinese Communist action was related to a general foreign political strategy, which had world-wide goals and which was intended to be coordinated with other actions by other communist powers.

Nevertheless the Chinese tried to limit severely both their costs and their risks. In 1954–55, they invested practically nothing. In 1958, they wasted some artillery to little purpose and exposed the weakness of their air force. On both occasions,

32

military force was used mainly in demonstrations, not in actual battle operations; the Chinese relied primarily on political methods to achieve their objectives.

In 1954–55, the Chinese Communists achieved some results. They did not regain Taiwan, but they forced the Nationalists to evacuate the Tachen islands and cut down interference with foreign ships destined for the mainland. They gained sympathy among Asians and started a dialogue with the United States which still continues. For two years this dialogue showed some promise of disposing of the Taiwan problem without reducing the People's Republic to a continued existence as a professedly rival regime. Since 1958, the dialogue has not shown such promise. Taiwan continues, as much because of the Chinese Communist position as for any other reason, to stand in the way of Sino-US relations and the PRC's participation in international organizations.

The results in 1958 were disastrous. The operation was a failure. It raised issues between Communist China and the Soviets regarding the usefulness of the Soviet nuclear deterrent, Soviet joint command or control of Chinese forces, independent Chinese nuclear capability, etc. It also brought to a head issues within the Chinese military command, and, as a result, both Su Yu and Peng Teh-huai lost their positions. The incident changed the Chinese Communist strategic outlook on Asia. Before October 1958, their policy was directed to rectifying a military imbalance against them in east Asia, while trying to neutralize south and southeast Asia. The outcome of the 1958 Quemoy crisis indicated to the Chinese leaders the limits of their ability to affect the over-all military situation in east Asia; since then they have been more or less resigned to adapting themselves to it. They became more concerned with south and southeast Asia as an area both of threat and of opportunity.

The Chinese Communists have consistently relied on political appeals to solve the Taiwan problem. Their propaganda efforts have varied according to the situation, and they have been particularly pointed at times when the PRC was putting on a show of force. These appeals have consistently failed, although the

33

cause is not obvious. The prospect of eventual success cannot be entirely ruled out, but the Taiwan problem can no longer be treated simply as a question of whether or when PRC political methods will bear fruit.

Taiwan continues to pose some military problems for the PRC. Attempts at infiltration of the mainland from Taiwan have been met primarily by action of the militia, in coordination with the regular armed forces. Air surveillance of the mainland from Taiwan has been conducted on a regular basis. The PRC's ability to interfere with it can be said to have improved. In the summer of 1962 it appeared that the PRC expected a serious attempt to invade the mainland. This did not take place, and it seems probable that if major force is not used by the PRC in the Taiwan area, it will not be used by others.

India

In 1962, force was used by the Chinese in the North East Frontier Agency of India. Events made it clear that China took the initiative. Preceding the event were nearly four years of developments in Sino-Indian relations, beginning with the discovery of a road built by the Chinese through Aksai Chin, and the 1959 revolt in Tibet. There were small-scale border incidents and Indian countermoves from late 1959 to 1962. Several efforts at negotiation during the period offered no promise of results.

By October 1962, the substantive stakes of the Chinese in this situation were rather small. It seems that their immediate objective was to end negotiations, while humiliating India and retaining control of the situation. In this they had short-term success. To carry off the NEFA operation, the Chinese must have had to solve some difficult logistic problems, but the resources of men and equipment needed were available in Tibet. By keeping the operation short and withdrawing while not under pressure, the Chinese could carry off the operation at minimum risk.

34

In a broader sense, the Sino-Indian conflict derived from a divergence of political ideals and policies between the two countries, and thus what was at stake was the influence of the two countries in Asia and in the "third world" (Afro-Asian and neutralist circles).

The Chinese made some political calculations concurrently with their military effort. The article "More on Nehru's Philosophy," published October 27, 1962, indicates some of them. The Chinese believed that India's economy and internal politics were due to deteriorate. How important it was to China to degrade India's image in the eyes of the "third world" remains debatable. One can rather confidently assume that the Chinese calculated the likelihood of a split in India's Communist Party and decided to provoke one. Further it is likely that Nehru's success at the Belgrade Conference in September 1961 crystallized in Peking the sense of political conflict between India and China.

In the international arena, the Chinese clearly disliked India's rapprochement with the West and with the Soviet Union. The NEFA engagement, far from diverting these trends, strengthened them. But it exposed something of which the Indians were apparently unaware—the thinness of Asian and African sympathy with India. Chinese policy departed from the line of friendship and cooperation with India and developed a power-political anti-Indian coalition, in which Pakistan and Indonesia were major partners. If one balances the gains and losses to the PRC in power-political terms to the present, the result is not negative. In the long run, however, it is not clear that Sino-Indian rivalry is advantageous for the Chinese. In terms of the effectiveness of the two countries in Afro-Asian councils, the outcome is equivocal.

Remoter Areas

Outside Asia—in Africa and Latin America—Chinese national interests are not directly at stake. Chinese intervention in such situations is normally limited to supplying small quantities of arms or political and organizational stimulation and support. The risks of direct reaction against China as a territory or a nation are practically nonexistent.

In what situation, at what times, and in what ways have the Chinese chosen to become involved? Their earliest involvement goes back to 1958, when they began supporting the FLN (National Liberation Front) in Algeria. Their direct material contribution was small, but in 1960, by promising more to the FLN they created a situation in which the Soviet Union had to increase its assistance in order to compete. The same tactic was used a few years later in Somalia, though with little military implication. To Cuba the Chinese could offer little material aid, but they constantly encouraged Castro and treated his cause as their own. Judging by the number of visitors between Cuba and China in the past five years, the Chinese may have been giving significant help at the organizational level, and there were some signs of cooperation between the two in some African countries. Direct Chinese material aid to the dissidents in the Congo came very late in the history of events there, although their political support had been made clear much earlier. The Chinese have also given aid and comfort to a number of African revolutionary groups in, for example, Angola, Cameroons, Mozambique, and Ruanda. This is not to say that Chinese help has, or will in the near future, put Africa into an uproar. What needs to be noted is that the Chinese are willing to invest the effort, just as they are willing to back the anti-British cause in Aden or the cause of militant revolutionary groups in Venezuela. Further, they are willing to supply ideological and organizational guidance to movements or individuals in the emerging countries who will keep alive the spirit of struggle, preferably armed, and avoid an easy accommodation with the former metropolitan powers.

There seems to be genuine sympathy in the Chinese attitude toward at least some of those they have helped. A regular reader of the Chinese press could not mistake the quality of Chinese jubilation after the Bay of Pigs incident in 1961, or the especially warm welcome given to Algerian representatives who visited China during the Ben Bella regime. Such things do not last forever and do not outweigh in Cuban or Algerian eyes the greater capacity of the Soviet Union to provide material help; but on the psychological level both Cubans and Algerians often showed a reciprocal affection for China. Conversely, in some parts of Africa—like Kenya, Malawi, Burundi, and Cameroons—a certain resistance to Chinese influence, especially when it has taken the form of supplying arms, has manifested itself.

Several conclusions are clear. The Chinese believe anti-colonial revolutions are advantageous to them. They are willing to support such revolutions and especially armed struggle. In some places a small amount of direct Chinese aid can make a considerable impact on a local situation; in others, Chinese aid, or promise of aid, improves the bargaining power of the recipient, who can then get more from other sources. The Chinese prefer to help those groups (like the FLN) who seem to show real revolutionary purpose, regardless of whether they bear the name of communist party or not, or even in preference to a recognized communist party. Further, the Chinese do not regard the success of nationalist independence movements as sufficient, but try to push them along a militant road.

Indonesia

The September 30, 1965 attempted coup in Indonesia is as yet an obscure development. Such facts as are verifiable indicate that here, too, the Chinese supported a revolutionary course which they thought conformed in spirit to their own. The PKI was their chosen instrument, but not their only instrument. They seem to see in Sukarno, as well, a figure whose motives correspond to their own. Indonesia is not remote, as Algeria and Cuba are, but the method of Chinese assistance conforms more or less to what they have done in anti-colonial situations. It can be established that Chinese weapons were put into the hands of the PKI and its paramilitary organizations. Very probably the Chinese were informed of the attempt to eliminate key

Indonesian army leaders and approved of it. Further, after the failure of the coup the Chinese have continued to support those who conducted it and to endorse their purpose, evidently feeling that the chapter is not closed. Specifically, they continue to represent D. N. Aidit as the authentic leader of the Indonesian revolution and angrily refute reports that Aidit is dead. It seems that at the very least he is a candidate for the list of martyrs of revolutionary armed struggle along with Lumumba, Malcolm X, and others.

Laos–Vietnam

This is the most complicated case, and many of the details must be omitted. The Laotian and Vietnamese situations are in my view inseparable, and the developments since early 1959 in the two countries are treated here as unitary.

As noted earlier, China's attention turned southward in 1958–59. The power situation there was potentially threatening. SEATO, which seems to some of its members and to outsiders such a weak effort, probably looked more serious to the Chinese and to the DRV (Democratic Republic of Vietnam). Both were aware of the American investment in constructing a "bastion of democracy" in Laos and in strengthening the military infrastructure in South Vietnam. In 1958–59, there were events which could be interpreted as an attempt to enlarge the effective area of action of SEATO by linking South Vietnam through Laos to Thailand.

In early 1959 initiative lay with the Royal Laotian Government, which tried to eliminate local communist influence. I believe the Chinese took a direct hand in this situation from the beginning. In 1959 they claimed that a threat to China's security was being manufactured, but they felt no need to meet it directly. Counteraction occurred when the fighting strength of the Pathet Lao was directly threatened, and it took little force to meet the threat and create a stalemate. Subsequently the initiative passed back and forth. With the windfall of the Kong Le coup in 1960, the balance swung to the advantage of the Communists. In the fighting that followed, Russian intervention forestalled Chinese action, but worked out favorably for the Chinese. The Geneva conference on Laos was scarcely a coalition effort on the Communist side, but the results contained almost everything the Chinese needed. In particular the 1962 Geneva agreement on Laos opened the southern part of the country as a supply route to South Vietnam.

The internal situation of South Vietnam in 1959 and 1960 showed signs of moving in a direction that would encourage internal resistance and external assistance to it. It seems certain that the DRV regime took the initiative in 1960 at the Third National Congress of the Vietnam Workers Party, with active backing from the Chinese. Probably this decision, along with other special tactical and strategic decisions of local communist parties elsewhere, was validated by the Moscow Conference of November–December 1960, though perhaps with cautionary conditions. The National Front for the Liberation of South Vietnam was organized December 20, 1960, and the pace of Viet Cong activities was stepped up.

The pattern of developments from then on was complex. In summary form, America's decision to treat Vietnam as an area of key importance was affirmed in 1961 and has been implemented consistently since then. Sino-Soviet rivalry for influence in the DRV sharpened about the same time, and by mid-1963 the Chinese had swung the DRV far over to their side. A factor in this development was that the Soviet presence was gradually reduced in both Laos and Vietnam, in part because the Soviets have apparently preferred and, in their own way, worked toward a nonviolent settlement in Indochina. During the critical period 1963–64, Soviet influence was at a minimum, while Chinese influence, thrown more and more behind armed struggle, was growing stronger. Since Kosygin's visit to Asia in February 1965, a certain measure of Soviet influence has been restored, although China tried to prevent it.

The material resources China has invested in Vietnam are not fully known, but they appear to be moderate, especially compared with the costs assumed by the DRV. They seem to conform to the formula of meeting what the DRV and NFLSV need, what they ask for, and what is effective. These criteria, in turn, are partly determined by Chinese encouragement of the North Vietnamese; thus the Chinese are raising the ante against themselves. It seems clear that the flow of Chinese weapons to Vietnam has steadily increased. Beyond this, however, there is little known investment of Chinese resources. There has been some redeployment of forces within China, but the Chinese at the moment have assumed few material risks and apparently jeopardized no manpower. These are not the only considerations, however. The Chinese are, as they have been notified, a potential target, not a safe sanctuary. It remains unknown how much they are prepared to risk in the contingency, admittedly unlikely, of a greatly expanded war.

Because of the interplay of American and Chinese interests, and for other reasons, Vietnam has become extraordinarily important to the Chinese. It is now at the center of their policy of opposing the United States; close to the center of their differences with the Soviet Union on strategy and tactics of revolutionary (or national liberation) war; necessary for the maintenance of a coalition of Asian communist parties; directly connected with China's drive for power in Asia; and a very important factor in China's efforts to swing the "third world" in the direction China wants. For all these reasons, the Chinese cannot afford a Communist defeat in Vietnam. For the same reasons, it may be necessary, from their point of view, to obtain a real victory.

Summary

Having reviewed a number of cases of the use of force in which the PRC has been involved—whether directly, by proxy, or through assistance to others—we are able to ask a simple question: Has force been a useful instrument of Chinese foreign policy? More bluntly: Do the Chinese have reason to think war pays?

If the calculations made in this paper correspond, even

partly, to those made by Chinese leadership, the answer would appear to be an affirmative, although not necessarily a ringing affirmative. The Chinese have not always gained their point, but they have at times accomplished through war what could hardly have been done by refraining. Their losses have not crippled them, and some might have happened anyhow. Exactly because the calculation of gains and losses does not yield a clear answer, there is a tendency to prize what has been gained and minimize what has been lost. Further, for revolutionary optimists, there is always the chance that things will work out well next time.

That, of course, is not all there is to it. If conflict is always a possibility, one may have to face it, whether one wants to or not. We turn, then, to a brief examination of the next topic.

Chinese Communist Strategic Doctrine

On matters that fall within the scope of strategic doctrine, the Chinese Communists have published a surprisingly small amount of the kind of material that gives an analyst a solid basis for making any statements. But in context—compared, for instance, with more or less contemporary Soviet publications or with the actual distribution of military power in the Far East—even that small amount can yield some conclusions.

For many years Chinese accounts of the international situation were largely propagandistic. The standard formulation was that the world was divided into two camps, the "socialist camp of peace and democracy" and the "imperialist camp of war and aggression." The propaganda was designed for a purpose and did not necessarily reflect a real calculation that war was imminent. Still, the concept of two irreconcilable worlds had a hold on the Chinese Communist mind. In 1957, when the Chinese took some bold and positive initiatives in communist countries, this concept was expressed by Mao in the slogan "The East Wind prevails over the West Wind"—a slogan later ridiculed by the Soviets as a meteorological interpretation of history. It did, however, sum up the Chinese appreciation of the meaning of nuclear parity and expressed their estimate that the world balance of power had shifted radically in favor of the communist world. It implied that pressure tactics, including some uses of force, could now be applied to communist advantage. The Russian appreciation was different and became apparent when Khrushchev, visiting Peking in October 1959, said publicly that now was not the time to test the stability of the capitalist world by using force.

The two-world concept continued to have a hold on Mao's thinking for several years. The East Wind–West Wind slogan was regularly repeated. Only in mid-1963 did the Chinese seem ready to accept the idea that world politics had moved towards a pluralistic structure. Even now the idea has been only partially accepted: the Chinese still maintain that any conflict between a revolutionary movement and an established government, or between a socialist and a nonsocialist country, is of concern to all revolutionaries, and that the revolutionary or socialist side automatically has a claim on the support of all communists.

As for China's own strategic situation, the concept of encirclement is still current. The Chinese have evidence to present. Military treaties bind the United States to many of China's neighbors, from South Korea and Japan to Australia, Thailand, and Pakistan. Apart from treaties, the United States, and to a lesser extent Britain, have shown themselves disposed to assist countries like India when they find themselves in conflict with China. There has been a continuous build-up of American military power in Asia. Since 1955, and more particularly, since 1957, this has included the establishment of facilities which make the use of atomic weapons possible. Most recently, Polaris-type submarines were introduced into the Pacific, and the Seventh Fleet was deployed in the Indian Ocean.

There is no doubt that a serious local imbalance of strategic military power exists, to China's disadvantage. Whether it constitutes a clear and present menace depends on many things, among them American intentions and the effectiveness of vari-

42

ous restrictions (whose existence the Chinese recognize) on the use of atomic weapons. The United States' military posture in this area may be purely defensive, designed as a deterrent, and there may be nothing more to it than that. But Chinese Communist ideologists evidently cannot bring themselves to believe this. Their statements on the subject cannot be dismissed as mere ideological dressing for some practical demand. They rather reflect a lively sense that China lives in a dangerous—though not impossibly dangerous—world. In this world some types of warfare are too adventurous to undertake, but some are still possible.

Following the collapse of the 1958 Quemoy operation and the open Sino-Soviet disagreements on peaceful coexistence, the Chinese found it necessary to make a statement on the strategic problems of the present period. The central question was the probability of war. On this point, the classical formulation was made in April 1960, in three articles published on the nineteenth anniversary of Lenin's birth (published as a pamphlet entitled "Long Live Leninism!").

These articles imply that the probability of a Third World War is low. (Later the Chinese formally stated that World War III can be avoided.) They insisted, however, that local wars are still inevitable and specified three types: "(1) wars among imperialists for redivision of the world, (2) wars of aggression and anti-aggression between the imperialists and the oppressed nations or civil wars . . . in the imperialist countries, or (3) of course, wars in which the imperialists attack the socialist countries . . . " The point I wish to make here is that there has been a good deal of agreement between Chinese theory and practice. The military incidents that have taken place since 1960 fall into their second category (with some necessary Marxist interpretation of Indian affairs); they have treated such incidents as "just wars" and thrown their support, within the limits of practicality, accordingly. What they still fear is the third category of wars.

The issue of war and peace became a major dispute in the international communist movement. Inevitably one of the central questions was the extent of risk, particularly the risk of escalation, inherent in local wars. The accusations leveled against the Chinese in Soviet and other polemical writings—that their understanding of modern war was inadequate, that they misjudged the probable reactions of the United States, even that they were eager to promote military conflict—undoubtedly contain grave overstatements. But two points in Chinese military doctrine are clear. One is that in local wars the area of the battlefield can be controlled by the decisions of their side. The other is that local wars can be prevented from escalating to the nuclear level. They have bolstered both points by citing recent cases which support them.

More difficult to summarize is the Chinese view on nuclear war as such. The essence of their position, as they have declared it, seems to be not that they welcome large-scale nuclear wars nor even that they advocate risking such wars under certain conditions. What seems to concern them is the attitude with which the risk is approached. If it is overestimated, they argue, the prospects of effectively manipulating force, not only at the nuclear but at much lower levels, are seriously compromised; thus many actions which might benefit the communist countries or revolutionary movements will be avoided. If the risk is faced boldly, then nuclear war is likely not to occur, and a number of uses of force at the subnuclear level can be undertaken or threatened. If these contentions are correct, nuclear weapons occupy a minor place among the factors which affect the possibility of using force to the advantage of their side, while factors like morale and home front organization are major.

Mao's basic strategic concepts, and Stalin's as well, therefore remain valid. The corollary, however—and this is the difficulty —is that one cannot bluff, but must be genuinely ready to face the worst possibility: the hundreds of millions of casualties that a high-level thermonuclear exchange would produce.

The major development in doctrine since 1960 has been that as differences between European communism and Asian communism became sharper, the Chinese emphasized underdevel-

44

oped countries, whether communist or not, and their influence in these countries. Thus the doctrine of "just wars," which should be supported by the world communist movement as a whole, grew into the doctrine of "national liberation wars," which the Chinese would support separately from or even against the Soviets, and finally into the doctrine that the under-developed countries correspond to the "rural areas of the world," which by following Mao's principles can surround and overcome the "cities of the world."

The Chinese Atom Bomb

In terms of China's military experience since 1949 and of its beliefs regarding the probability of war in the near future, is her decision to acquire a nuclear capability understandable? Or must we suppose that there were other reasons for it?

On this point also, the amount of solid discussion published by the Chinese is amazingly small. It is not only much less than what other nuclear powers put out, but less than what many non-nuclear powers say. On some points, therefore, one can only speculate.

It is likely that Chinese study of the effect on modern war of nuclear weapons goes back a long way. One can infer that serious study, as distinct from repeating Soviet formulae, was indicated not later than November 30, 1950, when President Truman noted in public that atomic weapons might be used in Korea. After 1955 the supply of Chinese manpower with the necessary skills to make a weapons program began to take shape. Concurrently, serious discussion of such problems as surprise attack began to be published, and various associated problems, like the relation of the military to the civilian budget, were debated. It seems likely, though, that international circumstances which made a Chinese nuclear weapons capability a concrete policy issue did not yet exist.

China's interest in acquiring nuclear weapons goes back at least to 1957. At that time they were apparently thinking of the strength of the communist bloc as a whole. Presumably they

45

were interested in a minor nuclear capability, which would give them some freedom of maneuver in Asia, but which would require integration with the strategic nuclear capability ("nuclear umbrella") of the Soviet Union. In 1959 they learned that the Soviets would not give them the technical assistance they wanted. In 1960 the Soviets withdrew all their technical aid, presumably including aid to the Chinese nuclear program. The Chinese decision to proceed anyway, which must have been made in 1961, was thus like the French decision—to obtain a truly independent capability.

I posit, then, a series of decisions, each with different content. The 1961 decision to go ahead in the face of Soviet non-cooperation was made in the context of serious disputes within the world communist movement on peaceful coexistence, the role of armed struggle, and the nature and probable policies of "imperialism." It was also a time of economic crisis in China. At the end of 1961 the Chinese stopped playing coy in public about the possibility of obtaining nuclear weapons and let it be known that the rest of the world might as well reckon with this probability.

What kind of reasoning would lead to such a decision? The possible political value of possessing nuclear weapons would not suffice by itself to determine the decision; that is to say, the critical calculations must have been of a military order. The Chinese have not been explicit about the "mutual balance of terrors," but as one poses the question, one arrives at the guess that they believe it works effectively. They do not, however, believe in deterrence, because this contradicts their analysis of the nature of imperialism. Since they do not trust the Soviet nuclear umbrella, they must have strength of their own. Evidently they do not accept the very strong arguments that a minor nuclear capability is a "license to commit suicide."

Apparently they believe a small nuclear capability has defensive value, and one can imagine circumstances in which this might be so. Unfortunately, a small capability has battlefield applications which do not necessarily risk drastic retaliation. The Chinese insist that many factors operate to restrain an "imperialist" power from using nuclear weapons against them or in local war. If so, there is some operational meaning to the contention that they have "broken the atomic monopoly." They refer frequently to "atomic blackmail" and claim to have eliminated it. If we take these statements at face value, it appears the Chinese do not believe all their problems of defense will be solved when they have a certain number of atom bombs, but do think their total defensive posture will be improved.

On the side of offense, the Chinese insist that socialist countries cannot be the first to use atom bombs in war, especially because the wars they are interested in are "national liberation" wars. On the question of blackmail, they are less exact. The possibility remains that they hope to eliminate the use of nuclear weapons in local wars by any side. This would increase freedom of maneuver for countries, like themselves, which rely on small arms and large manpower, but it does not solve all the purely military problems of local wars.

It is still possible that the Chinese will decide to acquire a real capability for strategic nuclear war. As long as this point remains uncertain, allowance must be made for profound changes in their military doctrine. These might precede the acquisition of a major capability, since strategic concepts everywhere tend to be based more on projections of future capability than on the forces one actually commands at the moment.

Disarmament

Alternatives to force have always had the attention of the Chinese Communists. Until early 1960, they consistently supported in public all the various disarmament proposals made by the Soviet Union. It is doubtful, however, that they expected disarmament negotiations to produce substantial results. Just as they do not believe in deterrence, they do not believe in the reliability of negotiated agreements which might hinder the maintenance of a strong power position. In 1953, not long after the breakdown of the London disarmament negotiations, the

Chinese said plainly that such negotiations were not to be conducted for the sake of results, but rather for propaganda, to expose the perfidy of the "imperialists" and to strengthen world-wide popular opposition to "imperialist" policies.

Khrushchev's visit to Peking in 1959 produced a new development in the Chinese position on disarmament. In January 1960 they announced that they would not be bound by any agreements in this area reached without their participation. In effect they denied the right of anyone to bargain on their behalf. Until the middle of 1962 they continued to express formal approval of a nuclear test ban, but when, in August 1962, they learned that an agreement was likely to materialize, they reversed themselves. Their condemnation of the 1963 tripartite partial test-ban treaty was clearly foreshadowed in advance.

The Chinese have on occasion put forth other peace-keeping formulae. One, brought up several times in the past decade, is a four-power circum-Pacific nonaggression treaty. In 1958 and later they several times advocated a nuclear-free zone in Asia. Both proposals have enough intrinsic pay-off for the Chinese to make one wonder if there might not be a possibility of using them as a basis for discussion. But whenever they put the proposals forth, they attached conditions which made it highly likely that they were seeking to provoke rejection.

China's entry into the nuclear club has not seemed to make her more seriously interested in disarmament negotiations. At the time the Chinese denounced the test-ban treaty, and again following each of their nuclear detonations, they circulated proposals of their own for world conferences. The core of their proposals was consistently a demand for the complete prohibition of nuclear weapons. The response must have been encouraging. They found few wholehearted backers, but on each occasion the replies from other governments—at least those they have published—showed an increasingly respectful attitude. Thus a situation has come to exist where China is being treated as a full-fledged nuclear power, her participation in disarmament discussions in that capacity is seriously solicited, while her actually demonstrated power is quite small.

48

Even so, the Chinese refused a recent invitation to join world disarmament discussions on the somewhat thin ground of her unwillingness to accept UN sponsorship of such discussions. A few voices now express the view that results can be achieved in this area without China's participation.

Meanwhile the Chinese have brought the question of nuclear proliferation to a new stage. They obviously know how they have affected it, and equally obviously were able to foresee that this would happen. How far ahead they foresaw it cannot be determined. Possibly they were aware of the problem from an early stage. In April 1958, Khrushchev sent an open letter to several communist states announcing the Soviet intention to, among other things, oppose proliferation. Chou En-lai's acknowledgment of the communication conspicuously omitted endorsement of nonproliferation. It is plausible that Chinese coyness about becoming a nuclear power had, as one of its motives, a desire to avoid stimulating other potential nuclear powers to acquire a capability before or at the same time as themselves. When they dropped their coyness, they were also ready to argue that proliferation was advantageous for world peace. The logic of this position has never been clear, even if one accepts a definition of peace as a condition in which "imperialism" has been eliminated or an equally obscure definition of peace as a condition in which the Soviet-American duopoly no longer disposes of more nuclear power than all other nuclear powers put together. There may, however, be a logic behind the Chinese position. If so, that logic might be a rather terrifying one.

It is difficult to come to a conclusion about the real Chinese position on disarmament. They themselves may not be quite sure how to proceed. Perhaps they are waiting to become stronger in nuclear armament before they take steps in the direction of disarmament. Other nuclear powers have not been notably quick in approaching the problem. It may be wise not to close the book on the Chinese just yet.

However, one can clearly see that because of China's nuclear capability, in being or in prospect, the Asian balance of power is in the process of change. Other Asian countries can be expected to develop their policies in view of the changes they anticipate. For many of them, at least those who accept the premise that in our times no minor power can assure its own security single-handedly, various aspects of their foreign alliances will have to be reviewed. With or without atomic weapons, the Chinese continue to advocate revolutionary wars. Such wars could occur and alter the status quo. Asian countries— and others as well—cannot avoid asking themselves how far the alteration can go before it brings about a situation they would prefer not to see.

Conclusion

In brief summary, the following points contribute to defining the Chinese view of the role of force in their foreign policy.

(1) Experience shows that war can be a useful instrument of policy. Total victory is not always necessary, and total defeat is not likely.

(2) War can be expected in the future. China's basic strategic situation is not good, and one type of war that may occur would be an attack on China. Another is revolutionary war outside China.

(3) China has an effective strategy for both types of war.

(4) China has a military requirement for atomic weapons. Her forward military planning envisages their possible use.

(5) The last point does not mean that all future wars in which China is interested will be atomic. Atomic weapons may be useful as a sanction against atomic wars.

(6) For the present the Chinese wish to avoid negotiations on disarmament and have little faith in other peace-keeping measures. This position, however, is not unalterably fixed. It may change in the future.

THE MINORITY NATIONALITIES
Josef Kolmaš

I studied in China for two years—from 1957 to 1959—as a postgraduate student at the Central Institute for National Minorities in Peking. I lived among the various national groups, studying their language, customs, history, and so forth. I chose the Tibetans for my main research; after my return to Czechoslovakia, I engaged in Tibetan studies in general, giving more attention to Tibetan history.

One of the many sayings of Mao Tse-tung that I used to see written in big Chinese characters everywhere in the Institute, and that I heard both from the Hans—who constitute the majority of the Chinese population [the Chinese majority]—and from the other nationalities, was: "China has a large territory, abundant material resources, and numerous population. Of these three the Hans possess one, namely, they are many in number; minority people possess two, namely, they have vast territories and rich resources."

I never checked Mao Tse-tung's Selected Works for the veracity of that famous saying; a glance at a map of China's nationalities is the best proof of it.

The question of non-Han national groups in China, like any other question of the reality surrounding us, can be looked at

51

from many different aspects and be treated in many different ways. It is not possible for me to present here exhaustive information on all aspects of China's nationality problem and try to analyze it in detail. I shall therefore limit myself, first to a short recapitulation of some basic facts about China's minorities, and second to an indication of some common features in the solution of this problem by the present Chinese government.

Until very recently, exact knowledge about these Chinese minority groups was very inadequate. One reason is that past Chinese governments kept the minority peoples so downtrodden that some were not even aware of their own group identity, while others often hid it to avoid discrimination. Before 1949, apart from sporadic academic work by Chinese and foreign ethnologists, not much reliable information was collected or analyzed. The situation was changed with the foundation of the Chinese People's Republic in 1949. Minorities officially gained equal status, the right of local self-government, and freedom to develop their languages and life. The central government, moreover, pledged itself to assist them in every phase of political, economic, and cultural advancement. All of this was embodied in the "Common Program" of the Chinese People's Political Consultative Conference and later, in 1954, in the Constitution of the People's Republic of China.

Let me briefly indicate some basic facts about China's nationalities. According to various Chinese sources, there are at least 40 million people—the equivalent of a large European nation—belonging to the national minorities, more than 6 per cent of the total population. These people constitute more than fifty separately recognized nationalities. Of these only ten have more than a million people: in order of size they are the Chuangs of Kwangsi province; the Uighurs of Chinese Turkestan; the Huis, sometimes called the Mohammedans, who are scattered throughout the country; the Is of the southwestern provinces of Yunnan, Szechuan and Kweichow; the Tibetans; the Miaos in Kweichow and Hunan; the Manchus, who are distributed among the Hans all over the northeast, their historic homeland, and have no special region; the Mongols of Inner Mongolia; the Pu-i of Kweichow; and the Koreans in the northeast.

With respect to their location the national minorities may be conveniently classified into two broad divisions: the northern and the southern. The northern group includes several nationalities in the northwestern part of the country, such as Uighurs, Kazakhs, Kirghiz, etc.; and the Mongols, Manchus, and some other northeastern groups. The greatest concentration of minorities, however, is in the south and southwest, mainly in the provinces of Kwangsi, Kweichow, Yunnan, and Szechuan, in Tibet, and on the islands of Taiwan and Hainan. Small as is the proportion represented by the minorities in the whole population of China, they occupy large territories—more than half the total area of the country. Generally, these territories lie along the inner Asian frontiers of China.

The main differentiating characteristics are language, occupation, religious belief, and social structure. Racially most of the minority nationality people belong to the Mongoloid type and resemble the Chinese majority. Only among the northwestern national groups is there a considerable influence of the Turkish element of Central Asia.

Language

Approximately 74 per cent belong to the Sino-Tibetan family of languages, divided into Sino-Thai, Tibeto-Burmese and Miao-Yao language branches; 21 per cent are of the Altaic family of languages (Turkic, Mongolian, and Tunguzic); less than 4 per cent are Koreans; one per cent speak Mon-Khmer languages; and one-tenth of 1 per cent are of the Indo-European family of languages.

Occupation

Nearly all the minority peoples get their livelihood from agriculture or raising cattle, although there are also merchants, craftsmen, fishermen, and industrial workers among them. The farmers are most numerous, comprising about seven-tenths of the total. Farming methods range from very crude to relatively efficient. Chinese agriculture, in the course of history, has owed much to the northern people called Hsiung-nu, often identified with the Huns who once invaded Europe. The Hsiung-nu no longer exist as a nationality, but may have been the ancestors of the present-day Uighurs or Mongols. They introduced the use of draft animals for field work in north China in the second century B.C. Again, melons, grapes, cucumbers, carrots, garlic, and other plants were introduced from Chinese Turkestan. Recent findings suggest that the Han people of the Yangtze valley acquired the techniques of planting, spinning, and weaving cotton from the Li people of Hainan island sometime in the thirteenth century.

Religion

The largest single religion among the minority groups is Islam, the faith of some eight to nine million people, mainly the Huis, Uighurs, Kazakhs, Tadjiks, and others. The Hui people, who are thought to be partially of Arab descent, gave China many scientists and technicians. They built an observatory in Peking for which they made all the astronomical instruments, and the imperial governments, up to 1911, maintained a department of calendar and astronomical affairs staffed mainly by Huis. Similarly the Uighurs, situated on both sides of the famous "silk road" connecting China with central Asia, India, and the Middle East, played a prominent part in two-way exchange, both economic and cultural, which among many other things brought Buddhism to China.

The second largest group are the Lamaists. Lamaism—or the Tibetan form of Buddhism—is found mostly among the Tibetans and Mongols. Owing both to their geographic location and religion, the Tibetans have always represented a strong link between China, India, and other Himalayan countries, such

54

as Nepal, Sikkim, and Bhutan. Similarly, the Mongols of Inner Mongolia are connected, racially, linguistically, religiously, etc., with the Mongols in Outer Mongolia and in the Soviet Buriat Autonomous Republic. There are also Hinayana Buddhists, Taoists, different types of polytheists, ancestor worshippers, and a small number of Christian converts. All without exception enjoy the freedom of religion guaranteed to all citizens of China under the constitution.

Social Structure

According to Dr. A. Palát, a Czech Sinologist who traveled extensively in the minority nationality areas of China, the social structure of the different nationalities—still existing in the first years of the Chinese People's Republic—can be divided roughly into four categories. (1) Nationalities with a rather developed system of feudal landlordship, sometimes interwoven with certain elements of capitalist economics. Such was the case with the Huis, Chuangs, Manchus, Uighurs, and most of the Mongols. (2) Nationalities with a prevailing system of feudal serfdom. The Tibetans are an example. (3) Nationalities where slavery still existed as a system. This category includes the Is of the Yunnan-Szechuan marches. (4) Nationalities living in primitive communes as well as in various stages of transition between primitive communism and class society. They live mainly in the border regions of Yunnan, on Hainan island, and in northern parts of Inner Mongolia. Of course, since 1949 many kinds of reforms changed or began to change the social status of the non-Han population.

Official Policy on Nationality Problems

The problem of policy toward minority nationalities in a multinational state is always extremely delicate. History shows many cases when its incorrect application has endangered even the existence of states. Past history and present political situa-

55

tion are closely connected, and it is not always easy for the governments involved to find a proper way out of all intricacies of a problem.

Throughout their long history relations between the Hans on one side and the minority peoples on the other were those of the dominant and suppressed, persecutors and persecuted, with hatred as the inevitable consequence. The formerly dominant classes in China used to foster what is called "Great Han chauvinism," i.e., a contempt for all nationalities other than the Han majority. Part of their policy was to sow discord among different groups of people, with the age-old aim of "divide and rule." China's many nationalities never lived together in peace. One of the most urgent domestic tasks facing the Chinese government after 1949 was to unite all peoples in a common effort to wipe out the inequalities inherited from the past and to help establish the best conditions for the distinctive development of all non-Han population groups. The characteristic feature of the Chinese government's new attitude was that its policy was not confined to theoretically prohibiting discrimination and oppression, but provided for regional self-rule in minority areas. Moreover, the central government pledged itself to their political, economic, cultural, and educational development. In the beginning this new policy was often first applied by the army, which entered isolated national minority areas to mop up remnants of the old regime. At the same time the soldiers were ordered to aid minority people with both agricultural work and medical service.

With the passing of time, as the Chinese government consolidated its position at home and abroad, as industrial and agricultural production increased, and as new specialist cadres grew, it was possible also to increase the amount and to improve the quality of help given to national groups. From the psychological point of view it is important to note that the Hans did not conceive of the development of the nationality areas only from an economic interest, nor was it undertaken solely because of the strategic importance of these areas. (One must bear in mind that most nationalities live in regions bordering

56

on the countries of southeast, south, and central Asia, and the Soviet Union.) Rather, those in the highest positions strongly emphasized that the Han people should repay the debt they owed to the minorities. Official Chinese propaganda at home and abroad always acknowledged, and still acknowledges, that the contributions of the minority peoples to various phases of Chinese civilization have been very considerable. This was indisputably a new element in the approach of the Han population toward the national minorities.

Apart from the reasons which led and still lead the Chinese government to implement this concept of minority policy, it remains true that during the past fifteen years the minority regions underwent essential changes which altered fundamentally their traditional patterns. Let me document this with some concrete examples.

Agricultural production was reorganized, local agriculture was equipped with modern agricultural implements, all of which led to a moderation of the chronic shortage of food and clothing.

Chinese trade with the nationality areas, which before 1949 had been mostly a weapon of exploitation, has been gradually transformed into a means of helping the minorities. State-owned trading organizations supply whatever is necessary at low prices, sometimes even at a loss.

The minority areas abound in industrial raw materials. Sinkiang yields petroleum; Inner Mongolia has coal; the southwest produces copper, tung-oil, camphor, etc. This forms the basis for industries which in their turn are providing new working facilities for the minority peoples.

A great deal of work has also been done to combat disease and increase population in minority areas. Diseases such as bubonic plague in Inner Mongolia and malaria in the southwest, which used to carry off whole villages, no longer exist. Measures against venereal diseases—for example, syphilis, which was prevalent in Inner Mongolia and Tibet and made many marriages sterile—have considerably increased the birthrate.

57

The cultural backwardness of many minorities is, and will perhaps remain for a long time, a serious handicap to their economic and social development. However, the government has taken a whole range of energetic measures, and the situation has changed rapidly. Special schools for children from the nationality areas, the Nationality Institutes, were established in Lanchow, Peking, Wuhan, Chengtu, Hsining, Nanning, and Kunming. A university was founded in Huhehot, the capital of Inner Mongolia. In the other territories lower schools have also been established. Young minority intelligentsia and qualified personnel, educated to be familiar with the conditions of the Chinese People's Republic, now amount to several thousand.

In order to attain a quick and general advancement of the backward minority areas and to raise the economic and cultural level of the population, the government, apart from the effective economic and technical assistance provided by the Han population, chose a system of self-rule and regional autonomy. This, too, represents a completely new phenomenon in the policy of Chinese governments toward the minority groups.

Regional Autonomy

The present government's constant policy in this respect has been to give whatever help the nationalities may require in moving forward at their own pace and under their own chosen leaders. It should be stated that the Chinese Communist Party acted upon this principle even before 1949. As early as 1929, autonomous governments were established in districts inhabited by the minority people of Kwangsi province, which was a part of the then-existing Chinese Soviet Republic. During the anti-Japanese War, autonomy was established among Moslems in the western part of the Shen-Kan-Ning Border Region. Regional autonomy is the basic policy which the government has adopted in its approach to the national problem. According to the Chinese Constitution, autonomy is to be exercised in areas where national minorities live in compact communities. In all other cases the electoral system is so arranged that they have suitable representation in local governments. Those nationalities which are sufficiently numerous or otherwise important have their representatives in the National People's Congress. Under the unified direction of the central government, autonomous groups not only exercise the functions and powers of local government organs, but also have rights in financial, economic, cultural, and educational matters, and in the organization of the local public security forces. These local autonomous organs are mainly composed of people from the minority nationality which exercises regional authority. The commonly used spoken and written language of the local nationality is an official language of the area. Various levels of autonomous areas have been set up according to the size of the population and extent of the territory involved. The largest of these are regions equivalent to provinces. With the establishment of the Tibet Autonomous Region on September 9, 1965, there are now five such regions. The four previously established are: the Inner Mongolian Autonomous Region in northern China, the Sinkiang Uighur Autonomous Region in the northwest, the Kwangsi Chuang Autonomous Region in south China, and the Ningsia Hui Autonomous Region in northwest China. Smaller groupings are represented by autonomous *chou*—administrative regions consisting of several counties; there are at present twenty-nine *chou*. The smallest units are called autonomous counties, numbering sixty-five by now.

These are, roughly speaking, the main common features which have characterized the policy of the Chinese government toward national groups. The results, attained over the seventeen years since the proclamation of the Chinese People's Republic in 1949, are certainly not negligible; we may even say that for China they represent something which is really new and unusual. I may cite as evidence several non-Han people gratefully acknowledging assistance they have received from the majority Chinese. Nevertheless, we cannot

59

say that the Chinese in their policy toward national minorities have always been successful, that they never met with difficulties or even failures. Of course, some of these failures have been limited and local, and consequently have not always been noticed abroad. However, cases such as the Tibetan revolt in 1959—and even troubles before this date—and recent signs of disquieting activities among the Uighur and Kazakh population of Sinkiang certainly cannot escape attention both at home and abroad. As I have said, the solution of nationality problems where the differences between the standard of social structure and technical civilization are sharp is always very delicate and sometimes even dangerous. Moreover, New China had to solve many of her domestic problems in the circumstances of a rather complicated international political situation which inevitably influenced many of her decisions. Without trying to enumerate all the instances when Chinese efforts among minority nationalities failed or almost failed, and without going into details in analyzing reasons for certain setbacks, I would point out two factors which in this connection deserve attention.

I am not sure, for instance, whether the concept that every national area is an integral and inseparable part of the territory of the People's Republic of China is absolutely correct: perhaps for the time being, but certainly not forever. History shows us quite a few cases when the economic and cultural advancement of a population has been followed by a rise in its national consciousness, and at the same time by the growth of strong separatist tendencies. It goes without saying that such tendencies are absolutely incompatible with the idea of territorial integrity, and sooner or later lead to conflict. Such was and is the case of the Tibetans, for instance. However, if I understand the Chinese leaders' psychology, and if I am to be absolutely frank, I have to say that I do not see any practical solution to this dilemma. To cite again the case of Tibet, it is known that the question of Tibet has never been, nor will ever be, a partisan issue in Chinese domestic politics. As a Chinese delegate of the Nationalist government once explained before the UN delegates, Tibet has been and still is a part of China; all Chinese, whatever their party or religion, regard it as such.

Another problem I would like to consider in this connection is represented by the fact of a noncoerced, day-to-day Sinification of the minority people. This is now far more more effective than ever before. As Dr. Palát says, "The market [in the minority areas] is flooded with Chinese standard factory goods much cheaper than homemade petty wares, highways and railroads are being built connecting these areas with the rest of China, and if we add to it all the means and devices influencing the opinion of broad masses, such as press, film, radio, television, general education, etc., as well as the much closer contact and intercourse with other parts of China, it is no surprise that not only the way of living but also the way of thinking of these nationalities is less differentiated from that of the Chinese population than it was yesterday." However natural and even inevitable a phenomenon it is, this progressive Sinification represents, in the final analysis, a danger of full absorption of a relatively weak non-Han element by a stronger Han element. The history of China shows not a few such examples.

Even though the main role in the reshaping of Chinese society is played by the Chinese proper, who constitute more than 90 per cent of the population, an important part is contributed in this complicated endeavor by the minority nationalities as well. True, they are mostly shaped by the Hans, but to a certain degree they are also shaping the Hans. Thus they are co-shapers of the great Chinese civilization.

Impressions of
the New China

THE RESHAPING
OF CHINESE SOCIETY
Jan Myrdal

T HE TITLE makes the subject dangerous. The bland objec-
tivity of the words is misleading. Taken at their face
value, they imply that the writer considers himself able to
encompass all things Chinese (history, social history, structure
of Chinese society in ancient times, during the last days of
the Empire, in 1950 and in 1965), that he has a grand and
global theory of the reasons for change and "reshaping" of
societies, that all known or knowable facts fit this theory,
and that he thus can clearly perceive and plainly explain how
Chinese society today is changing, from what to what, by
whom changed, why and how. Now, such a man does not
exist. If he did exist he would be the sage of the ages. And
even if the words of this title are taken at a token value and
the demands become more human, that a writer, through a
thorough scholarly knowledge of Chinese society and a deep
experience of China today, would attempt to present a clear
picture of the reshaping of Chinese society, even then I have
to point out that I am no such expert. Thus I understand the
title as if it had begun with three unwritten words: "Some
notes on. . . ."

If the subject had been a different one, one concerned with the natural sciences, this reservation would have been pointless. Nobody expects the scientist talking about "the structure of the atom" to do more than give a contribution. But when it comes to contemporary social and political questions that directly concern all of us and our future, there is a strong social pressure on the social scientist, the historian, the writer, to stand up and with clear voice and (scientific) Greek words state the "truth." Where formerly the preachers stood up in their pulpits on the eve of war, like the chaplain of Gustavus Adolphus saying, "God with us," when the troops marched off to war in Germany, now in a more scientific age it is we who are granted the privilege of rationalizing the irrational.

Speaking about contemporary China in the United States today is not, and cannot be construed as, a piece of disengaged scholarly work. Such disengagement would be either pretense or lack of consciousness. There is a very real danger of war between the United States and China. Such a war would be utter madness. If it can be prevented—and I am not at all sure it can be—I believe that one of the factors preventing it would be a better understanding in the United States of the social reality in China today. This belief is possibly the strongest motivation for my being here. To state this does not—according to my ideas—make me subjective. If superficial scholarly disengagement is dangerous, it is because it serves as a cloak for subjectivity; only by consciousness of the subjective motivation can words be made to function objectively, be detached in a rational and not rationalized sense. The role of the clerk—the conscious treater of words—remains the same whether he is a poet, a Sinologist or a journalist.

Li Kuei-ying, a peasant woman and a *kanpu* of Liu Ling village, said when talking about the discussions leading to the forming of the People's Commune:

Li Ying-teh, who is an old man and Li Hsin-chen's father, then said: "We should not listen to women when it is a question of serious business. They understand nothing.

66

After all, they are only women and ought not to disturb our discussions. We do not need to concern ourselves with what they have said." But my brother Li Hai-tsai replied to this: "Why shouldn't we listen to the women? Every other Chinese is a woman. There is a lot of sense in what they've just said about investment and production and land interest and joint effort. I am entirely with them." . . .*

The social role of women is changing. Chinese society is changing. When I presented (in *Report from a Chinese Village*) material of this sort, interviews and statements, I got some reactions that fascinated me. Especially from certain professional experts on contemporary China. Before going any further, I think it is necessary to understand these reactions. This is not a private necessity, but a precondition for talking rationally about China in the United States.

China is the most populous country in the world, America the mightiest economically. There is a bitter and real conflict between them. Listening to Radio Peking and the Voice of America, reading the popular press of the two countries, it is striking how rational arguments become irrational and emotional. Thus even though there is a real conflict with real issues concerning us all, we from other countries, inundated with this flow of words, often get the feeling that we are witnessing the performance of a Strindbergian marriage play.

This emotionalism in the two countries is one factor in our misunderstanding of China. Another is the unhappy circumstance that American experts on contemporary China have had no chance to see the reality they are supposed to study. Even though there are more experts on China in the United States than anywhere else in the world and although the number of facts they collect is enormous, their picture of life tends to be dehydrated. The simple truths—that Chinese lovers walk in the Pei Hai park in Peking, that Chinese laugh at jokes, that they work and marry, that they die and get cried over—get

* All quotations in this essay are from Jan Myrdal, *Report from a Chinese Village* (New York: Pantheon Books, 1965).

lost. I do not say that the experts on contemporary China in America are dishonest. Far from it. But the political circumstances, the distance, the impossibility of their seeing, hearing, smelling, touching, tasting China have put them in a theological or metaphysical relationship to the realities of China.

Thus if I describe a village by letting the villagers talk, they are apt to say that I am no Sinologist—which is very true but slightly beside the point; that the story of the Chinese peasant is still unwritten—which is also very true but still more beside the point; and that it is uninteresting to hear what the peasants say because the peasants do not state the deeper motives for change in China—and there our roads part. For two reasons. One is that the way a village in China lives —what food the people eat, how they work, what kind of shoes the women wear in winter, the difficulties the children have in school—are to me infinitely more fascinating and enlightening than the analysis of a banquet speech by a "prominent public figure." Secondly, I always find what people say interesting, even though I never believe that they say more than they want to say: I don't expect peasants in any country to give information about the "deeper pattern." Neither in China, nor in Sweden. (We know, for instance, that the yearly bank savings of the Swedish farmers exceed their declared incomes. Local, regional and state tax authorities and financial experts have for many years tried to clarify this. Without results. For political reasons—the farmer vote—the question is not discussed openly. I don't know any normal and decent interrogatory method that would make the Swedish farmers talk on this subject. That does not stop us from listening to what they say and even from believing them.) Deeper patterns are to be seen when one listens to what people say. It really surprises me that so few saw the implications for the economic development of China in what Liu Hsin-min, the party secretary of Liu Ling People's Commune, said about labor exchange between the brigades:

. . . In the winter of 1959–60, Liu Ling Labor Brigade carried out a very big water-regulation project. This cost

68

a total of 14,772 days' work, of which Liu Ling Labor Brigade itself contributed only 4,172. Liu Ling Brigade first repaid a total of 1,568 days' work to the other two brigades which had collaborated: Chungchuan Labor Brigade and the Sun Rises Labor Brigade. They got roughly 800 days' work each. After that, it became difficult to repay in days' work, and after lengthy meetings and much discussion, we agreed that Liu Ling Labor Brigade could pay in cash. Negotiations took a long time. In the end the parties agreed that payment should be at 0.80 yuan per day's work performed. That was roughly 0.30 yuan below the current valuation of a day's work. It was a matter of 8,532 days' work. Since then, no labor exchange project of this magnitude has been carried out between brigades.

I want to qualify the word "few"; few experts. Because local politicians, municipal councilors, farmers, trade union officials and businessmen in Sweden understand it. Because of their own practical experience, they are able to see Chinese problems realistically as soon as they understand that China is an existing reality.

People in Liu Ling village said about Li Hung-fu:

He is good-looking. He is an ordinary person. He is taciturn and never speaks unnecessarily. He is quite respected, but the women don't like joking with him. He does not understand joking, and laughing and that sort of thing. "Though he doesn't like chatting and never jokes, and though he can go days at a stretch without opening his mouth or saying a word to anyone, there is a lot in his head." He is a good organizer. He understands how to get people to work. He himself spares no effort and is always an example in any situation calling for energy and endurance. His manner of living is that which the Party recommends: hard work and a simple way of life.

If one changed "party" to "church" this could be people in Willmar, Minnesota, talking about a farmer fifty years ago. And this simple reality, that Liu Ling in Shensi is as normal as Willmar, Minnesota, should not be hidden.

69

I make three assumptions about China:

(I) The aims of the Chinese government are those professed by most governments in the world today—to increase the material well-being of all citizens in order to achieve greater freedom. These aims are not only professed aims but they are real. That is; the Chinese government is not a conspiracy to enslave the Chinese people. And, professed and real, these aims are shared alike by the governments of Sweden and the United States. There is thus on one level a greater ideological affinity between the American and Chinese governments than between, for instance, the present Swedish government and the Swedish government of 1705. There is, of course, real conflict between China and the United States. And the policies of these governments might bring about atomic holocaust and the destruction of the human race. But when this basic harmony of aims and ideals is hidden or forgotten, any discussion of China in America or of America in China will be transformed into a metaphysical discussion of Buddhist hells, and real and existing conflicts will be interpreted as conflicts between good and evil, light and darkness.

(II) My second assumption is more hypothetical. The first I could prove; this I can only surmise—that there has been no break in Chinese continuity, that the current reshaping is a phase of Chinese social development. To prove this I would need a knowledge of Chinese tradition and Chinese social history that I lack. Others have this knowledge and have in different ways also stressed this continuity. But what is needed is empirical study in the field. At the moment, this is difficult. And the cleavage today between Sinologists who are learned about Chinese culture and social history and those experts on contemporary China who are working with a restricted political model of Chinese society, where one of the main points in their *profession de foi* is that there has been a break of continuity, makes any study of the question still more difficult.

My assumption about continuity is based partly on my first-hand impressions of China, discussions and reading, and partly on my general belief in the continuity of cultural patterns. To explain this, let me take an example from Sweden. It has been said that the attitudes toward premarital intercourse and suicide have changed in Sweden as a result of the welfare state. Even one of your presidents believed in this break. But any study will show that there has been no break at all. Society is changing. This changes the life of all its members, but a certain set of attitudes persists throughout the centuries. What has changed is that the small, educated, urban middle class of the nineteenth century, who professed the official continental attitudes on these questions, have to a large extent lost their power. The attitudes of the large peasant majority are becoming the official attitudes, in a social change that swept away the peasant majority and is transforming the few remaining farmers from peasants to agricultural technicians. But if you want to understand the attitudes towards premarital intercourse among students in Stockholm today, then you have to go to the villages that began breaking up 150 years ago. I want to take another Swedish example to prove the defectiveness of a purely contemporary political reasoning. Some years ago a law was introduced in Sweden making it an offense to build houses on the shorelines of our lakes. Everyone was to have the legal right to walk and bathe along every shore. The political discussion was intense. But the law passed. Now beautiful political analyses were made of this—socialistic government and what not. But what really had happened was that a part of the old common law, "every man's right," had to be made written law due to the increased number of summer houses. Swedes have—together with Norwegians and Finns but in distinction to the continent of Europe—"always" had the right to walk, pick berries, bathe and so on, whether the land was private or public. Most Swedes—by the way—are not even conscious that this is a social phenomenon. They believe it is "natural."

Without an understanding of continuity the description of the political development of any country becomes unreal. And

71

even where there are breaks, as in revolutions, the continuity is not broken. The old secretary of Liu Ling village, Li Yiu-hua, speaking about the revolution in the thirties, said:

> Another thing that had a lot of significance was that we heard of the revolution from members of our own family. We had most trust in the family, and when the family started saying that the revolution was necessary, this was better propaganda than anyone coming from outside to talk to us. An uncle can say things that an outsider cannot say.

(III) My third assumption is that Mao Tse-tung led his peasant armies to victory in a Chinese peasant war. I want to make this assumption explicit because the nonrecognition of China by the United States has its ideological counterpart in the widespread popular myth that the victory of Mao Tse-tung was due to some kind of accident. That "it should not have happened." This myth is influential. To prove that the Chinese government today stresses the peasant misery of former times in order to gain support for its policies is correct and scientific; but to go one step further and prove this so well that the reader gets the impression that the Chinese peasants were not living in a misery that motivated them to revolt, but were hoaxed into revolution and civil war, is ideological reasoning, metaphysics.

Viewing the reshaping, the change, from above as a process directed and manipulated by individual leaders makes the picture hazy and unreal. The official policies and statements will prove to change continuously; the contents of the slogans will prove to slide away from underneath the words, until in the end the words themselves erode and are replaced by new signs. I do not underestimate governmental policies or social theories. If I did I would not be a writer. But I think it is more fruitful to take a large concrete question, place it in a concrete village, and use that as a starting point. I will thus take the question of population control, leaving out the ideological battles, the different theories (Malthusian and

72

anti-Malthusian, Marx and Malthus, early and late Marx),
the changes in the official line.

As in every peasant culture the prime demand on any man
is that he continue the family, not break the biological chain:

> The most serious thing one can say about anyone is: "he
> has been so bad and behaved so immorally that he has no
> young generation." To die without anyone to continue
> the family is the most dreadful thing that can happen to
> anyone. That almost happened to Li Yu-teh. He has his
> family grave on Loushan, for he belongs to the old land-
> owning family. He never had a son of his own, only two
> daughters, and they, of course, would leave the family as
> soon as they married. His elder daughter is Li Kuei-
> fung and she is married. She married Wang Fung-li. Only,
> instead of her leaving home, Wang Fung-li moved to her
> home. That was arranged when the marriage was being
> settled. Li Yu-teh wanted Wang Fung-li to come and live
> with him and give him a young generation. . . . Thus
> Li Yu-teh's family will not die out . . .

But this craving for a "young generation" is not "human
nature." Neither is it just an ideology shared by peasants in
China, India and all over the world. It satisfies a practical
social need. Ma Chen-hai said:

> But now I am getting old and my son has to take on re-
> sponsibility for the family's affairs. But I talk a lot with
> him. Life is good now. I do household work and sometimes
> I go down to our private plot and do a little work there.
> Mine is a peaceful old age. My two daughters are married
> and have children. My son is married and has children.
> I believe that I have thirteen grandchildren now, and
> my eldest granddaughter is twenty and married and has
> children of her own. I have a calm and peaceful time of
> it. I spend the daytime with my grandchildren. But I
> don't see well. My eyes are almost finished and my teeth
> ache all the time. It is difficult for me to chew. I have
> toothache the whole time, especially in my left lower
> jaw. . . . I have my coffin all ready. It's made of proper
> thick wood. It's a very fine coffin.

73

In Liu Ling people said of Ma Chen-hai: "He is respected. He's an old man and respected. His son, Ma Juei-ching, works very hard and is a capable person." The family is the peasant's security, more important even than land. To grow old without children is not only theoretically and ideologically dreadful; it has always been, and still is, physically dreadful. The family is the security of a peasant culture. Tu Fang-lan, a fifty-six-year-old woman, said:

> There were six of us children, three sons and three daughters. Mother is still alive. She is seventy-two. Father was drowned. I send Mother money. In 1961 I gave her twenty yuan. All six children send the same amount and this means that she has proper pocket money. She lives alone up in Hengshan, but her daughters-in-law go and cook for her. She still hears well and still makes quilted jackets for the family.

If the family is large, if there are many children (boys), the security is greater. Children are also (leaving aside the question of girls for the moment) an economic asset. Even if the income from the collective in principle is given to each individual, in fact it is still delivered to the head of the household. This is not only for survival; it is in plain fact practical. And there is a very real difference in economic standard between the rich family with many working members and the poor family with few workers.

Certain aspects of the social and political changes in rural China after the revolution also strengthen the motivations for large families: as income is given for work only—not for land or capital—the family gets richer only by hard work and increase in numbers. That the role of women is changing also by and by transforms the girls from liabilities to assets.

Together with better sanitation and reduced mortality, these are the factors working for marked increase of population. They are also ideologically reflected in the policy statements that a greater Chinese population means more work done and thus greater prosperity. The ideology does not work the other way around.

74

Before going any further there is one point I want to make clear. There is, as far as I know, no human culture in this world that is without knowledge of contraceptive or abortion methods. Their methods might be less reliable, but they work. That is, even if Western medicine now has given us methods 98–99 per cent reliable, the popular methods that are only 75–80 per cent reliable will still be effective. Let us not forget that most people in our countries still use traditional contraceptive techniques, and that the birth rate went down before the use of modern contraceptives became widespread (while the official ideology—even the laws—of our countries were strongly against birth control, and most people officially condemned it). Science and technology will make it easier to implement a decision to avoid conception; but the decision does not depend on technology. The question of population control is not a question of new contraceptive techniques or of ideological propaganda. If there is a strong private or social motivation the popular techniques will be used—even without, or against, propaganda—and will be effective.

In Liu Ling the tendencies to increase the number of children is further strengthened because there still is land to be cleared.

> When I came here twenty-five years ago, only the valley was cultivated. All the fields you see up there on the hillside have been cleared since then. . . . Up there on the hillside is where we cleared new ground.

Ideologically the population problem on the Liu Ling village level could be stated: Wealth comes from work. More people means more manpower means more work means more wealth. And even though the newly cleared ground gives but little:

> It is good soil down there in the valley. It yields ten times as much as that on the slopes.

One of the results of the government's propaganda for increased harvests and new agricultural techniques has been that the peasants believe, rationally and correctly, that the good land in the valley could yield more in the future. But the belief that the good land will give more if more work is put into it also strengthens the motivation for many children.

And despite the revolution—rather because the revolution was a peasant war—the perspectives of the village remain rural. During the revolution of thirty years ago in Shensi the peasants had held chiliastic ideas rather than socialistic (in the urban sense):

> We had meetings at which we talked of how all humanity was to be freed of all oppression and all misfortune and need, and how all peoples were to become brothers and live as equals all over the world.

Such ideas are still—as can be seen in any Chinese paper—very much present in Chinese thought. The perspectives of the village remain rural. The "good life" that is to be built is the "good village life." Speaking about housing Mau Ke-yeh said:

> . . . an earth cave seldom lasts more than two or three generations. Often only thirty years. . . . A stone cave calls for more careful planning and considerably more work. You can take it that each stone cave takes roughly four hundred work days. The three caves in this row took the work of seventy men for a whole month. They are thus considerably more expensive to build than both earth caves and ordinary houses; but, while an ordinary house won't go for more than thirty years without major repairs, a stone cave will stand four or five hundred years and not need a thing done to it. . . . We are planning to rebuild the whole village with stone caves. . . . In a few years the whole village will consist of stone caves and they will stand for five hundred years without needing repair. That is what makes stone caves the most economical.

On the national, or policy level, the need to develop Chinese economy necessitates a change from the familial to the social, and in the longer run, from rural to urban, agricultural to industrial-technological.

In the stricter sense, this is not a question of politics. It is as necessary for China as it has been necessary for us. Education, health, even security in life, have become social responsibilities. By and large this trend is the same whether the government is a Labor government (as in Sweden these last thirty years), a Republican or Democratic one (as in the United States), or carries another label. As the family loses economic importance in China, the strong motivations for population increase will weaken. Collectivization facilitates the change from family to society. But even so, this reshaping is not so much a question of government leadership. The government (party) has a very narrow field in which to maneuver. The choice of policies is limited. Decidedly much more limited, for instance, than in Sweden fifty years ago. Production is low, resources are meager. And even when change has economic and social results, including a fall in the birth rate, society must have the economic means to ensure these new social functions. As the peasants of Liu Ling said: "Nothing comes from heaven. Everything comes from work." Their work.

According to the figures I was given (and even if I doubt that they are absolutely correct—the bookkeeper had difficulties in keeping his figures straight—they are at least indicative), grain production in 1961 had been 326,784 pounds. The state grain tax had been 23,680 pounds; 22,060 pounds had been sold to the state. On these 45,000 pounds (together with the equivalent deliveries from all other villages of China) rests not only the whole Chinese state with armies, atomic weapons, universities, diplomats, and national monuments, but also the new industrial development. If China is to develop and survive these deliveries must increase.

Of the remaining grain, 48,680 pounds were used for seed and fodder, that is, went back to production. The rest was eaten up by the 212 villagers. And 56,799 pounds were divided among "merit workers" and labor groups who had exceeded the planned production, 159,265 pounds were given for work according to workpoints, and 16,300 pounds were "social grant."

77

These 16,300 pounds are not taken from any stored surplus. They have to come from what otherwise would be consumed by the families. But on these 16,300 pounds rests the social security in Liu Ling. The change from familial to social will be very long and very hard. The ideology of this change, of course, bears a striking resemblance to that of the "welfare countries" in the beginning of the shift from familial to social responsibilities for security. Feng Chang-yeh:

> The year before the formation of Liu Ling People's Commune, 1957, we in the East Shines Red Higher Agricultural Co-operative handed over as social help 3,360 jin of corn and 6,000 of fuel. During 1958, when Liu Ling People's Commune was formed, these figures rose to 13,900 and 14,000 respectively, and, in 1959, the first whole year with the commune, when we had stabilized the position, 13,300 and 16,000; and last year, 1961, we had got up to 16,300 and 18,000. There you have the development. I consider this one of the most important changes of recent years. Illness, death, and accident are no longer catastrophes. Citizens now have security.

The important thing is not the figures—they might be more or less correct—but the proportions and the evaluations. It would be false to say that the citizens in Chinese villages now have a social rather than a familial security. But this is in process, and security is expressed in social terms.

The problem of social security in a Chinese village would be well understood by any local politician in Sweden who had worked in one of the poorer rural areas. The money for security must come from people who themselves have no abundance.

> Those who work must themselves agree what proportion of their work they are prepared to hand over to their neighbors, for whom things are difficult. That is a question of social responsibility and solidarity. You can't solve that question by taking the possibility of deciding this away from the workers. That would . . . be the end of solidarity.

78

The people's communes were a part of this change to the necessary social organization of society:

> . . . with the introduction of the people's commune and the big propaganda campaigns we had during that time, the members' consciousness increased and their responsibility was strengthened so greatly that it was possible to introduce rational social care. This is also one of the main points in our propaganda: the mutual responsibility of members.

Both objections to and reasons for social welfare were expressed in the village in terms closely resembling those of the discussion in Swedish rural areas:

> At the same time, we have to see that the social grants don't become so big that social help is greater than the workers' incomes. One must not undermine the value of work. But one has to see that everyone, even those who for various reasons have got into difficulties, has the possibility to live a decent life.

The process of change from familial to social can only be carried through during a period of increasing production. At the same time it is one means of raising production. But the process is slow.

Thus the question of birth control and population in China is not an ideological discussion between different "schools of thought" in Peking. It is only to a limited degree a question of government or party policy. Such policies can help—or hinder—the development, but they cannot make the development. What is decisive is how the village sees and formulates social needs. Even if the government were to become quite convinced of the necessity to limit the growth of the Chinese population, this conviction would have but little effect in the villages—that is among the majority of the population—until the peasants themselves had a personal conviction; and they will not feel this as long as the family structure provides the primary security. But to make security social, production must increase. This is a very real dilemma, one which holds not only for population but also for industrialization and economic growth in general. Breaking off at this point, the argument would lead to a most depressing conclusion: the reshaping of Chinese society, undertaken with great difficulties and at great costs, checkmates itself.

But, still keeping within the bounds of birth control and Liu Ling village, there are other factors changing the village. Ideas are taken seriously. The statement that all men are created equal was not only a theory. It was, and still is, an explosive force. And the idea of equality of rights between men and women set loose a tremendous wind of change in the Chinese villages. The old secretary Li Yiu-hua, speaking of the revolution, said:

> We made propaganda for the equality of women and free choice in marriage. There were lots of divorces in those days, for most people's marriages had been arranged for them and they did not care for each other. We held meetings about love then. Most did not go back to their former marriage partners, but looked for new ones with whom they would be happier. The class enemy then slandered us and flung mud at us, saying that we had no morals. But we wanted everyone to be free and equal and the new marriages were both happier and more enduring than the old.

But the new freedom—that of choice in marriage (which the authorities try to ensure) and the right to divorce—becomes in the setting of the village a strongly puritanical force. Even if the old secretary is worried lest the enemy slander their ways ("The upper classes still tell lies about us"), this worry is more significant for the village than the slander is for the "enemy."

> Nowadays divorce is very rare. There having been no free choice of partner under the old system, there was a sudden rush of divorces when the new order began. But that is a thing of the past. If there are children, people think it immoral and wicked to leave them. Even if the marriage is childless, people still consider divorce immoral, because now that people can choose whom they will marry,

80

they will have chosen each other and should put up with the consequences. One can always adopt a child . . . proceedings for a divorce . . . has not yet happened in Liu Ling, nor have any divorces been heard of in the neighboring villages for many years, for it is a long time now since women have been granted equality and marriages have been entered into voluntarily.

Freedom becomes an obligation: "They will have chosen . . . and should put up with the consequences." The idea would not have been foreign to a New England settler. The right to love and the freedom of love become one thing in an urban middle-class environment in Europe and something quite different in an Asian village. The new freedom for women becomes the full expression of peasant morality—with the need for stable family groups of working members. The puritanism of the village is not something enforced by the government. Rather the village puritanism now molds the government.

Our press now and then reports that one or another Chinese paper has written about revolutionary purity. We quote writings about soldiers who, with pure hearts, sing revolutionary songs and abstain from contaminating luxuries. This says something about China. But Western laughter says more about us. My revivalist great-grandparents in any case would not have understood why Swedish readers are expected to laugh. Puritanism is closely bound to peasant traditions and village needs. And security becomes social inside a puritan framework. This transition, too, can be stated in terms we rarely use in our countries except on formal occasions. A peasant in Liu Ling whose neighbor is old and ill and poor is expected to understand that if he asked: "Am I my brother's keeper?", the village would answer: "Thou art."

The changing role of women, of course, leads to conflict between generations. Li Kuei-ying said:

> . . . the old women find it difficult to understand that nowadays women laugh and joke with the men. They scold their daughters and daughters-in-law and grand-

81

daughters for not observing decent behavior. When that happens we have to speak with the old women about the equality of the sexes. . . . But in their heart of hearts they always feel uneasy and uncertain when they see girls joking with men. But we are patient with the old people. They can't help their attitude. Perhaps not all old women are like that, but most, I'm sure, think it indecent and immoral and shocking that young people talk with each other. The young people, of course, are all agreed. None of the young people think like the old ones on this question. So it will solve itself in time.

And the problem of freedom of choice in marriage is not just an abstract question. Li Kuei-ying told of one case:

> . . . Tuan Fu-yin's eighteen-year-old daughter, Tuan Ai-chen, fell in love with a boy from Seven-mile Village. But her parents refused to let her marry. They said the boy was poor and that they wanted to marry her to somebody better off. One evening Tuan Ai-chen came to me and wept and complained. I went with her to her cave and talked with her parents. I said to them: "You have no right to prevent your daughter from marrying . . ." Tuan Fu-yin tried to stand up to me. He said: "I had to pay dearly for my wife. Now I have been giving this girl food and clothes. I have brought her up and she just goes off. It isn't right. I just lose and lose all the time. I must get back something of all the money I have laid out on her. If she can't fall in love with a man who can pay back what she's cost, then it isn't right for her to marry." . . .

There is much to be said for Tuan Fu-yin. Even though the marriages are voluntary now, they of course still tend to be voluntarily arranged.

The young women who have been swept along in this new movement of liberation do not have an easy path; even enthusiasm does not fundamentally change the old ways. Li Kuei-ying came back to the village from the party school in 1951. She had learned how to read and write:

. . . in the winter I began organizing the women to study. . . . I told them all how good it was to be able to read and write; that she who could read could see; and she who couldn't was blind. That winter I taught ten women to read and write a hundred characters each. . . . They have gone on with it since, but it has been difficult for them. They can't read much more now after ten years, though I have been working with them the whole time.

And when Ching Chi, an intellectual from Sian who had been in Liu Ling for voluntary labor during thirteen months, was criticized before leaving:

I was told that I had said that I would teach the leaders of the women's group to write and read, but when it came to it, I had only been able to teach one of them to read.

Despite great efforts in education and literacy campaigns, my impression was that only the generation now going to school would become literate. This of course makes progress slower than was hoped for in the early days of the revolution.

In this situation the birth control campaigns become questions of women's rights and public health:

We have continued our work with hygiene and public health all the time. . . . We instruct them (the women) in birth control and contraceptive methods. . . . Birth control is primarily a question of propaganda. Firstly many say: "We want to have more children"; secondly, after all, birth control is voluntary. . . . In certain families with lots of children, the women would like birth control, but their husbands won't. In those families the husbands say: "There's not going to be any family planning here!" Then we women go to them and try to talk sense into them. We say: "Look how many children you have. Your wife looks after the household and sees to the children and she makes shoes and clothes for both you and the children, but you don't think of all she has to do or of her

83

health but just make her with child again and again." . . .
But there are, too, families where both husband and wife
agreed that they want to have children all the time. We
can't do anything there. The whole thing is voluntary.
The chief thing is to have a healthy family, and that the
mother feels all right.

The discussion of birth control is conducted not in political
or economic terms, but in moral terms. Speaking about cases
where the woman wanted birth control but the husband
continued to refuse, Li Kuei-ying said:

Then we women speak to him every day, till he agrees
to birth control. No husband has yet managed to stand
out for any length of time when we are talking to him.
Actually, of course, they know that we are right. They
know, of course, that they are responsible. It's only their
pride that stands in the way, and we have to tell them that
such a pride is false and not all right.

This puritan, moral approach to life is a part of the liberation
of women. In the long run this change in the social function
of women together with the slow change from familial to
social security can—and will if China is not a victim of large
agricultural catastrophies—lead to the strengthening of the
small family, the final break-up of the large family, and a
reduced birth rate.

Viewing the reshaping from this angle—one that, by being
outside the usual framework, saves us from our own conditioned ideological reflexes—we will see that the situation is
fundamentally different for the intellectuals, the administrators,
the engineers and skilled workers. For them both the government's needs and their own social situations call for family
limitation.

One point in the (theologically expressed but nonetheless
real) conflict between the Soviet CP and the Chinese CP
has been the Russian accusation that the Chinese Communists
have fallen into un-Marxist and bourgeois errors by their
attitude towards voluntary sterilization.

The social need for limiting the families of these groups of

84

intellectuals is evident. A large part of the meager resources of China must go to education. If China is to survive, the country must quickly get a whole new generation of engineers, administrators, skilled workers, and scientists. The investment in each such student is equivalent to the surplus of a whole village like Liu Ling. If this investment is to be productive, the new educated generation has to work hard: Hence the accent on duty instead of private love and raising a family. It becomes immoral to enter into early marriages. Where villagers marry at eighteen, intellectuals tend to marry at twenty-four to twenty-eight. This has two effects. One is that the intellectuals, with slight success, try to spread the idea of late marriages even in the villages, where early marriages satisfy an economic need. The other is that the puritanism of the intellectuals gets overtones that the village puritanism does not have. In the villages they marry rather soon after sexual maturity. The intellectuals are forced into a situation—not unknown in our cultures—of having to repress their sexuality during their whole youth. This makes their puritanism more feverish—and often much less realistic.

For a girl to leave her work after having got an education just in order to raise a family would be thoroughly immoral, a sign of personal weakness and truly antisocial behavior. I too would consider it antisocial, because, whatever my ideas about Utopian society, I cannot see how in the economic situation of China early marriage by students could be reconciled with the needs of the country. Puritanism is no choice: it is a necessity.

For these groups the new contraceptive techniques, voluntary sterilization, pills and other methods, carry meaning. According to Sture Källberg (*Kamrat med 700 miljoner*, Ab Rabén och Sjögren, Stockholm, 1964) in the rubber factory of Canton 3,200,000 condoms were produced monthly in 1963, and the production was to increase by 50 per cent in 1964. Counting in a Lutheran fashion this means that 400,000 couples in 1963 and 600,000 couples in 1964 were supplied from Canton. According to the same source the production cost for each condom was 3.6 *fen*. The retail price even in Liu Ling was 3 *fen*. The state was subsidizing the sale of contraceptives. More clearly, the peasants were subsidizing the contraceptives used by the administrators, engineers and skilled workers. I said, "in a Lutheran fashion." That was not meant to be a joke. The puritanical background remains. The marriages are late, but society does not encourage celibacy: "It is better to marry than to burn."

The puritanical values of this group are different from those of the older scholars. In some cases—the role of women, the role of the family—they seem antithetical. But at the same time, by stressing still more strongly the social responsibility of the individual, the values of social thrift, self-abnegation, hard work, honesty, they are inside the classical tradition of Chinese values.

A Chinese intellectual, a writer who had lived and become well-known abroad, said:

> We had a small dog. We loved it. The neighbors wrote on our door that the dog was fed with chicken every day. That was not true. But it did eat. And people were hungry. We killed the dog and we all cried. It hurt very much. But it was correct. Do I have the right to give food for my private enjoyment when there are people who need the food? Am I a man worth so much more than other men? It is a very difficult thing to remold one's thinking. But it is necessary. If I do not do it I have to accept that I do not belong. That I consider myself a superior being. What right have I to do that?

That the puritanism of the intellectuals is of a different order than that of the peasants could have dangerous social effects. Among the peasants social forces motivate for large families, early marriages and working children (it still is a certain problem to get children to school—as it was fifty years ago in Sweden); among the intellectuals social forces motivate for late marriages, small families and school-going children. The situation could easily get out of hand. The intellectuals still have privileges—not only subsidized contraceptives—which are intimately bound to their social role. These privileges could easily take on material form and become institutionalized.

It is not without reason that the Chinese political leaders time upon time utter warnings against the possibility of a cleavage in Chinese society. Especially at a time when the number of engineers and scientists is rising—has to rise— sharply, such a development could lead to the establishment of a new, highly privileged group of "scholars," administrator-bureaucrats. The weight of Chinese tradition is on the side of such a development. In China—as in most Asian countries —the gap between peasant and scholar has always been wide. But unlike India, in time the gap could be bridged. There were periods of social mobility. The scion of the peasant could— in theory and often in practice—rise to the highest posts. But once there the gap between him and the peasants would seem unbridgeable. This gap could once more open during a phase of new social mobility.

Now, if one does not consider an egalitarian society to be the primary social goal, one could say that this might be an interesting problem for the Chinese Communists, but that it only proves that social development follows other laws than those the Chinese Communists have adopted as social laws. One could say that such a gap is only natural in a developing country. A Russian could say that "material incentive" is necessary for building a country. I could point out that incomes in Sweden were being equalized between 1912 and 1948, but that the gap widened between 1948 and 1965, coinciding with a general increase of productivity that increased living standards and gave a much higher level of minimum security. I believe the reasoning to be false (even on the Swedish level—but that is quite a different story). It does not take the real situation in which China finds itself into account.

The economic needs of China are tremendous. Even if the international situation were quite different, it is unlikely that the capital could be supplied from abroad. (The United States and, to a certain extent, Sweden were developed by capital investment from Europe and capital import in the form of skilled manpower.) In the final analysis the responsibility for supplying capital rests on the peasant of China. His productivity is low. To accumulate capital means a long period of "hard work and plain living," to use the words the Chinese use. Every political mistake, every bad harvest can cost years of work. If the gap really widened between the "scholars" and the peasants, this could mean the end of any possibility for economic development. It would result in misery and famine. Talk of propaganda, brainwashing and political control should not hide the truth that the peasants can, more or less willingly, bear heavy burdens as long as they generally are convinced that there is a rational motivation for those burdens, that society is "honest." The Stalinist road of squeezing capital out of the peasantry by force is impossible, partly because there is so little to be squeezed out and partly because the danger of peasant unrest is so much greater than it was in Russia during the thirties.

China can only develop if the peasants actively strive for increased production. After these years of peasant war, international war, civil war, and revolution, they would not bear this burden if they became thoroughly convinced that they were only carrying a new group of "scholars" on their backs. A widening gap would lead to peasant unrest, to revolt, to the end of capital formation on the village level. And, as we know, that capital formation is already dangerously low.

The main economic question is thus not that China can "afford" to provide some hundred thousand refrigerators for the higher echelons of the administration. That could easily be done without materially changing the economic picture. But politically China cannot do it. The repercussions could be serious. Equality thus takes on the form of a continuous moral struggle: "Thou shalt. . . ."

There is one more factor: disrespect for manual work is traditional among the Chinese intellectuals, as it is in all poor countries. This has been—and is—one of the great impediments to technological and economic development. The Scandinavian and Yankee tradition is different, a difference that

88

came out of a struggle against European "aristocratic thought." It might be good to reread Mark Twain: *A Connecticut Yankee in King Arthur's Court* to recapture the spirit of this:

> . . . So I am a Yankee of the Yankees—and practical, yes, and nearly barren of sentiment, I suppose—or poetry in other words. My father was a blacksmith, my uncle was a horsedoctor, and I was both, along at first. Then I went over to the great arms factory and learned my real trade; learned all there was to it; learned to make everything: guns, revolvers, cannon, boilers, engines, all sorts of labor-saving machinery. Why, I could make anything a body wanted—anything in the world, it didn't make any difference what, and if there wasn't any quick new-fangled way to make a thing, I could invent one—and do it as easy as rolling off a log.

In China, the scholar must change to an intellectual having knowledge of, and thus respect for and power over, manual work. At the same time he must become this new type of intellectual in a strictly puritanical and social setting. This change is necessary if China is to develop, as Gandhi saw that it was necessary for India.

These two factors, the necessity for equality and the necessity for a new type of intellectual, have been the rational motives for the remolding. And in the economic and traditional situation of China this remolding becomes a moral shift, a change of values, a puritanization. Ching Chi said:

> After the winter harvest was in, that was December 1959, there was less work in the fields. That is the time of year when life in the country quiets down and people occupy themselves with minor jobs. We then embarked on serious criticism and self-criticism. For two months we kept at this and held discussions about it. We went through each one's faults and judged whether they had corrected them and how. We probed into ourselves and examined each other and tried to get at the bottom of all our personal problems and each of our incorrect attitudes to life and work. Sometimes, these meetings lasted half a day, and we

went on day after day. Altogether we had seventy or more meetings. This meant that each of us in the group was analyzed and corrected for anything up to fifty hours. . . . Often enough the criticism hurt, but it helped. . . . You know the old person has to go, so that the new can emerge and take her place.

I believe that this shaping of young intellectuals ("The old person has to go so that the new can emerge") is far more important to China than the more spectacular remoldings of former generals or of the "Emperor" of Manchukuo. We ought to understand why it takes on this intensely—nearly religiously —puritanical form. But also to understand that the process is necessary if China is to survive.

There is every possibility that China will fail. The icy international climate has shut her out from contacts with large parts of the world. The new and remolded intellectuals who now have to take over may, through lack of knowledge, steer the country in a dangerous foreign policy course. The People's Communes, which are able to utilize China's only capital, manpower, even during the slack season, might prove unable to produce enough grain. The population growth might outrun the increase in production—and thus lead to an increase in birth rate and so either lead to increased hunger—and catastrophe —or severe authoritarian measures against the peasantry in order to check the increasing birth rate, which will inevitably lead to peasant risings—and catastrophe. The strong puritanical framework that has been erected might break, since the generation now taking over has no memory of the heroic times of the Long March and the civil war. That would—as the economy is strained and the possibility of failure always present—in its turn lead to catastrophe. On the other hand puritanism itself, by becoming a rigid framework, might make the Chinese policy less pliable and thus once more lead towards catastrophe. The choice of the Chinese government— any Chinese government—is severely limited.

One might object that all this may be correct, but that there are other types of economic development. A free enterprise system could save China. I am not so sure. Capital, after all, has to come from somewhere. Capital formation on a private property basis in an agricultural country like China does not easily lead to economic growth, but rather to capital flight and landlordism. But even if the accumulated capital were to be invested inside the country in productive enterprises—and not only in conspicuous consumption—it would mean that equality would be broken, the heaviest burdens would be shifted to parts of the population. Not only would that make England of 1830 look like a paradise by comparison; it is also doubtful whether that burden could be carried in the general poverty of China. And even if it could, the harsh social conflicts that would ensue would inevitably lead to a government still more authoritarian than the present, presumably a military government ruling directly with might.

Western experts on contemporary China gleefully report its failings, but I have never been able to understand what they are expecting. After all, a breakdown in China is the breakdown of nearly a quarter of the world's population. It is possible. But if it occurs it is a catastrophe not only for China.

SOCIAL TRANSFORMATION IN CHINA

Han Suyin

THE TRANSFORMATION of a social group or community is a many-sided affair, involving changes on both material and psychological planes. This predicates not only a change in the means of production, but an irreversible process of change in attitudes towards many arbitrary or accepted "values." It is this process which took place in Europe at the Renaissance and during the Industrial Revolution; it is now taking place in China.

But whereas the process of change, from feudalistic means of production and modes of behavior and beliefs to capitalistic ones, took place in a haphazard fashion in many Western countries, in China today the process of transformation is a conscious, aware, and deliberately wished for reshaping. It employs, therefore, the highest concentration of both self-conscious planning on the philosophical and material scales, as well as the greatest demand in self-awareness and spontaneous, wilful self-remolding in the social group involved. It is this double, interlocking evolution, a deliberate, speeded advance towards what is regarded as a higher stage in the evolution of mankind which is the theme of China's revolution.

This conscious speeding up of a process of physical and spir-

93

itual awareness, the self-changing of a whole society, involving in this instance one-quarter of mankind, is a phenomenon of such import that its implications cannot be ignored. It is based upon the most fundamental attribute of Man, that which distinguishes the conscious, purposeful human being from the unconscious nonhuman: the learning aptitude. It presumes also that Man is perfectible and can evolve into a higher form of himself. The implications of such a process, not left to chance but taken in hand and made conscious and purposeful, are enormous for humanity itself.

Physical Changes

The processes of physical change are usually the most obvious and the ones most widely accepted in the world today. We all speak of "modernization" and of "industrialization"; we all accept the fact that two-thirds of the world is lagging behind in the attainment of scientific techniques and their application to production, to the lives of individuals as well as to the nations involved. These countries are usually spoken of as "undeveloped" or "underdeveloped," terms which obfuscate the necessity of keeping in mind that physical change, unless accompanied by a thorough educational process, will remain only surface application of techniques and will not thoroughly penetrate, remold, and change the attitudes and behavior of large masses of the population involved. On a substratum of superstition, ignorance, and feudalistic reactions, there will then be grafted in a few cities some "industrial achievements," such as factories, airports, etc.; this will only emphasize the complete dichotomy between a small elite or "educated" upper class, cognizant of and habituated to modern techniques and modes of thinking, and a large mass, the greater number of the population, still living in the Middle Ages as far as physical standards and spiritual attitudes are concerned.

To turn China from a feudal, backward, impoverished state to a modern, industrialized socialist state with a modern economy, was one of the avowed aims of the Communist revolution when it came to triumph in 1949. The last sixteen years have seen development toward this aim; and although no one in the government in Peking today would claim that this is entirely accomplished, as Edgar Snow has pointed out in his interviews with Chinese leaders, they figure that it will take China at least another fifty to one hundred years to become a thoroughly modern, industrialized, technically advanced state in the modern sense of the word. Yet it is obvious to even the most superficial observer that everywhere in China—and not only in a few cities—the signs of putting into gear the whole of the material production of the country for an ultimate break-through into a modern industrial economy are present.

Collectivization, Electrification, Modernization of Agriculture

Taking due account of experimental errors which, however, measured against achievements, cannot be deemed fundamental, this aim has been steadily pushed by concentrating upon the agricultural 80 per cent of the population, their means of production and livelihood, their education, and the gearing of industrial potential to their needs and advancement.

Collectivization of agriculture, ending in the commune system, has been achieved after fifteen years, and terminates in a workable, decentralized, yet controllable system. That this system has its weaknesses is recognized, but that it is the correct way in China to achieve the ultimate aims—electrification of the countryside, control of irrigation, increase in productivity, retooling and mechanization, and ultimately an increase in cultivated land and food production with a decrease in the total and percentual population employed in agriculture—is also becoming evident. Its successes have now been consolidated by the organization of a financial banking and credit network covering every commune. The operation of a credit system, governed by the workpoint, which is the intermediate between the crude labor estimate and its financial equivalent, is proving satisfactory. It has also had its effect in changing the attitudes of both men and women in the countryside towards the valuation of their own labor, and has resulted in bringing into circulation both money and consumer goods among the bulk of the population, thus turning millions of peasants, for the first time, into moneyed consumers.

The commune system has permitted large-scale projects of irrigation, combatting floods, constructing dikes on rivers and damming reservoirs; it has allowed for a greater and more efficient exploitation of available resources, and the opening up of new ones. It is also laying the groundwork for more adequate systems of distribution of goods and transport, for the mechanization of tools, and for electrification. The most striking visual image of these improvements is conveyed by the number of electric pumps now in use, and also the lathes in the small factories and flour mills which are found in the communes.

The designing of improved tools, the production of farm equipment and machinery, the erection of fertilizer plants, together with improved and better usage of natural fertilizers, have made for more efficient output on the cultivated land already in use. The Third Five-Year Plan, promulgated this year, does not envisage an increased area put under cultivation so much as increased attention to efficiency and output on the land already under cultivation, which altogether amounts to 13 per cent of the area of the country. Another 15 per cent can be cultivated, and these virgin lands will no doubt be utilized in the coming decades; but the government estimates that self-sufficiency within the next decade can be reached with the area now under cultivation, and no great increase in area of cultivated land is envisaged at the moment.

With the introduction of the commune system, formation of accumulation funds (capital formation) in the countryside is now possible. Freed from the land rent, from onerous and multiple taxes which were current until 1949, and also from the burden of usury, the peasant communes plan their production and accumulate money and reserves. Apart from an agricultural tax of 7 per cent (sometimes only 4 to 5 per cent, when it involves perishable goods whose turnover is quick, such as suburban communes producing quick-spoiling fruit), the central authority does not levy other taxes in money: it buys the production quota of the commune at a stated and fixed price; out of this sum, which is the revenue of the commune, the cost of agricultural production, amounting to about 20 per cent, is met, and the welfare and capital accumulation funds are replenished. The commune utilizes about 40 per cent of its income on its running expenses: of this, 5 per cent is kept as a reserve; the remaining 60 per cent must be paid out to the members of the commune as remuneration for work done.

The labor value of the individual family is estimated by the number of workpoints accumulated by the individuals in the family. In this system there is equal remuneration for the male and female worker, depending only on the amount of work done, and in general families like their workpoints to be totaled: husband, wife, older children, grandparents, all pitching in to accumulate workpoints. The establishment of the value of the workpoint is done by common agreement and consensus, arrived at in open general meetings of all the members of the production teams. This provides for a basic democracy within the commune which was not possible under the old system of exploitation.

New Attitudes and Liberation

The importance attached to spiritual transformation is not alien to Chinese culture: the whole of Chinese civilization is founded precisely on the idea of the perfectibility of man, of his becoming "civilized" through an educational process, of an ultimate "better" man who will come into mankind's full heritage through wisdom, understanding, and the practice of brotherhood.

The word "education," therefore, in the Chinese language, is not restricted, as it has become in other cultures, to the acquisition of technical skills designed to make a living, but comprises the Renaissance idea of the "whole man," including

97

moral behavior; attitudes towards fellow men, relatives, parents, and country; public responsibility; and so forth.

This process, it is stressed, is inseparable from the more obvious process of the banishment of illiteracy. It is spoken of as "the liberation of the mind." After fifteen years it is possible to survey what has been done in this dual aspect of enlightenment.

Campaigns against illiteracy, or rather nonliteracy, which affected 90 per cent of the population, have been a prominent feature of the new regime's educational policies. But these campaigns are not only drives to teach reading and writing; they are also extended, especially within the last two years, to reinforce what is called "socialist education," a combined political-moral-social-ethical reshaping of attitudes.

The eradication of the feudal mind is not an easy process; it is a multisided one. It means getting the masses away from the anchored belief that natural calamities are "fixed by heaven" and that therefore nothing can be done to remedy one's lot; it means teaching and making acceptable the scientific explanations of such phenomena as rain, floods, typhoons, and disease, not as a mark of the displeasure of the gods but as part of the geographical, climatic components, which can be controlled or alleviated by the will and the combined efforts of mankind. All that is rational and accepted in Western society is by no means known or accepted as logical and evident in a feudal society; to bridge the gap between scientific, modern man and feudal man, the prey of superstition, and to do it within the compass of one generation, is a formidable task.

It is this process—providing a rational, scientific explanation for what had been regarded as the wrath of the gods, or immutable—which is also known as "education." It has its political overtones, of course: it is brought in evidence that it is the Communist Party, under Chairman Mao, which puts to flight the old ignorance and replaces it with knowledge, and especially with the will and the power to control the processes of nature and men's destinies, rather than to be controlled by forces beyond the power of mankind.

Moral education, which is not distinguished from political education in that it is spoken of as "socialist morality," is as important as the acquisition of technical knowledge. With centuries of despotism and corruption, with habits of sloth, nepotism, and venality in the very recent past, a complete moral rehabilitation of the attitudes associated with power or knowledge had to be undertaken: not only the reform of one class, but even down to the grassroots, the peasant level. For centuries the peasant had regarded officialdom with feelings of hatred, terror, but also of envy: to become an official, to have a son educated to become an official, seemed to him the acme of success; and when universal education became available, the danger of creating a new class of literates, who in turn despise and oppress the working people, was evident.

The Communist regime in China applied itself to this problem energetically. We can arbitrarily divide its action into three planes: (1) rectification campaigns among Party members themselves; (2) remolding and re-education of the intellectual class; (3) education and socialist morality campaigns among the workers and peasants.

I have personally counted four large rectification campaigns among the Party members since 1950, although I shall not detail them here. The remolding and re-education of intellectuals has attracted most attention in the West. The main theme of this re-education into socialist morality—to do away with venality and especially with the tremendous superiority complex, with its attendant grotesque vanity, of the "mandarin scholars"—has been through rehabilitation of the dignity of manual labor.

Manual labor, employed as a means of socialist education and re-education of intellectuals, must be viewed in the context of China. It is impressive to understand the profound contempt and revulsion towards physical labor which animated the educated in China and is still found among the educated in India, Africa, and other regions of the world. I have always contended that in this respect, the middle classes in Western nations have enjoyed one advantage: manual work, in one form or another, has never been considered below the status of an individual to perform, as it has in Asia, as it is still among the Westernized elites of the new African nations. This conditioned complex takes the most excessive forms: doctors will refuse to lift an accident case in the street in Nigeria; in India and Pakistan the sight of hideously mutilated beggars on the street awakens no compassion in the breasts of educated intellectuals; in factories in certain countries trained engineers refuse to dirty their hands manipulating the engines. I know a trained pathologist who refused to perform postmortems and had them performed by "coolies" under his eyes, while he pointed from a distance with a stick at the organs to be opened and inspected.

The establishment of the notion of the dignity of labor, physical labor, was to become and remains the main preoccupation of the Chinese leadership. The inculcation of the principle of manual work as part of education forms a most important part in the moral-political-sociological behavior change. Manual labor, started early on in the 1950s, has now become an accepted pattern of life, an integral part of the new education system, known as the part-work part-study system.

Part-Work Part-Study System

The thorough reform of the educational system has been contemplated for some years, but it got its real start in 1964. As usual, a period of trial and error preceded it. By January 1966, when I interviewed the educational authorities, a large-scale scheme was already functioning. It was emphasized that there were still many shortcomings, but that these were small in comparison with the main successes.

It was in 1958 that a plan for education on a wide-ranging scope and conforming to the concrete situation—that of an agricultural country, in the shortest time possible, pulling itself out of backward feudalism into economically advanced, modern socialism—was first enacted. But it was in 1964 that a real start was made. The slowing down was due to the "three bad

100

years" suffered by the country as a whole from 1959 to 1962.

The first institutes organized along the part-work part-study schemes were in Tientsin and Shanghai in connection with factory areas. A vast number of workers and workers' children could be educated, but at the same time this education could become part of their training for factory work or technical and engineering skills, with the factory as training and experimental laboratory. These institutes having proved successful, the scheme is now extended to agricultural areas. As a result there are now two Education Ministries: one is the Higher Education Ministry (for universities, high grade colleges and institutes, higher research institutes, etc.), and one is for Ordinary Education (below and up to university standard).

The part-agricultural-work part-study primary agricultural school is the basic educational unit for the peasantry in the communes, the grassroots instrument of political and technical training as well as behavioral change.

In these new-type schools, both factory and agricultural, the processes of work and of education are dovetailed. To the communes and to the factories also go the university students, lecturers, and professors to labor and to keep in touch with the bulk of the population. I have interviewed university professors who some years ago would not have dreamed of working in a field, but who now look forward eagerly to a month in the country. "I only began to learn how my own people lived the first time I went down to the fields, and I was astonished that for so long I had remained so ignorant of the true conditions in my own country," one of these, a Western-educated professor of physics, said to me.

And finally, by this part-work part-study scheme, the cost of education to the commune, factory, region, province, and ultimately to the state is much reduced. Many of these part-work part-study schools in agricultural regions become almost self-sufficient in the production of basic foodstuffs, vegetables, etc. The cost of transport is also reduced.

This restoration of the dignity of manual labor, and the link it creates between book knowledge and actual practice, the

101

emphasis on "experiment" by testing theory against practice away from the ancient abstractions, promote a scientific turn of mind in these schools. "Let us try" and "Nothing is impossible" are now common slogans.

Socialist Debate

The first few years of Communist rule in China were characterized by meetings at every level. These meetings partook of the character of emotional revivals, in that people were criticized, and encouraged to criticize themselves, the whole emphasis being on a moral and spiritual awareness, confessions of past misdeeds, repentance, and the emergence of "new men and women," purified through self-confession and awareness, and ready to become better human beings. However repugnant all this may seem to a Western mind, the time was not so long ago when the same things happened in western Europe, but with religious, rather than moral and political, emphasis. But one component which has gradually emerged in the Chinese meetings is the debating or argumentative aspect.

The value of these get-togethers has been to break down the walls of "face" and concealment, to bring out in the open misdemeanors which could not otherwise have been dealt with, above all to provide platforms for defense as well, which did not exist in Old China either. To say that these meetings are wholly one-sided would be wrong. The authoritarian attitude was not only rooted in the feudal mind, but very often was exemplified by the attitudes of the Communist cadres themselves, and the encouragement of the population to speak up has led in the last few years to repeated exhortations to the cadres to abstain from "commandism, not listening to the people, judging arbitrarily and impulsively."

Since 1963 a great deal more attention is being paid to "criticism from the masses"; an increasing trend towards debate as such is manifest. The picture of a monolithic, rigid, authoritarian dictatorship, to be obeyed without dispute, is not quite what emerges from a close study of the newspapers and the

102

journals from China. My feeling is that to indoctrinate a whole people with the habit of analytic, scientific, and dispassionate argument is a task which will take many years, with many ups and downs. But a proper perspective on "education in debate" concerning China must also be established in the West. It should, for instance, be pointed out that in its theoretical disputes—disputes on Marxist-Leninist theory and practice with the Soviet Union—the Chinese government has gone to the length of printing *in toto* all the speeches, sayings, etc. of Khrushchev, "to educate the people in what revisionism is." This does not quite fit into the picture of blind indoctrination.

It is claimed that within the last fifteen years the power of thinking, of grasping scientific detail and analysis, has been considerably augmented among the population. The encouragement to study Mao Tse-tung's works is not only in order to reinforce political attitudes, but also to promulgate scientific analysis.

The setting up of "heroes" is also part of this deliberate creation of an atmosphere, a climate of high endeavor and morality.

The breaking down of old modes of thought is to be achieved not only on the private and group scale, not only within the national framework, but internationally as well.

In this respect, the treatment of China's national minorities, of which there are some thirty, comprising about 50 million people within the boundaries of China, may be mentioned. The minorities were always subject to persecution and discrimination in China before 1949. Today they are given particular attention in autonomous regions, their cultures sustained and maintained. For instance, the unofficial interdiction against Han Chinese males marrying the women of minority areas is terse from the previous impression created by the kidnapping and ill treatment of minority women by Kuomintang officials. In some regions of Szechuan province, women of the Miao minority used to be sold for a sack of rice. These memories go deep and are not easily eradicated.

Great Han chauvinism and racialism are severely discour-

103

aged; although cases may still occur, they are minimal, deemed relics of the feudal past to be eradicated.

The emphasis on the "international duty" of the Chinese people towards the "two-thirds of humanity still suffering exploitation" is also a prominent phase of the past two years. In several communes I have come across exhortation to achieve habits of thrift, work, and frugality "for the two-thirds of humanity." The repeated statements of the Chinese leaders that China will "fulfill her international duty" are also to be envisaged in that context.

To teach people to think objectively, scientifically, philosophically, dialectically; to teach the use of abstract thought in its concrete applications; to renovate morality; to inculcate responsibility and good citizenship; to teach modesty, frugality, outspokenness, fearlessness: all this is summed up as "Follow and study the thinking and teaching of Mao Tse-tung." All this is to produce another kind of motivation than that based on "face" and "prestige," or "money" and "advancement." "Doctors who go to the countryside to practice must learn that it is in the praise of their community, their affection and esteem, that lies their highest reward," said a doctor to me, a doctor once head of a large city hospital, and now on a tour of a remote area of the country.

The transformation and reshaping of Chinese society is a twofold process of change, both material and spiritual, the one interacting with and influencing the other; both are cumulative, and become self-propelled by the process of an extended education which never dissociates the abstract from the concrete, the moral and spiritual from the material. Liberation of the mind is to be the essential concomitant of physical liberation, for one cannot exist without the other. The revolution to make China a modern, scientific socialist state goes hand in hand with a cultural revolution which will transform the attitudes and motivations of 700 million for the better.

CONTEMPORARY CHINESE HEALTH, MEDICAL PRACTICE AND PHILOSOPHY

G. L. Willox

WHEAT SALES to China, for several years a major customer for Canadian wheat, have greatly assisted the economy of western Canada. In the fall of 1964, the Farmers' Union of Alberta organized a good-will tour to China with a view to maintaining and fostering trade relationships. A group of thirty-two Canadians, mostly heads of farm organizations and farm cooperatives, were invited by the China Council for the Promotion of International Trade to Peking to attend the fifteenth anniversary celebration of the founding of the People's Republic of China. Although I am not a farmer, I had the privilege of accompanying the group.

I went out of curiosity. I knew little or nothing about this country, comprising one-quarter of the world's population, and I had the impression that much of what I was reading in the press and in magazines was not entirely within the realm of truth. We visited the major cities of China, factories, steel mills, kindergartens, high schools, universities, and six or seven communes. In addition to having a "cram course" in farming, I was able to visit seven or eight medical establishments, observe surgical operations, and see for myself the many and varied facets of contemporary Chinese health and medical practices.

I realize fully that a visitor to China cannot pose as an expert on that country. He can see what the present regime in China has done for its own people, but he cannot answer the most pertinent question of all: What are China's aims in relation to the rest of the world?

We were impressed by the extreme friendliness of the people, which we had no right to expect considering the shabby fashion in which our forebears treated the Chinese. We were overwhelmed at the Peking station by a reception, with bands and bouquets of flowers. Charles Taylor, the Peking correspondent of the *Toronto Globe and Mail*, told us that for one week before our arrival rumors had spread through Peking that a group of Canadian peasants were on their way to join in the October 1 celebration marking the fifteenth anniversary of the revolution, which in China was a peasant revolution. Apparently in Chinese a farmer is a peasant. Mr. Taylor told us that in spite of the fact we looked more like a who's who of Western Canada, he still would say "Welcome peasants."

I found conditions in China far better than I had been led to believe. I saw no evidence of malnutrition or starvation. We were impressed by the youth and by the enthusiasm of the managers of factories, plants, and communes. They date everything from the Liberation, a term which they use incessantly, referring to October 1, 1949. At that time China closed its doors to clean up the internal corruption and stop the exploitation by all outside countries. The Chinese found themselves without very many trained or educated people, but they have come a long way in the last fifteen or sixteen years. They have the highest moral code of any nation I have ever visited. Their honesty is almost pathological; we never locked our hotel room doors and lost nothing. We had difficulty in disposing of used articles such as empty cigar holders, and so on, as these were returned to us on the station platform. One of our group dropped a Canadian one-cent piece in the station at Peking, and it was returned to us in Shanghai as we were the only

Canadian group in China at the time. In our travels throughout China we were always asked what we wanted to see. To my knowledge we were not denied anything.

Medicine and Medical Training

My first encounter with Chinese medicine was in the hotel in Peking. Some of the group visited a young woman doctor in the hotel because of chest colds which they had picked up on the train. They received expensive antibiotics, drugs largely of French origin; both the drugs and the professional advice were free of charge. It was the same type of overtreatment of minor complaints that Canadians administer to their distinguished visitors. I do not know how the ordinary native would be treated for similar complaints. During the October 1 parade, this same doctor set up a first-aid station along the parade route to look after any of the crowd who might be overcome by the long standing. The parade was one of the most spectacular and colorful performances I have ever seen, with 750,000 people, between 100 and 150 abreast, marching for two and one-half hours. Following the parade groups of men and women with brooms cleared up the litter and debris. The streets are as clean as any I have ever seen. The Chinese are extremely conscious of health and sanitation. Masks are frequently seen on the street, worn by people with coughs and colds.

I visited the Peking Medical College. As on my other official visits to a plant and a commune, there was a brief introduction. The director told me of the great increase in student enrollment, staff, and teaching facilities that had occurred since the time of Liberation. Students have a six-year course which, in essence, is similar to our own, with the addition of courses in politics and traditional Chinese medicine. The director said it was desirable that the students be both "red and expert." By red, he meant politically conscious and loyal to the cause.

Political indoctrination is a part of all Chinese education, from kindergarten through high school, university, and even medical school. I have some doubts about the value of spending so much time on political studies at the medical school level. It might result in my profession taking a more active role in politics, even if just to defend ourselves from the constant encroachment of government. Yet adherence to a central party line creates an atmosphere of conformity which, in my opinion, is less desirable than one of independence and originality.

I visited the classrooms and laboratories in the basic science buildings. They were very well equipped, and the training appeared to be very similar to our own. In the Neuroanatomy Department they showed me excellent slides and preparations and told me that Dr. Wilder Penfield of the Montreal Neurological Institute had visited their laboratory about two months before.

In Chinese medicine and in medical training, great emphasis is placed on public health and preventive medicine. Disease was a major problem in China, and they have accomplished a great deal in preventing the large epidemics. The infant mortality rate has dropped until it now is similar to our own. Cholera, smallpox, typhoid, typhus, and venereal disease have been almost eliminated. Schistosomiasis, a parasitic infection seen chiefly in southern tropical China, has been brought under control. Human excrement is processed to make it safe before it is used on the fields. The doctors are well trained in public health matters, but their efforts would be useless without the intensive radio propaganda and group talks to enlighten and direct the entire population in a mass program of health and sanitation consciousness. Chinese methods in this field could be followed by the rest of the world.

I visited several of the newer hospitals in Peking. The number of available beds has increased tremendously. The wards were bright and airy and a little austere by our standards as far as the frills and conveniences were concerned. The medical care was excellent. Charting was identical to our own. On the general surgical ward I found the kinds of operations and the pre-operative and post-operative care almost the same as in my own practice. The instruments were from many European countries, as well as from Shanghai. The whole routine and environment was such that I felt right at home and thought I could have carried on a surgical practice in any one of their hospitals without changing my pace or taking time out to get accustomed to a different situation. Local anesthesia is used a little more in China than in Canada, largely because of the lack of sufficiently trained personnel. When any medicare scheme expands as rapidly as it has in China, there must inevitably be such a shortage of trained personnel. However, the general anesthetics and the equipment that they do have are first-class. I spent a very interesting afternoon on the wards with two young surgeons, both of whom had been trained in China, but who spoke a smattering of English. We conversed initially through an interpreter, later discarding the interpreter and using mostly medical terms.

For many years I have examined medical students for higher degrees in surgery, and I virtually gave these two an oral examination for over two hours. They read all the same surgical journals which we obtain. They were acquainted with all the big names in American and world surgery. They were aware of all the recent advances in surgery. I saw all the latest American medical journals in their library. I would have passed both these men for higher degrees in surgery. In my own hospital we have recently been using the anterior approach for fusion of the spinal vertebrae. In one ward alone I saw that two such operations had been performed.

At the conclusion of any interviews or discussion in China it is customary for the Chinese participant to make a small incantation to the effect that all this is due to the correct leadership of Chairman Mao Tse-tung, the Communist Party of China and the three red banners of the correct party, the Great Leap Forward, and the People's Commune. Most of our hosts were able to say this little speech without difficulty. I was amused to find that my Chinese medical confreres kept forgetting to finish with these remarks, and I had the occasion to prompt

109

one of them in the final sentence. I had heard it said so often in the factories and communes that it was becoming second nature to me.

Research Facilities

The facilities for research in Peking Medical College were excellent. The latest medical equipment was available. In my own hospital the equipment we use to test pulmonary functioning comes from Holland. The makers of the equipment told me that they have sold more of their machines to China than to any other country, and I saw the equipment in use in Peking. The caliber of the medical practice in Peking was of the highest quality. There is really no reason why it should not be so. The Chinese have good brains, good hands, all the equipment they need, and the medical literature of the world is available to them. It would be to our mutual benefit if we could attend each other's medical meetings and conventions. I would very much like to see a delegation from China attend the large Clinical Congress of the American Congress of Surgeons in Chicago in October, 1967.

Salaries

I repeatedly asked how much a surgeon was paid for his services. At this the interpreters always looked pained, as though I had mentioned a bad word. I finally found that workers are paid 90 yuan a month, good surgeons about 250, and the top administrators and scientists of the country between 350 and 400 yuan (approximately half that amount in dollars). Our interpreters, all college graduates, earned only 60 yuan. The fact that workers earned more than they did not seem to bother them because, as they explained, they needed less food than a man or woman performing heavy manual labor. I finally came to the realization that I was in a country in which money was of small value anyway, as there was so little to spend it on, and therefore not much sense in accumulating it. I wondered if

110

intelligent, ambitious, and educated people might not ultimately tire of the self-denial and austerity of their puritan regime and eventually establish an aristocracy, not based on money like our own, but on such things as position, power, and prestige.

Norman Bethune

In one of the main hallways I noticed a large picture of Dr. Norman Bethune and underneath it an inscription by Mao Tse-tung praising the international spirit of Dr. Bethune. I subsequently found similar pictures and statues of Bethune in hospitals throughout China. In the large Museum of the Revolution in Peking a section is devoted to his mementos, portable X-ray machines, and so on. Dr. Bethune was a Canadian surgeon. He is almost unknown in his native Canada, but he is a national hero and a household word to one-quarter of the world's population. In the introductory remarks to our group in Peking we were told that China and Canada had two things in common—wheat and Dr. Norman Bethune. Soon after graduation in medicine, Bethune almost died of tuberculosis. As a result, he became interested in chest surgery. He rebelled against the lack of active treatment given to tuberculosis chest cases. In the twenties his radical proposals for tuberculosis treatment, and for medicine in general, were far too advanced for his time. All of his proposals have since been realized, but at that time he was branded a communist. He went to Spain and helped to pioneer in the administration of blood to frontline casualties. Subsequently he went to China to help Mao Tse-tung in his fight against the Japanese. He organized the care of the wounded, and subsequently died a hero's death from septicemia (blood poisoning) contracted while operating without gloves or antibiotics. As a Canadian surgeon, I found myself, as it were, traveling on this man's passport and welcomed in hospitals across China. I do not know if Dr. Bethune was a communist. He seemed to me to be much more of a humanitarian than someone who was concerned with the finer

111

points of communist ideology. We now have Bethune Exchange Scholarships in Canada, and this summer another member of our medical staff visited China to give lectures in their medical colleges under this exchange agreement.

Hospital Visits

Our visits to Chinese hospitals did not have to be arranged in advance. Before leaving Canada the Medical Health Officer of Regina, a Chinese who had graduated from Peking before the Liberation, asked me to visit his younger sister who had just graduated in medicine in Peking, and who was interning in one of the city's hospitals. I asked our interpreters to arrange for me to meet her. They said they would look into the matter, and nothing happened. Before going to China we were told that we would be allowed to see only what the Chinese wanted us to see. Still in this suspicious frame of mind, my wife and I set off to find her. With nothing more than her name written in English and Chinese, we hired a taxi for the day for two or three dollars and set off for the nearest hospital. Without an interpreter, we soon found ourselves drinking copious quantities of tea with the director and other members of the medical staff. The piece of paper with her name on it was passed around to various people in the hospital, and suddenly a young man recognized it. We were taken outside and put back in our taxicab with another name written on a piece of paper. In short, we went through three hospitals, drank what seemed like gallons of tea, and finally found her in a tuberculosis hospital on the outskirts of Peking. The director spoke some English, and he showed us through his entire hospital. Having treated Indians and Eskimos, I have some familiarity with tuberculosis; I found that treatment of tuberculosis in the hospital in China was identical to that which we use in Canada. The disease is gradually being stamped out. In fact, the Chinese do not have the same reservoir of disease that we have in our native Canadian population in the northern parts of the country. The director was rather amused at the number of inocula-

112

tions and injections we had to obtain before visiting China. He told me he had not seen a case of cholera for years and that typhoid and typhus were almost nonexistent. Trachoma, a disease of the eyes causing a good deal of blindness among older people in China, is now being brought under control. Survey teams go through the rural areas looking for the early symptom of the disease, which is intense itching around the eyes.

The doctor in Regina had given us a good deal of penicillin and other medications to smuggle to his sister for use in his own family. She was rather amused at this, because she showed us that she had free access to all these preparations.

A few days after the visit our interpreters told me that they had finally located her and had arranged for my wife and me to pay her a visit. It was obvious that they had no idea where we had gone, or that we had already visited her. And I like to think that my free-enterprise system had found her faster than the government channels.

Traditional Chinese Medicine

I wanted to see the practice of traditional Chinese medicine, and I visited the Research Institute of Acupuncture and Moxibustion at the Academy of Traditional Chinese Medicine in Peking. During the brief meeting that preceded this visit, I had the impression that my host was feeling me out, and it took four or five cups of tea to convince him that I had not come there to be amused and that I really was very seriously interested in this form of medicine. When he was convinced of my seriousness, he blossomed like a rose and spent most of the day with me. "Acupuncture" means needle puncture, and "moxibustion" means the burning of a *moxa*, or a dried herb, not unlike the punks we used as children for lighting firecrackers. They are part of the traditional Chinese therapeutic methods which have been handed down for centuries. Stone needles were used some 4,000 years ago. Solid, stainless steel needles are now inserted into points along about eleven pairs of lines, or channels, on the body. These channels, or meridians,

113

are reputed to conduct vital energy. Depending on the diagnosis, needles are inserted at various points corresponding to the organ involved. Harmful excesses of body humors and moribund essences are drawn off. Stagnating vital forces flow freely again, restoring the balance between *yin* and *yang*.

I really don't understand what all this is about. Being a surgeon trained in the West, I do not understand such terms as "essences," "vital forces," and so on. I cannot conceive of channels which cannot be demonstrated, even by the electron microscope. I saw a bronze model of the human body from the Ming dynasty with holes in it on which the medical students practiced inserting needles. This was about the time Columbus was discovering America. I saw very modern displays of equipment in which the channels light up with colored lights. These marvelous demonstration machines were manufactured in Shanghai. And finally I saw some fifty people treated by acupuncture or moxibustion, or a combination of both. The waiting rooms and hallways were jammed with patients waiting their turn. I saw hypertension treated by needles inserted into the forehead and in the wrists. A lady with a protruded intraverbal disk had needles inserted into her forehead and both ankles. Small portions of moxa, looking like bits of cigarettes, were placed on the ends of the needles and set on fire. I was permitted to take numerous pictures, and I have shown them to many of my medical friends who would not believe that I was telling the truth.

During his regime, Chiang Kai-shek tried to abolish traditional Chinese medicine. In 1944, Mao Tse-tung promised to restore it, and he gained a good deal of popular support from the people by this promise. At the present time, all medical graduates spend some of their time learning traditional Chinese medicine, and the institute which I visited was trying to investigate scientifically what was until now an art rather than a science. Every year more people are treated by these methods than there are people in Canada. I was given a set of needles, moxa, and numerous charts when I left the institute, but I have not yet used them in my practice. Dr. G. B. Ong, the very capable Chinese-trained Professor of Surgery at Hong Kong, told me that he thought that the Chinese were especially susceptible to this form of treatment and implied that the treatment was particularly useful in functional disorders.

When I visited hospitals in Moscow in 1958 at the height of the Sino-Soviet friendship, traditional Chinese medicine was being demonstrated in Russian hospitals. I understand, however, that in recent years this form of treatment has become much less popular.

The Communes and Local Medical Facilities

With the rest of my group I visited numerous communes and found them to be large cooperative farms, sometimes including a whole township, and frequently encompassing several small villages and towns. Their organization was quite similar to the organization of cooperatives in Canada. I found no evidence of segregation of men and women in the barracks. For the most part, more attention was paid to improvement of barns and facilities for farm production than to housing. There seemed to be little question, judging from the numerous statistics, that farm production has increased since the advent of the commune system in 1958. However, I wondered how much of this increase was negated by the population increase of over 100 million since that time. When the farming problems became too technical, I wandered off by myself, and, being more interested in people than in pigs, usually managed to visit the local medical establishment. In one small village I saw a red cross over the door of a private dwelling and walked in without an interpreter. The lady of the house served me tea and showed me her two-room home. Most of the family lived in one room in which were a radio and pictures of Mao Tse-tung and Liu Shao-ch'i, as well as of her immediate family. The entire family slept in one room; the cooking and living facilities were in the other. I went back and got an interpreter and found that the lady was a nurse and that she was running the first-aid station in the town. In this and many other instances I never ceased to be amazed at how easy it was to get along in the country without being able to speak the language.

In one of the larger towns I visited a small medical center equipped with all forms of treatment, including the traditional Chinese medicine. This small center was built and furnished by the commune. The doctor, however, was posted to the commune and paid by the state. I tried to find out how he would go about becoming a surgeon in a city hospital if such was his desire. He finally told me that it was a privilege for him to serve wherever he was sent. This reminded me of what I used to hear when I drew a particularly poor posting in the army. It seemed to me that much of China was run like an army, and, while I tolerated the army style of regimentation in time of war, I would not care for it in time of peace.

In many of the communes housing had been removed to make better use of the land, and the people were housed in new apartments. These were mostly one or two rooms. Each had its own toilet, but frequently a kitchen would be shared by as many as two or three units. However, the facilities in each kitchen were usually separate, because of the health and sanitation problems.

Surgical Practice

I visited the Sixth People's Hospital in Shanghai to see the patients who had had severed limbs restored to their bodies. I saw a very good movie of the first patient whose right hand had been amputated just above the wrist and successfully restored. I saw a patient whose left arm had been amputated just below the shoulder and successfully restored to the body. I do not wish to enter a discussion as to the value of preserving paralyzed anesthetic limbs, but what I found thrilling was the fact that surgery of this caliber was now available to even the poorer people on the outskirts of Shanghai. Shanghai now makes all forms of surgical instruments. Some of them are direct copies from those of other countries, but many are of Chinese design and manufacture. I saw a very good heart-

116

lung pump and understand that some 300 patients had had open-heart operations up to that time. The cobalt bomb unit was similar to that designed in Saskatoon, Saskatchewan.

Conditions in Shanghai

Shanghai, like the rest of China, has been cleaned up; prostitution, vice, and venereal disease have been almost eliminated. We visited some of the old slum areas of Shanghai, where thousands had died of starvation and disease at the end of the war with Japan. In Shanghai alone, according to foreign estimates, as many as 20,000 bodies each year were picked up from the streets—adults and children—victims of starvation and disease. This was the area where disease was rampant, where half-clad coolies had slept under straw mats called dragon huts. We talked to one old lady who had lost six of her eight children, some dying of starvation in her arms. This was the area where some form of upheaval had to occur, and I could understand how even the present regimented life was considered an advance. Starvation was no more. Disease was almost wiped out. Infant mortality was near our own.

We found the neighborhood and its homes clean, with almost a total absence of mosquitoes or flies. We visited homes and saw happy, healthy children. We heard the remark that living in this area before was like living in hell; now it was like living in heaven. It didn't look much like heaven to me, but it was heaven to them to have enough food to ward off starvation, to have a suit of clothes to wear, to sleep inside a house, to see their children have a chance to survive and even get an education, and finally, the height of luxury, to obtain water from an open tap half a block away instead of having to bail their water out of the rancid, polluted waters of Soochow Creek.

Birth Control

The interpreter on this trip was a young lady who had been married two years before and as yet had no family. From her I managed to obtain information about birth control as practiced in China. She told me that the state advised late marriages and limiting the number of children to two or three. She pointed out that even in the commune I was visiting lectures were held at regular intervals and information regarding birth control was available to all the people. Mechanical devices were available, but they did not at that time have oral contraceptives. (I understand that the pill is now available. Its late introduction was due to the fact that the Chinese Medical Association had not completed its study on the safety of the drug.) My informant told me that sterilization could be obtained by a male or a female at any time, with no questions asked. As far as I could ascertain, legalized abortion was not practiced as it is in Japan. However, the Chinese freely follow the leadership of their government in so many matters that I would think that birth control in China will probably be accomplished. Unlike some other countries in Asia, they are not handicapped by religious taboos.

Christianity

One afternoon in Nanking, largely to escape visiting a fertilizer processing plant, I visited the Protestant Seminary of Nanking. Bishop Ting, Dean of the Seminary and Bishop of the Anglican Church in China, had spent a year in Canada as secretary of the Student Christian Movement. He told us that there are some 3 million Catholics and about 750,000 Protestants in China, about the same number as before Liberation. However, he thought their position in China was stronger than before, in that they were united for the first time. He said they were self-supporting, self-propagating, and self-governing, and were not, as he had thought before, small islands under foreign

118

influence or domination. He said that Article 88 of the Constitution guaranteed them religious freedom, and that he had found this to be the case. He said that Christianity was no longer a status symbol, that it neither helped nor hindered them in government, and pointed out that a governor of their state was a Christian. When I asked how he, a Christian, found his life compatible with that of Mao Tse-tung, a communist, he stated that he had no quarrel with any man who had done so much for his country, who had largely eliminated crime, vice, and prostitution, and who had elevated the moral standards of his people higher than he had ever thought was possible.

In Retrospect

The hospitality of the Chinese was tremendous. Their enthusiasm was contagious. They are not afraid to work. They have come up off the deck by their own efforts, not relying on foreign aid. These attributes I cannot help but admire.

Whenever I say anything complimentary about China, people ask me if I would like to live there. The answer is "No." While they have come a long way, the Chinese are still far behind, and I would find the complete government control intolerable and even frightening. China's problems of overpopulation, starvation, and disease are not our problems. We do not need Chinese methods in our part of the world, and the adoption of their system would, in my estimation, be too radical a solution—or rather, a very retrograde step.

I do not understand the isolation of China. I feel that even if China is our enemy, the more we know about her the better. Ignoring China will not make her change or go away. I believe, however, that on the scientific and educational level some of the isolation is disappearing. My group of farmers found no difficulty in talking to farmers in China. As for my own profession, doctors the world over speak a common language. Medicine knows no international boundaries. When you meet your opposite number, it is easy to get his point of

119

view and see the world through his eyes. I believe that it is better to obtain information about a foreign country through friendly contacts at first hand, than through analysis of data derived from a distance, or from spies, or expatriates. I believe that a freer exchange of people with common interests—doctors, nurses, engineers, farmers, or anyone who speaks with a common language of his own interest—would help break down some of the barriers that exist between us.

Economy

*W*hen the Chinese Communists came to power in October of 1949, they faced three immediate and crucial economic problems: restoring production to its prewar level and rehabilitating the transport system; controlling the rampant inflation; and securing the indispensable foreign exchange required to tackle the first two problems. That these needs were met in the first three years is a tribute to the organization and dedication of the revolutionary leaders. But what has happened since?

We know that the period from 1953 to 1955 was one of remarkable economic growth under the stimulus of considerable Soviet assistance. We know that the efforts during the Great Leap Forward to concentrate on heavy industry and to improve agriculture by the increased mobilization of labor was not successful and ended in the agricultural crisis of 1959-61. What have the Chinese leaders learned from their mistakes and, in particular, from the catastrophic Great Leap? What are the prospects for economic improvement, given available resources and restricted foreign trade? If Soviet aid was an important factor in the early years, what are the implications of the Sino-Soviet split for the future?

123

At the China Conference, economists seemed in general agreement that the New Plan gives priority to agricultural development with a more selective investment in industry, primarily where it is related to agriculture. The major exception to this general approach, not surprisingly, appears to be investment in heavy industry necessary for military requirements.

Robert F. Dernberger of the Department of Economics, University of Chicago, and James S. Duncan, author of several books on China, offer a critical review of Chinese economic development.

Audrey Donnithorne, lecturer in Chinese economics at University College, London, advances the theory that the Chinese economy is much more decentralized and differentiated than commonly thought—a cellular rather than a monolithic structure.

Dick Wilson, former editor of the Far Eastern Economic Review, *considers China's economic prospects.*

124

ECONOMIC REALITIES
Robert F. Dernberger

Perhaps the most pressing economic realities in contemporary China can be dramatized by saying that approximately one out of every four people in the world today is a Chinese, that this one-fourth of the world's population lives on approximately 7 per cent of the world's available land, and consumes only 4 per cent of the world's output; or by saying that the citizens of a hundred countries of the world enjoy a per capita income greater than that of the Chinese, who have a per capita annual income of less than 75 dollars.

The trouble with these statistics is that they are very crude and ignore the great regional diversity of China's economy and the rapid changes that have taken place in the past fifteen years. Nonetheless, China's major economic realities are the problems of too many people, limited fertile land, and too low a level of output. In examining these realities, I propose to present a brief consideration of the specific way in which they limit China's ability to achieve sustained economic growth, and the various ways in which the Chinese Communists have attempted to alter them. I will then assess the major economic problems the Chinese Communists face today and, finally, offer some opinions of their future prospects.

125

One of the reasons Americans are so concerned with the Chinese today is that there are so many of them. In terms of area, the United States is almost as large as China, and Canada is larger; West Germany produces a greater amount of goods and services each year than China does, and France produces almost as much; but, in terms of people, China is almost 60 per cent larger than India and more than three times larger than any other country in the world. The Chinese Communists are aware that their population is one reason for their emergence as a world power. In addition, they argue that their numbers are an economic asset, an important resource for their development effort, as well as a valuable asset in their military strategy. That labor is the only productive resource is one of the basic axioms of Marxist economics; but most economists, communists and noncommunists alike, would agree that surplus labor is desirable in a rapidly developing economy. Furthermore, given the labor-intensive methods of agricultural production employed in China, the present level of output depends on the present large work force. Any attempt to foster economic development by reducing total population would only lead to an equivalent decline in output.

The real problem associated with China's population is its rate of growth. The Chinese must increase output by 2 per cent a year merely to keep per capita income constant. While there are sixty-four countries with a higher rate of population growth, every year China adds the present number of people in Czechoslovakia to her population.

The Chinese Communists do appreciate, and at different times have emphasized, the benefits to be derived from reducing the birth rate, while attempting to increase the per capita income of those Chinese already alive. A vigorous campaign to reduce the birth rate was launched in 1956. This initial attempt to change the Chinese attitude to family planning overnight ended in failure, and the attempt to reduce the birth rate was abandoned during the enthusiasm of the Great Leap Forward in 1958. When the Great Leap ended in failure, however, the Communists introduced a less direct, yet more meaningful, campaign to reduce the birth rate, using books and pamphlets on family planning, and advocating late marriages, abortion, sterilization, and contraception. Medical services and birth control devices are provided at low prices or are free. Family planning is still up to the individual Chinese family, however, and it will be some time before the lasting effects of this new and less direct campaign can be determined. The results of a new census, reported to have been taken in the summer of 1964, have not yet been made public. Some wags suggest the census results were kept secret so as not to scare the Westerner; some suggest they were kept secret so as not to scare the Chinese.

While its rate of growth is the most important economic problem of China's population, its absolute size also presents a serious problem to the Chinese Communists in their attempt to organize and mobilize that population. When they came to power in 1949, only one out of every seventy-five Chinese was a member of the Party. Thus, the Chinese Communists faced a monumental task in their attempt to organize, mobilize, and gain the support of the uncommitted Chinese for their economic development plans, as well as for all their other economic, social, and political policies. The Chinese peasants —the bulk of the population and the base of the revolution— were rewarded with land distributed during the land reform in 1950–52, and by the liquidation of the hated landlord. Shortly after receiving his land, of course, the peasant lost it as he was pressured into joining first a cooperative in 1954 and then a collective in 1956.

The Marriage Law, the first law promulgated by the Chinese Communists, was an attempt to appeal to the women in China. It freed them from any marriage they had been forced into or, within limits, no longer desired. The creation of equal economic and educational opportunities for women was another important factor in improving their lot under the Communists. The young were freed from the traditional family system, and educational, economic, and even political op-

127

portunities were made available to those willing to transfer their loyalty from the family to the Party. Finally, soldiers and factory workers were given preferential treatment in all economic and social welfare legislation. Initially, intellectuals and businessmen were merely tolerated; the persecution of these two groups did not come until the mid-1950s, when the Party's control over the rest of the population had been made secure. The mobilization of all Chinese to obtain their cooperation and loyalty was promoted by means of the many nation-wide propaganda campaigns, meetings, mass organizations, public demonstrations, and the thought-reform, self-criticism, and brainwashing meetings that have become an essential part of life in China.

By 1956, the economy and the people of China were completely under the control of the Communist Party, and people were aware that their material and social well-being depended upon their compliance with its demands. It is important to note that this control had been achieved without the social and economic crises that had occurred in the Soviet Union. The available evidence suggests that while the agricultural difficulties in 1959–61 seriously damaged the enthusiasm and morale of the Chinese people, including those in the lower echelons of both the Party and the army, there is nothing to indicate that the Party has lost its control.

Land Shortage

The second major economic problem in China is the shortage of land: not a shortage of land *per se,* but a shortage of arable land or land that is *presently* available for use in agricultural production. Forty-one countries, including almost all of Europe, have more people per square mile than does China. But in China, only 15 per cent of the total land area is cultivated. Even in terms of people per square mile of agricultural land, however, the pressure of population is greater in thirty-two countries, including the Netherlands, West Germany, the United Kingdom, and Luxembourg. The

128

real problem in China is that a very small proportion of the total population, about 10 per cent, live in cities with over 20,000 people, and a large proportion of those living in rural areas are crowded on alluvial plains—the North East Plain along the Sungari and Liao Rivers, the Yangtze River Plain, the Canton Delta of the West, North, and East Rivers, the North China Plain along the Yellow River, and the Chengtu Plain in Szechuan. It is on the fertile land of these plains that the population densities are exceedingly high, making labor abundant and land scarce. The exceedingly high labor-to-land ratio has led to the adoption of labor-intensive methods of production, resulting in high yields per unit of land, but low yields per man.

Several alternative means to increase agricultural production could have been adopted by the Chinese Communists. First, additional land could have been brought under cultivation, but the necessary expenditure for these land reclamation projects would have been very large. The Chinese Communists rejected this alternative, and the cultivated area increased by only 7 per cent between 1950 and 1958, while over the same period China's total population increased by more than 15 per cent. A second alternative would have been to mechanize agriculture, but the Chinese Communists considered the necessary expenditure involved to be prohibitive at the present time. Furthermore, mechanization would have reduced the need for farmers, and those released from farming would seek employment in the city. Despite the rapid increases in industrial production in China, the increase in factory employment during the 1950s did not keep pace with the growth in the labor force, even without the mechanization of agriculture. While the Chinese Communists regard mechanization as a long-run goal, the peasants had only one tractor for every twenty-five square miles of cultivated land in 1958. A third possible means of increasing yields would have been to adopt the successful model of Japan: to retain labor-intensive methods, but greatly increase the use of chemical fertilizers and the area under irrigation. Production of chemical fertilizers and construction of large-scale water conservation projects, however, also involve large expenditures. According to one observer, the total increase in irrigated land during the First Five-Year Plan, 1953–57, amounted to only 10 per cent of the total area under cultivation, and more than nine-tenths of this increase was accounted for by small-scale irrigation projects undertaken and paid for by the peasants themselves. The major indigenous source of fertilizer continued to be the traditional Chinese fertilizer factory—the pig; in 1958, imports were still almost twice as large as domestic production of chemical fertilizers. Imports and domestic production together amounted to less than 5 per cent of the quantity of chemical fertilizer applied per unit of land in Japan.

A fourth means of increasing yields, and the one chosen by the Chinese Communists, was to reorganize agriculture. All communist governments, at one time or another, have believed that, even with limited investment and minor changes in the actual methods of production in agriculture, it is possible to increase agricultural output by forming cooperatives or collectives. Thus far, history shows that these organizations do succeed in giving the government greater control over both the peasant and his output, but offers little evidence that they succeed in achieving the required increases. Nonetheless, during the early 1950s, whenever a favorable harvest had led to a period of optimism on the part of the Chinese Communists, they abandoned the existing form of organization in agriculture for an even more centralized one. The good harvest in 1952 was followed by the introduction of the cooperative. In this instance, the Chinese Communists proceeded slowly, and only 14 per cent of the peasant households were members of the collectives by 1955. Another very good harvest in 1955, however, led Mao Tse-tung to call for more speed in the socialist transformation of agriculture; those who preferred a slower pace he compared to Chinese women with bound feet. In the collective, the peasant lost title to his land and was forced to depend largely on workpoints earned through labor for his income. Mao originally believed it would take until

130

1960 to persuade at least half of the Chinese peasantry to join these collectives. The local Communist cadres got the message, however, and almost 90 per cent of the peasant households had become members of collectives by the end of 1956. The introduction of the commune system did not follow a favorable harvest, but, on the contrary, was a reaction to the very poor harvests in 1956 and 1957. In the collective the peasant had been given a small private plot and had been able to supplement his income by raising vegetables, pigs, and chickens; in the commune, the peasant lost all independent sources of income and had to rely completely on his labor for the commune. In other words, he had been transformed into a rural proletarian. When the commune movement ended in failure with the severe agricultural crises of 1959–61, the Communists were forced to re-examine the basic premises of their development policy.

The Chinese Communists had failed to invest heavily in agriculture because of the priority they had placed on the development of heavy industry. Heavy industrial production is a prerequisite for the needs of a modern military establishment, for the supply of chemical fertilizer, for the mechanization of agriculture, for the creation of a modern transportation system, and even for the supply of equipment and materials to expand the capacity of the consumer goods industry. All of these needs could be imported in exchange for Chinese exports of agricultural products, but the Communists desired to reduce their dependence on foreign sources of supply and to change China from an agricultural to an industrial nation. These goals are clearly reflected in investment during the First Five-Year Plan, when almost half of the state's investment was in industry and only 3 per cent was in agriculture. Furthermore, of the total investment in industry, 85 per cent was in heavy industry. When faced with the problem of the agricultural crises following the commune movement, however, the relative importance of the various sectors was completely inverted, and agriculture was given top priority.

While the commune remained as an administrative organization, decision-making was decentralized to the lower level production units. The private plot was restored to the peasant, and he was allowed to sell its produce at rural fairs. Unemployed and nonessential urban dwellers were put to work in agriculture, and agricultural needs were given priority in investment and the production of industry. Almost one-half the land under cultivation had been irrigated by the end of 1963, while the supply of chemical fertilizer and the total number of tractors available were double what had been available in 1958. Agricultural production has undoubtedly been restored in the last few years to a level slightly higher than that achieved in 1957, but otherwise the results of the new agricultural development program have not been particularly significant and indicate that the Chinese have only begun to tackle the problem of agricultural development. Furthermore, the increase in population between 1957 and 1965 has required China to import approximately 6 million tons of wheat annually in recent years to maintain food consumption at the near-minimum level of approximately 1,900 calories per day.

Savings and Capital

The low level of per capita income and consumption is directly related to the third economic reality in China: the low level of voluntary savings and capital accumulation. In other words, the large population with limited fertile land leads to high labor-to-land ratios and low productivity per worker; low productivity per worker means low incomes; low incomes mean both low levels of consumption and low rates of savings; low savings mean limited capital accumulation; and limited capital accumulation means low productivity —the typical vicious cycle one finds in the underdeveloped countries. If each Chinese saved only a small portion of his income, of course, total savings for the economy as a whole would not be insignificant. Nonetheless, available studies indicate that the Chinese were actually dissaving and using up their accumulated capital stock during the early 1930s.

Therefore, one of the major tasks of the People's Republic during the 1950s was to divert resources from the production of consumer goods to the production of producer goods, military equipment, and export. They were eminently successful in achieving one of the highest rates of savings and capital accumulation in the world—between 20 and 30 per cent—but they did so by restricting consumption, and per capita consumption has not grown significantly over the last fifteen years. To an economist these are forced savings. Perhaps the form of forced savings most familiar to us is taxes. The Chinese Communists did not rely exclusively on direct taxes, however, to acquire the needed funds for investment in industry. Two important sources of funds for this purpose were really hidden taxes—forced deliveries of grain to the state at less-than-market prices, and the profits of state enterprises. Another hidden tax was levied on factory workers and consumers simply by keeping increases in wages far below increases in productivity and by maintaining existing prices when productivity increased and costs declined. A somewhat less important source of funds was bond sales to the public and individual savings deposits at the State Bank. In this country, the bond sales and savings deposits would be called voluntary savings, but there is some doubt as to the extent to which they were voluntary in China. The Chinese did not, however, resort to one of the most onerous and inequitable forms of forced savings: inflation. The financing of development by inflation has been very popular throughout the world; possibly because it is so simple, it appeals to irresponsible governments. The government prints paper money and uses it to purchase the necessary resources for investing in heavy industry, leaving the public to scramble for the available consumer goods with money that soon loses its value as prices rise. Despite the various taxes, both direct and hidden, utilized by the Chinese Communists, the public still had sufficient

133

income to buy more than the available consumer goods, and it was necessary to resort to rationing as early as 1953.

Technical Ability

Even though the Chinese were able to increase the rate of savings to an extremely high level, they still faced the fourth major economic reality in China—the low level of technical ability. In real terms, savings were in the form of agricultural products such as grain, soybeans, peanuts, and pork, and consumer goods such as cotton textiles. To convert these savings into investment in heavy industry, it was only necessary to provide commodities to domestic workers and technicians who would build the steel mills, the airplane plants, the automobile factories, the bridges, etc. The problem was, of course, that China lacked technicians and workers who had the ability to build and equip many of these heavy industrial plants, and it was necessary to export these commodities to those foreign countries willing to accept them in exchange for the necessary technicians, machinery, and equipment. In the early 1950s, the Soviet Union greatly assisted China's economic development program by building complete plants in China and sending its technicians to train the Chinese technicians; Soviet assistance was paid for not only by Chinese exports, but also by the proceeds of Soviet loans. Thus, the high rate of savings, the Soviet loans, and Soviet exports of technicians, machinery, and equipment enabled China to achieve a very rapid rate of growth in the domestic economy—about 11 per cent during the First Five-Year Plan. Even after correction of the official statistics, the estimated rates of growth for this period remain very high.

The Chinese found it very difficult, however, to maintain this pace of economic growth in 1956 and 1957, because of several important developments. Soviet loan proceeds for 1956 and 1957 were very small, and no new Soviet loans were negotiated. Repayment in 1956 and thereafter of the Soviet loans of the early 1950s made Communist China an exporter

134

of capital only five years after it had come to exist, truly a remarkable phenomenon for an underdeveloped country. Added to the burden of these Soviet loan repayments were the capital exports to southeast Asia that began with Communist China's own foreign aid program in 1956. Thus, Communist China's imports of machinery and equipment after 1955 were limited by the current export earnings, and a portion of these earnings had to be used to repay the Soviet loans and to pay for China's foreign aid program. The export earnings themselves were limited, however, by the poor agricultural harvests of 1956 and 1957. Finally, the heavy industry plants that the Soviet Union had agreed to build in Communist China were being completed in 1957, and the slow growth in exports made future large-scale purchases of complete plants from the Soviet Union unlikely. At the end of 1957, therefore, the Chinese Communists were forced to make a serious choice: they could accept the inevitable low rate of growth that resulted from their inability to build modern, heavy industrial plants themselves or to purchase them from the Soviet Union on a large scale, and also from the slow increase of agricultural output; or they could adopt a new strategy for development.

Great Leap—Great Failure

The Great Leap Forward in 1958 and 1959 can be understood as an attempt by the Chinese Communists to provide the required new strategy of development. The commune movement and the "walking-on-two-legs" campaign were attempts to use the surplus work force in agriculture and native technology to build small-scale factories throughout the countryside. The commune organized the peasants on a sufficient scale—each commune including between 25,000 and 100,000 people—to employ the available surplus labor in these native industries. Moreover, the native industries would not rely on the import of machinery and equipment from abroad. As far as industry is concerned, the commune movement ended in failure, resulting from the overestimation made by the

135

Communists of the number of available surplus workers who could be taken away from agricultural production to work in the native industries and on large-scale water conservation projects. It also failed due to the waste of resources used to produce poor-quality products that were later determined unfit for industrial use. The failure of the commune movement caused the Chinese to abandon their emphasis on the rapid development of heavy industry and concentrate on the development of agriculture.

This discussion of the four major economic realities in China—the large population and its rate of growth, the limited amount of agricultural land and low output per man, the low rate of voluntary savings and capital accumulation, and the low level of technical ability and dependence on foreign assistance—need not lead to the conclusion that the situation is hopeless. While China has a low level of productivity in agriculture because of present labor-intensive methods of production, I have no doubts concerning the potential of the land already within China's borders to support a population perhaps three times as large as the present one. To support such a population it will be necessary to increase the area under cultivation through land reclamation projects, increased use of chemical fertilizers, and mechanization of agriculture. All of these developments will take a long time and involve very large investments, and it is essential that the growth in population does not exceed the increases in available fertile land and its productivity. In other words, the Chinese must continue their present emphasis on agricultural development and their current efforts to reduce the birth rate. To achieve the necessary expenditures for agricultural development, they will also have to maintain a high level of savings and capital accumulation, and they have already proved their ability to cope with this economic reality. Even though much progress has been made—especially during the recent agricultural crises when they diversified much of their industrial production, and in connection with the development of nuclear weapons—the Chinese must further elevate the level of technical ability.

136

Economic Realities

The recent reduction in emphasis on the development of heavy industry and the increase in emphasis on agricultural development lessens to some extent the demands on their limited supply of technicians and scientists. But China still depends on the foreign supply of certain types of machinery and equipment, and on technical assistance. Finally, inasmuch as her exports still consist of raw and finished agricultural products, foreign loans and aid will be needed if China is to import these required materials and technicians on a large scale. I see no reason why a responsible government could not successfully solve all of these problems.

Responsible Government

But is the present government of China a responsible government? I cannot answer this question with certainty, although in many instances reality has forced them to be responsible. The Chinese Communists clearly desire to make China a self-sufficient industrial and military power, yet they quickly abandoned their emphasis on heavy industry and turned their attention to agricultural development, and even used scarce foreign exchange to import foodstuffs, when the commune movement ended in failure. Now that agricultural production has been restored to the pre-1958 level, will they return to their long-run goal of industrial development? Again, I cannot answer with certainty. A new Five-Year Plan has been announced, but the Communists have not released any information about it that would help to obtain an answer. Yet, the five-year agreement with Canada for large-scale imports of wheat on credit, the many contracts with western European firms for the building of industrial plants in China on credit, the continuous neglect of agricultural development throughout the communist world, and the need to provide a modern military arsenal for their international ambitions, lend support to the view that the building of heavy industry and a modern military establishment retain unalterable priorities in Communist China.

137

We may say that these are the priorities of an evil or an irrational government, but this would be a useless semantic argument. Given the present international power struggle in Asia, I would argue that these priorities could well be the priorities of any responsible Chinese government. The Chinese peasant, of course, is bearing the costs of this international power struggle. But we must never forget that we, as Americans, are also bearing the costs. The only difference is that, as a developed nation, the burden on us is easier to bear.

This article represents an extension of the author's testimony before the Subcommittee on the Far East and the Pacific of the Committee on Foreign Affairs, House of Representatives, on January 25, 1966, which was circulated at the Chicago China Conference and delivered as an address at the Tenth Annual Institute on United States Foreign Policy at the University of Wisconsin-Milwaukee on March 12, 1966. The address will be included in the proceedings of the Institute of World Affairs of the University of Wisconsin-Milwaukee, and is used here with their permission.

RED CHINA'S ECONOMIC DEVELOPMENT SINCE 1949

James S. Duncan

PROBABLY NEVER BEFORE in the world's history has so much progress been made so rapidly by a country newly emerging from internal strife and foreign invasion, and reeling under the ravages of the galloping inflation that occurred in China during the first ten years of the Communist regime, from 1949 to 1959.

Surprising progress was made in all fields: industry, education, public health, construction, communications, and to a lesser degree, agriculture. These felicitous results were due to many factors of which I will cite only three.

First, an atmosphere conducive to progress was created by the capable if ruthless government of Mao Tse-tung, which, having ensured military control of China, brought about for the first time in the memory of her citizens, internal peace, law and order, enforced unity of purpose, and a sense of achievement. Second, there was massive aid from the USSR in every field of endeavor, and third, the intelligent, resourceful, and hard-working Chinese themselves proved to be apt pupils and applied themselves to the lessons learned with unprecedented energy, resourcefulness, and skill.

It is important to realize that, despite the splendid qualities

139

of the Chinese people, had it not been for the USSR, China would still be struggling to emerge from a primitive agricultural economy into the first stages of a modern state.

In their all-embracing aid to China, the USSR made the kind of error which, fortunately for the West, totalitarian governments, lacking the checks and balances of democracies, so frequently commit.

The original purpose of the Soviet Union was to transform China, in the shortest time possible, into a modern, industrialized, educated, and scientifically developed state. Their aim was to confront the West with a solid communist bloc comprising over a billion people, stretching from the frontiers of Western Germany to the China Sea, under the leadership and control of Moscow. They had reckoned, however, without Mao Tse-tung, who, while eagerly accepting and profiting by Soviet aid in the early stages of China's development, never had any intention of playing second fiddle to Moscow, with whose policies, especially after Stalin's death, he fundamentally disagreed.

It was only in 1957, when Khrushchev began to realize that they were helping to create a Frankenstein monster on their eastern border, that he initiated a policy of gradual withdrawal, especially in the delicate areas of scientific development. But it was already too late; China had done her homework. When, in July of 1960, the USSR cancelled her contracts and withdrew her experts, China's economy suffered a considerable setback, but she was able to carry on her scientific and industrial development unaided.

Totalitarian China also made an error of historical significance. In 1957, buoyed up by successes during the revolutionary war and since Liberation in 1949, and filled with unbridled self-confidence, she disregarded the counsel of her Russian advisors and the muted disapproval of some of her own leaders and decided to step up radically the tempo of her already remarkable progress. She made what was termed the Great Leap Forward to achieve major power status. This was an ill-planned, frenzied, and overambitious drive which

140

reached its peak toward the end of 1959, at the time of my first visit to China.

Mao Tse-tung's government argued that, by correct thinking and heightened ideological fervor, the already harassed masses could be pushed to greater effort, enthusiasm, and sacrifice; and that achievements heretofore considered unattainable could be realized. As Mao Tse-tung put it: "Every kind of miracle can be performed by communism if the people are suitably led."

Not a miracle, however, but a catastrophic breakdown in China's economy took place in 1960. It was a bitter lesson for the government. Their planning had proved faulty. Their conviction that the already overworked masses had been so molded and transformed that they were ready to accept further sacrifice and perform any task with abnegation, even with enthusiasm, proved to be wishful thinking.

Coincidentally, the country experienced three bad crops in succession; and in the midst of mounting difficulties, China's fraternal partner, the Soviet Union, walked out. By 1960 China was experiencing a full-blown depression of staggering proportions, a phenomenon which, according to Lenin, Stalin, and Mao Tse-tung, was exclusively reserved for the capitalist world.

Agriculture, the fundamental factor in China's economy from time immemorial, had been relegated to second place. Industry, the emblem of great-power status, was to occupy the leading position. As a result of these miscalculations, the difficulties which arose in the communes, and the poor crop in 1959, the grain production, which had been officially estimated by Chou En-lai in May, 1959, at 520 million metric tons, was finally estimated at a total of between 140 and 150 million tons when the harvest was brought in that fall. As a result of a scarcity of food for the animals and a scarcity of meat for the people, livestock herds were radically depleted. Rigorous rationing was instituted. Capitalist wheat was imported. But everywhere hunger stalked the land.

Industry, dependent as it was upon the resources generated

141

from the export of agricultural surpluses and the production of such crops as cotton, sugar, and vegetable oils, dropped to one-half of the 1959 forecast. The prolonged depression following the cataclysmic failure of the Great Leap Forward was shattering. A bewildered government eventually took courageous and energetic measures to meet the situation.

Many of the measures involved repudiation of the government's most cherished communist doctrines. By the middle of 1963, aided by a series of good crops from 1962 through 1965, the economy began to recover and has been slowly gathering strength ever since.

During my visit to China in 1964, two factors governing the economic life of the country stood out. In all the areas I visited during a six-week tour which covered over 12,000 miles, food was more abundant than during my previous visit in 1959. Industry, on the other hand, and heavy industry in particular, was substantially lagging behind not only the 1959 but also the 1957 production figures.

In assessing the improved food situation, it is evident that the total grain production has increased remarkably slowly despite the excellent crops of the past four years. Total grain production from 1953 to 1957 averaged 172 million metric tons, whereas in 1964, an excellent harvest year, it amounted to but 182 million metric tons; and in 1965, it is claimed that production will drop back to 180 million tons, or only 8 million tons better than the average of 1953–57. As for the production of wheat, the estimated 1965 crop, at 20.5 million tons, fell short of the 1953–57 average by approximately 1 million tons. In this respect, it is interesting to note that while the importation of 5.5 or 6 million tons of Western wheat per annum appears small in relation to a population of 730 million people, it is the equivalent of over 25 per cent of all the wheat China produces.

The greater abundance of food to which I have referred is undoubtedly due in some measure to the importation of Western wheat, but much more to the salvage measures adopted by the government during the height of the depression, of which the most significant was the return of private plots to the peasants. This capitalist measure enabled the peasants, who represented some 530 million people, not only to provide the largest part of their own subsistence, but to sell their surplus to cooperative agencies set up for this purpose.

The importance of the produce obtained from private plots is illustrated by the fact that, although it represents only 5 to 7 per cent of the cultivable area of the communes, 80 per cent of all the hogs and 95 per cent of all the poultry in China come from this source.

On the other hand, it is acknowledged that as a consequence of the almost superhuman effort exerted by tens of millions of peasants, mobilized by the government for this purpose, considerable progress has been made and is still being made, although at a greatly reduced tempo, in water conservation programs. The acreage thus saved from periodic floods and benefitting from irrigation has ensured, in some measure, the regularity of crops in important areas. These benefits have, however, been partially offset by waterlogging and saline deposits, resulting from lack of drainage.

Great efforts have been made to supplement organic fertilizers with chemical fertilizers imported from abroad and produced locally in increasing quantity. But the requirements of China's impoverished soil, which has been cropped for centuries, are great and progress is slow indeed, and dependent on foreign exchange and important capital investments, both of which are hard to come by in present-day China.

China's dilemma is that, although her people are increasing yearly by numbers approximately equal to the population of Canada, she is growing only a little more grain food than in prerevolutionary days. Some authorities claim that her grain production is less than the pre-Liberation average of 186 million metric tons.

Apparently the explanation of this disappointing production in the face of the superhuman efforts wrested from the hardworking population is to be found in the communist system itself. By taking the land from the farmers and turning peasants

143

into laborers, it decreased their incentive, discarded the experience handed down from their forefathers, and discouraged their initiative.

The government's policy of commune management by committees made up largely of cadres and political appointees—strong in communist indoctrination, but weak in farm management experience—added greatly to the problems. These were further aggravated by the decisions handed down periodically from the central government, decisions which were accepted and applied without question.

When I was in China in 1959, two ultimata had been handed down to the communes: (1) deep ploughing and (2) close planting. This, the communes were told, would result in increased production. Chairman Mao had said so, and Chairman Mao knew. Both measures resulted in decreased production and have since been abandoned: the one because the impoverished and unsuitable soil was brought to the surface, the other because it increased the foliage, but decreased the seeds.

The solution to China's food problems resides in a radical increase in the productivity of her limited amount of arable land. In the pursuit of this goal, the government will always be handicapped because much of China's agricultural land does not lend itself to large-scale mechanization, and the communist approach will always prevent her from reaching those heights of productivity enjoyed by the farmers of Taiwan and Japan, under a system where initiative, experience, and freedom of choice are rewarded.

Industrially, China has paid a heavy price for her quarrel with the Soviet Union. In July, 1960, the USSR withdrew all her experts, tore up 343 contracts, discontinued her cooperation in 257 scientific and industrial projects, cancelled the supply of equipment and machine tools on order, and placed an embargo on the supply of all critical raw materials. This was undoubtedly a blow of major proportions to China's socialist economy. Coming at a time when China's agriculture and economy as a whole were in deep trouble, the Soviet defection

144

precipitated an industrial crisis which few governments, other than that of Mao Tse-tung, could have survived.

The situation, politically speaking, was aggravated by the fact that the government had not only published, but widely distributed among the people for study in their weekly discussion groups, industrial and agricultural figures for 1959 and 1960 which turned out to be wildly inaccurate and unbelievably inflated. These soaring production forecasts which were to be "fulfilled and overfulfilled" were a source of pride and exhilaration to people in all walks of life. I recall how impressed I was in 1959 to observe that a peasant in a commune, a worker in a factory, a waiter in a hotel, or any high school girl or boy could reel off figures concerning China's steel, coal, cement, or electrical production with the accuracy of a lesson well learned.

When, toward the end of 1959 and throughout 1960, realistic production figures began to filter through to the public, when they saw plants closing down or operating on a part-time basis, when all building projects were halted and hundreds of thousands of city workers were returned to the communes, the disillusionment of the people was great indeed.

There was unquestionably a lot to be disillusioned about.

Steel production, officially estimated at 18 million tons for 1960, dropped to between 7 and 8 million. (Canada, with her 20 million inhabitants, produced 11.1 million tons.) Coal dropped from 425 million tons estimated to 190 million, and cement from 13.5 million tons to 6, as compared with Canada's 7.7. Electricity, always an excellent barometer of a country's prosperity, dropped from an estimated 55 billion kilowatt hours to 30 billion (Canada: 134.3 billion), and trucks decreased from 29,000 to 3,000 (Canada: 110,400).

The government, shocked by the enormous dimensions of its miscalculations, was slow to react, but when it did move, it was with courage, energy, and determination.

Among the salvage measures taken was the wise decision that, for the foreseeable future, priority would be given to industries serving agriculture, such as chemical fertilizers,

145

simple farm tools, synthetic fibers (to relieve the cotton short-age); and to industries supplying the machine tools and equipment required by those given priority. Military arms and equipment (including MIG aircraft), nuclear development, trucks, and transportation vehicles were included in the priority list.

There are those who feel—and the Soviet authorities with whom I discussed this matter in Peking were among them—that a concentration on priority industries rather than on a more orderly program will retard ultimate industrial recovery. My own view is that, bearing in mind the necessity of pro-ducing more food as rapidly as possible in the face of limita-tions due to lack of capital, the government's decision was probably the correct one.

At all events, it resulted in a substantial increase in the production of all priority industries working 24 hours a day, and relative stagnation in heavy industry, as can be seen from these 1964 production figures:

Steel		8 to 11 million metric tons
Coal		220 million metric tons
Electric power		35 million kilowatt hours
Cement		8 to 8.5 million metric tons
Priority industries {	Chemical fertilizers	3.6 million metric tons (1.24 in 1958)
	Crude oil	6.9 million metric tons (2.26 in 1958)

Further modest industrial progress was made in 1965, both in heavy and priority industries, and it is assumed that China's overall industrial production will have regained the totals of 1957, although her heavy industries will still be lagging con-siderably. In this respect, China is probably the only important country in the world where industrial output is no greater than it was eight years ago.

China's industrial base has, however, been very considerably broadened. The Soviet Union's defection in July, 1960, stimulated the resourceful and energetic Chinese to develop their skills and produce a variety of raw materials, alloys, machine tools, and equipment which were previously imported. China has become remarkably self-sufficient. Her scientific development in metallurgy, radar, and instrumentation is noteworthy, and her knowledge and understanding of nuclear science has progressed beyond earlier appraisals. She has also benefitted greatly from the wider range of more modern industrial and scientific equipment which her present tendency to trade with Western countries has brought her. Her purchase of complete plants from the United Kingdom, France, Italy, Holland, and Japan will prove beneficial.

In the development of all aspects of her economy, China's great asset lies in the remarkable intelligence, resourcefulness, and serious-minded application of her students, scientists, and technicians. Invaluable, too, is the broad range of her workers, their zeal to catch up with and surpass the achievements of Western countries—and now of the USSR—and particularly their willingness to accept the sacrifices which such dedication entails.

Aided by an improvement in agricultural and industrial conditions and stimulated by a 15 to 20 per cent increase in experts to noncommunist countries, China may witness in 1966 the end of her recovery period in industry and the commencement of a gradual expansion. Basically, however, her industrial potential, dependent as it will continue to be on the resources generated by agriculture, will continue to be insignificant in relation to the size of her country or her population.

It is difficult to see how China, no longer aided by the USSR, or by capital acquired from the dispossession of her prerevolutionary capitalists, both Chinese and foreign, will be able to generate the resources necessary to build an impressive industrial structure, particularly when the govern-

147

ment is determined to divert a growing share of the country's national income to the expansion of its military potential at home and its political ambitions abroad.

There is a limit to the capital which can be generated by excessive sacrifices imposed upon the people. China has already gone too far in this direction, as the failure of the Great Leap Forward policies proved, and it is doubtful whether she can go much further. In this regard, one of the most interesting and significant developments of modern China is her belated recognition that the physiological and psychological excesses of 1957, '58, and '59 resulted not only in decreased production, but in the exhaustion and discouragement of the overworked masses, as well as in costly damage to the country's physical plant. Emphasis is now being placed on "labor and leisure." More important, attacks are being openly launched against the government for regimenting not only the working hours of the masses, but their leisure hours as well.

Authoritative Chinese articles are currently expressing views which we in the West have long since held, but which Mao Tse-tung and his colleagues brushed aside in 1957 and 1958 as "retrograde capitalist thinking." The following are but a few examples. One writer proclaims: "Man's physical power is limited. Continuous practice of overtime will make people overexhausted, damage equipment, cause accidents; not only will quality decline, but eventually output also." Another writer describes the practice of "voluntary" unpaid overtime as the policy of "well-fed bureaucratism." Others attack the "excessive collective spare time activities" and write of the need to guarantee eight hours sleep and adequate leisure. And finally, another writer states that "Championism and medalism are harmful to production and should be stopped, and we must not launch large-scale mass movements, hold rallies, make reports, engage in plenary discussions over everything."

This new approach—which is in complete contradiction to the policies which prevailed during the Great Leap Forward and indeed, insofar as mass movements and incessant flag-

148

waving rallies are concerned—is indicative of a reaction among the sounder elements in the government to the excesses which were largely responsible for the failure of the 1957–59 policies. It is conceivable that such statements could have been made fifteen months ago, and it is hoped that this saner attitude is an augury of the gradual process of attrition which inevitably dampens the early enthusiasm of all revolutionary movements.

This significant change in attitude appears to justify the hope which I have always held that in the fullness of time, the intelligent and fundamentally peaceloving Chinese people, tired of overwork and poverty at home and of adventurism abroad, will gradually influence their leaders to abandon their policies of belligerence in favor of one in which China will seek and be given an honored place in the community of nations, and work with it toward policies of cooperation, mutual aid, and better understanding among all people.

CENTRAL ECONOMIC CONTROL IN CHINA

Audrey Donnithorne

WESTERNERS COMMONLY ASSUME present-day China to be a monolith under tight control by the central government in Peking. This article questions that assumption and discusses the degree and manner of central control, particularly in economic matters, although these cannot be dissociated from political factors.

We will first detail those categories of economic undertakings still remaining under the direct management of the central government, and those economic targets which the center still lays down. Most of our information about these dates from the decentralization measures of 1957–58.[1] Since then information has, of course, been scantier, but had there been a radical change of direction it is unlikely to have been completely concealed. We will then discuss the extent to which central authorities have been able to maintain control of the economy, despite administrative decentralization, through the instrumentality of the Party and the army. Finally we shall consider features of the Chinese scene which render close control difficult by any level of government, central or local.

The decree of November 1957 on the reform of the industrial management system was implemented faster than originally

151

anticipated. By June 1958 no textile factories remained under the direct control of the central Ministry of Textile Industry, and all but five of the factories under the Ministry of Light Industry had similarly been handed over to the management of local authorities, primarily to those of the provincial level. (By the "provincial level authorities" is meant the administrations of the twenty-one provinces, five autonomous regions, and the cities of Peking and Shanghai, all of which come directly under the central government. In this article these will often be referred to as "the provinces.") By the middle of 1958, therefore, the central government directly controlled virtually no manufacture of consumer goods. In producer goods industries, most undertakings of importance were, by terms of the decree, to remain under direct control of the central ministries. These undertakings included large metallurgical and chemical enterprises; important coalfields; large power stations and electricity grids; oil refineries (no size qualification specified for these last); factories making large and precision machines, electric motors, and instruments; and the whole of the military equipment industry; and other technically complex branches of industry, together with experimental plants and other special cases.[2] The decentralization of heavy industry was reported to have covered a wider range than indicated by the original decree.[3]

The group of state farms, factories, mines, and other undertakings operated by the People's Liberation Army Production and Construction Corps in Sinkiang is under the immediate control of the Ministry of State Farms and Land Reclamation, as is the important group of state farms (also founded by ex-servicemen) in Heilungkiang, and another group of farms in a frontier district of Inner Mongolia. This gives the central government a close hold over certain strategic areas, as well as providing sources of grain supplies under its immediate control.

In transport, the main railway system, other than small local railways and lines built to serve individual coalfields, factories, or lumber areas, is under direct central control, together with the major civil aviation services. Road transport is mainly under local control, but the central government has been responsible for building—and presumably maintaining—certain major highways, notably some of strategic importance. The main coastal shipping services are directly under the central government (although there may be some difference in this respect between shipping services along the north China and the south China coasts), while a central government organ—the Yangtze Navigation Administrative Bureau —exercises general supervision of shipping on the Yangtze. In addition to the Bureau's own vessels, local authorities and joint state-private companies also run ships on the river. Trans-ocean shipping under the Chinese flag, whether Chinese-owned or chartered, may be presumed to come directly under the central government, as would the China Ocean Steamship Agency, which handles the clearing of foreign ships and agency work at all ports at which foreign ships are accustomed to call.

The main national-level organs of radio, telecommunications, and the press come directly under the central authorities.

The central government has direct control of the river conservancy commissions, of which the chief are the Yellow River Water Conservancy Commission, the Huai River Water Conservancy Commission, and the Yangtze River Planning Office. These commissions span several provinces and are charged with the multipurpose development of the respective rivers. Similarly, the Grand Canal Committee, established to improve the Grand Canal for purposes of both navigation and water conservancy, was placed under the chairmanship of the Minister of Communications.

The banking system, coming directly under the central government, and especially the ubiquitous People's Bank, is an all-important instrument of supervision and control over the entire economy. The main foreign trade corporations also fall under direct control, although local foreign trade corporations appear to have some independence in their dealings.

The chief institutions of higher learning and scientific research have been maintained as national, rather than provincial, organs and their subordination to the central government has furthered its control over both the economy and the armed forces.

Reduced Central Control

After considering those economic undertakings which remained directly under the central government after the 1957–58 administrative decentralization, our attention must now turn to the economic indices which the center announced its intention of still controlling. After 1959 their number was reduced to the following seven:

1. Output and transfer balances to and from provinces of certain major industrial products (e.g. steel, iron, coal, lathes, cotton yarn).

2. Output and transfer balances to and from provinces of major agricultural products (e.g. grain, cotton, vegetable oil, pigs).

3. Total exports and imports and the volume of important export and import commodities.

4. Volume of freight of railways and of transport undertakings directly under the Ministry of Communications.

5. Total investment, new productive capacity, major projects, and scale of capital investment. (The phrase "scale of capital investment" is vague in Chinese. It may mean the investment ratio in the national income.)

6. Total wages and average number of staff and workers.

7. Enrollment in higher educational institutions and allocation of graduates.

Other targets which ceased to be fixed by the central authorities included total value of industrial output, irrigated acreage, arable acreage, total circulation of commodities, total retail sales, local transport, rate and total of cost reduction, and volume of building and installation work. These targets were in future to be settled by the local authorities and the ministries among themselves. In order to provide flexibility, even the centrally controlled targets might be adjusted by local authorities so long as state plans were fulfilled and more especially those plans concerning construction projects, productive capacity, level of production, transfer balances, and revenue.[4]

With respect to material allocations, the central government since 1959 appears to have concentrated on trying to control interprovincial transfers of certain major commodities, both agricultural and industrial (notably grain, cotton, vegetable oil, pigs, steel, iron, coal, lathes, and cotton yarn). It is true that the list of centrally controlled indices includes the output as well as the transfer balances of such commodities. However, in agriculture from 1956 onwards the intention has been to change from unrealistic production planning to procurement planning, at least as far as central government plans were concerned.[5] And in grain procurement, the main concern of the central authorities is not with what happens within any province so long as that province meets its external obligations, i.e., so long as it delivers its required quota for interprovincial transfer or for export or, in the case of a grain-deficient province, so long as it does not demand more than its stipulated inward transfer.[6] While the circumstances of agriculture make production planning particularly hazardous, this is also very difficult with that substantial proportion of China's industrial output which comes from small enterprises. As far as coal is concerned, the central government does not attempt to allocate, much less to enforce, a close output plan on that considerable part of the country's total production which comes from the smaller and less accessible mines.

Provincial control over allocations of raw materials was extended when it was laid down that from 1959 on, even central government enterprises were to apply to the planning organs of provincial level authorities for supplies. Exceptions to this were made in special cases, such as materials for the armed forces, armament industries, and the railways; fuel for civil aviation; and goods for export, for which requisition would continue to be made to the central ministries concerned.[7]

Overall control of the rate and direction of investment is, as we have seen, one of the targets retained in the hands of the central government, as it must be if any claim is made to have a planned economy. Central control of enrollment in institutions of higher education and of the allocation of graduates can be seen to be a special instance, and a vitally important one, of the control of investment. Closely connected with central control of investment is another centrally controlled target—that of total wages, which, if inflation is to be avoided, must be kept in step with the supply of consumer goods. Joined with the target for total wages is that of the average number of employees: together they constitute control of wage levels and, given the system of urban residence permits, of immigration into towns. Control over the disposition of the country's foreign exchange reserves strengthens the central government's control over investment, and also over allocation of certain key commodities, notably (in the past few years) grain and machinery. Central control of the volume of freight carried by railways and the major modern transport enterprises helps to reinforce central controls over other targets.

Among those targets specifically listed as continuing under central control from 1959 are the figures for revenue transfers between the central government and the provincial level authorities. From 1959 onward the centrally approved figure for a provincial level authority's budgetary expenditure was to be compared with the figure for the total revenue the authority was responsible for raising (i.e. all the revenue from its area, except for customs duties and the profits of enterprises under direct central control). Approved deficits were to be made up by the central government, to which also a proportion of estimated excess revenue had to be transferred. Figures for these balances were the only financial targets at provincial level still to be directly controlled by the central government.[8] Apart from these block transfers of revenue, the central government makes budgetary grants for major investment projects and also *ad hoc* grants for emergency and other special purposes.

Price Control

Decentralization was also applied to price fixing. According to regulations of October 1958, the appropriate ministries of the central government were to continue to control the procurement prices of major agricultural products: grain, raw cotton, vegetable oils, jute, ramie, tea, tobacco, timber, and live pigs. They were also still to control the selling prices (presumably both wholesale and retail), at important commercial centers, of grain, edible oil, pork, timber, cotton yarn and cloth, woolen cloth, edible salt, sugar, coal, petroleum, chemical fertilizers, and wrist watches. The centrally fixed prices of both kinds—procurement and selling prices—were to apply to standard types of the goods in question while prices of other types, and of standard types at places other than the main commercial centers, were to be determined by the local authorities, with reference to the prices of standard types. The prices of all other goods, both agricultural and manufactured, were also to be under local control.[9] This list of centrally controlled prices excludes those industrial goods subject to central allocation, the allocation prices of which would also be centrally fixed.

Another important item supposedly determined by the central authorities has been the annual budgetary allotment of additional credit funds to the banks. However, it was found difficult to keep the total of bank loans down to the figure in the budget, and in 1957–59, the last years for which figures have been published, budgetary funds expended for this purpose greatly exceeded estimates.[10] The estimated loanable funds of the Agricultural Bank in 1965 were at the beginning of the year allocated among various provincial level authorities.[11] It is likely that a similar division of loanable funds was also made by the People's Bank.

This account of targets under the control of the central government dates largely from the decentralization measures of 1957–58. Since then the ban on the export (and possibly on the open circulation within China) of journals on economic planning, and the paucity of other sources, makes it difficult to speak with assurance about the regulations in force at later dates. In 1961–62 reports were current of a move back toward greater financial centralization.[12] This however, as far as can be seen, consisted mainly of improving accounting procedures. If such improvement was successful, it would do more than any organizational change in actually increasing the financial powers of the center, for one of the chief limits on central control or control by lower levels of the government lies in administrative and accounting weaknesses.

In general, instead of greater centralization, such evidence as we have suggests that in the 1960s relaxation (whether *de jure* or just *de facto*) of central control occurred even in the cases of some items, such as procurement prices of grain,[13] which earlier had been reserved to the central authorities. This, too, might have been expected after the decentralization of 1957–58 gave great powers to the provinces, powers which it would have been difficult for the center to circumscribe within the limits it had propounded.

The vital economic matters between the provinces and the central government are, therefore, net transfers of revenue (including *ad hoc* central grants for investment and other purposes); net transfers of grain and other major commodities, agricultural and industrial; and the allocation between provinces of banks' loanable funds. Another item of transfer between provinces and the center is manpower for the armed services. Provinces are responsible for carrying out conscription.[14] The fact that a large part of the central government's revenues is collected by provincial organs and forwarded by the provinces to the central Ministry of Finance is likely to strengthen the provinces' position in negotiations with the central government, at least in those provinces which have a net outward transfer of revenue. Those authorities, such as Sinkiang, which are subsidized by the central government are, of course, in a weaker position in this respect.

The only revenues directly collected by the central government are import duties, profits accruing from foreign trade, and profits of those enterprises under direct central management. In the 1958 budget local authorities were responsible for collecting 77 per cent of the budgetary revenue, but for spending only 44 per cent of total expenditure. These figures are for the *ex ante* budget of 1958, and not for the realized budget of that year, for which a similar analysis is not available.[15] The Chinese state budget, like that of the Soviet Union, is an aggregate of the revenues and expenditures of all levels of the government. As the 1958 budget was balanced, it can be seen that in that year the central government's estimated direct revenues sufficed for only 41 per cent of its budgeted expenditure. The center's dependence on the provinces is therefore very marked.

The economic relations between center and provinces are concerned only with marginal transfers. The great bulk of production, consumption, and exchange is intraprovincial, if not intra-*hsien*. What goes on within a province is of little direct concern to the central government, so long as the province meets its external obligations. The Party, of course, demands more. It demands from its provincial and other local branches, and thus indirectly from the local administrations they control, obedience to policies, programs, and campaigns. The degree of verbal obedience it receives is overwhelming. A slogan launched one day in the capital will be repeated on the morrow throughout the country. It was intended that, after administrative decentralization, control by the Party should ensure enforcement of central policy throughout the country. This did in fact occur in 1958. However, it is by no means so certain whether the local branches of the Party still remain dependable agents for carrying out central policies which may conflict with local interests.

The Party Role

The role of the Communist Party, as the instrument of the center's control over the country, demands that its branches be omnipresent, extending into all administrative and economic units of the country, and yet that it maintain its own separate identity; that it be amenable to central commands and yet on good terms with the masses. These requirements have often proved incompatible.

The two hierarchies, that of the Party and of the government administration, are supposed to run parallel to each other through the political and economic systems right down to the lowest units of local authority and to individual enterprises and institutions. The Party hierarchy ranks the higher of the two. The system of dual hierarchies is, of course, copied from the Soviet Union, where the Party committee at each level has usually been more influential than the corresponding government organ. The tendency toward direct Party control in economic matters has been stronger in China because that country has had proportionately fewer educated people than the Soviet Union, even than the Soviet Union in its early days; hence the maintenance in China of fully staffed dual hierarchies is difficult, if not impossible. Another reason for the tendency, no doubt, is the more recent date of the Chinese revolution and the necessity of continuing to employ as managers and professional personnel many members of the old bourgeoisie who cannot be considered politically reliable. The Party therefore keeps a tight rein on their activities.

Direct executive control of political and economic life by the Party was especially evident during the Great Leap. This period saw an increase in provincial autarchy. Despite the good harvest of 1958, in that year interprovincial transfers of grain declined.[16] Chaotic conditions in the allocation system and in transport made it more necessary than ever for each administrative unit to reach for the highest possible degree of self-sufficiency. The desire for self-sufficiency, whether industrial (by each industrial ministry), by enterprises, or by localities, is endemic in the type of economic planning practiced by China, where the complexities of allocating raw materials and the uncertainties involved encourage individual units to become self-sufficient. The decentralization measures

160

of 1957–58 provided the framework for greater autonomy of the provincial level authorities. In the circumstances of the time this meant increased authority for the provincial Party secretaries, who were supposed to be agents for maintaining the Party's centralized hold on the provinces. However, once a provincial Party secretary becomes *de facto* responsible for the government of a province, he necessarily becomes identified with the provincial administration, with its particular interests and problems. He also finds himself making his province's case, in negotiations with the central government, on the size of the all-important transfers of revenue and commodities, of which we have spoken above.[17] (This example of a First Secretary's opposition to central policy on grain procurement and grain transfers dates from the period of centralization, when his powers were less than in subsequent years.)

These considerations seriously weakened the usefulness of provincial Party committees as agents of the central authorities. It is thought that the chief reason for the re-establishment of the six regional bureaus of the Party, reported in 1961, was to restrain the growing independence of the provincial Party committees. In 1965 the role of the first secretaries of the Party regional bureaus as agents of the center was emphasized by the appointment of four of the six to concurrent high offices in the central government. At one time there were several cases of the first secretaryship of regional bureaus of the Party being held concurrently with the first secretaryship of the Party committee of the most important provincial level unit within the region. From 1965 the tendency was for the two positions to be separated, perhaps to prevent the Party regional bureaus from being absorbed into the general administration as the Party provincial committees had been. The fact that there is no governmental administrative unit corresponding to the region should lessen the danger of this fate befalling the Party regional bureaus.

At lower levels of the political and economic administration the same difficulty in preserving the separate identity of the Party has been apparent. At the time of the Great Leap the

161

tendency to direct Party control intensified. In some places Party organs merged with organs of *hsien* and communes, while in factories Party committees usurped managerial functions. After the Leap it was attempted to disentangle the Party from too close identification with the administrations of geographic units and of enterprises. However, in 1961 it was still necessary for *Red Flag* to oppose "tendencies that do not distinguish between the Party and the government and between the Party and the commune";[18] and for it to be urged that a Party committee in an enterprise should avoid involvement in routine matters, lest it be "demoted to the status of an ordinary operational department and its leadership role weakened." [19]

In 1957 Party cadres in enterprises were assessed for bonuses within the enterprises in which they worked, often by enterprise staff. This, and the fact that the bonuses were probably dependent, at least in part, on the fortunes of the enterprise, must have been an important factor in causing political cadres to identify themselves with enterprise management.[20] During the Great Leap, bonuses for all staff and workers were widely discontinued, but appear to have been resumed. No information is available about assessment of bonuses for Party cadres in enterprises after the Leap.

The attempt to prevent Party committees of enterprises from being absorbed into the ordinary administration was apparently not successful. In any case, from 1964 on, it was thought necessary to provide additional political leadership in economic life through establishing special political departments, first only at the national level, but before long at provincial and *hsien* levels as well, inside the ordinary administrative departments of finance, commerce, industry, and communications. New political departments were also formed inside some corporations, presumably alongside their Party committees. Sometimes a number of enterprises (*ch'i yeh*) are grouped under the control of a corporation (*kungsze*). ("Kungsze" is also on occasion appended to the name of and used to denote a single enterprise.) In some places special "guides" or "instructors" were assigned to individual enterprises by political de-

partments of *hsien* or higher levels.[21] Clearly it was felt that
the strictly political tasks had been neglected and that a stif-
fening of the political element was needed throughout the
economy.

Doubt may be permitted on whether these political departments, in their turn, may not go the same way as the Party
committees. As long as the main task of Party organs in economic sectors is to produce certain economic results—and even
if their tasks are expressed in political terms, success in these
may be measured by the degree of subsequent economic success, i.e., the attainment of targets is the most easily ascer-
tainable proof of ideological zeal—so long must the leading
elements in these Party organs concentrate their energies on
economic matters. "Whether or not an enterprise is able to
fulfill the whole of the plan laid down by the state is the chief
way of determining if theoretical political work in the enterprise has been done well or badly." [22] This inevitably involves
taking sides on economic issues, as, for example, which method
of production to prefer in a given instance. Before long these
problems engross the group which has to decide them and
mold it, rather than the group molding the economic matters
with which it deals. That the group in question continues to
repeat the approved political slogans may disguise, rather than
demonstrate, its chief preoccupations. This trend may be
hastened if, as often seems the case, new industrial recruits
to the Party are chosen in great measure for competence in
their jobs, so that their interests are likely to be more professional than political.

In any case, the new political departments can only be as
effective as the quality of their staff permits. Figures available
for one province, Heilungkiang, show that the majority (54
per cent) of the new political instructors assigned to the particularly sensitive sector of finance and trade were secretaries
of Party branches, i.e., from the category whose defects presumably made the new departments necessary; 10 per cent
were chosen from administrative staff; and 32 per cent were ex-
servicemen.[23] It is on the last category that the most sanguine

hopes have been placed, yet the ex-servicemen's ignorance of economic affairs is likely to weaken their ability to enforce political control over economic life.

Managerial Elite

Altogether then, we must conclude that the Party will continue to become assimilated to administration and management at all levels. In this way the Party, especially in urban areas, is in process of being transformed from a revolutionary controlling group to a managerial elite, a club for meritocrats. The Party cannot, therefore, necessarily be depended on to be an effective instrument for enforcing central policies against the interests of provinces and lower local authorities, and of enterprises. It might be thought that the army could fulfill this role, or at least ensure that local Party branches accede to central wishes in these matters. While the army may be presumed to be under firm central control, it is a blunt instrument for carrying out central policies in economic matters. (I am indebted to John Gittings for the information that provincial first secretaries are concurrently political commissars of their provincial military districts, except for Szechuan and Shantung, which are military regions.) As we have just seen, the military men given economic appointments in the new political departments are seldom likely to have sufficient understanding of economic matters to be able to exert the desired influence.

There remains another channel of possible central influence and control. Within the Party, yet in some way additional to it, the public security system provides a potential centralizing agency. Its vertical lines of responsibility are thought to be especially strong, at least up to the level of the province; it is uncertain how strong they are above this level. (I am indebted to Professor A. Doak Barnett for allowing me to draw on the findings of his research here.)

The control of appointments is probably one of the chief means available to the central authorities for controlling affairs

164

within provinces, although it is by no means clear what degree of control over appointments is still exercised by the center. In 1954 the State Council was made responsible *inter alia* for the appointment and dismissal of directors and deputy directors of departments and bureaus of provincial level authorities, i.e., the local counterparts of central ministries; below these and the other officials under State Council jurisdiction came grades whose occupants fell under the jurisdiction of individual central ministries. The duties of the State Council in this sphere have been discharged by the Ministry of Internal Affairs since 1959, when it took over the responsibilities of the defunct Personnel Bureau of the State Council, which had dealt with appointments of officials of the rank of *hsien* magistrate and above, employed by ministries.[24] Presumably the administrative staff of state enterprises were included, subject to the provisions of the decentralization decrees. In enterprises handed down to them by the decentralization directive of November 1957, provinces were to have the same authority over personnel as they had in the enterprises they already controlled. Even in the case of enterprises that remained in the control of central ministries, local authorities were permitted "to adjust cadres appropriately" so long as they did not weaken the staff of major factories and mines. When transferring cadres of grades controlled by the State Council, approval was to be obtained from the State Council; similarly, consultation with the central ministries was required before transferring cadres of those categories falling under the jurisdiction of ministries.[25]

Behind the state apparatus for the assignment of officials lies that of the Party. In the Soviet Union the Party controls the distribution of cadres through the *nomenklatura* system, by which given Party committees are responsible for making particular appointments in the state administration, in enterprises, trade unions, and other bodies; the word can also be used to signify the list of persons qualified to hold these posts. Little information is available on this topic in respect to China, but it is probable that a similar system is in operation. A provincial report of 1958 mentions that "the appointment or dismissal of cadres must first of all be decided by the Party committees." [26] The context makes it clear that cadres in all sectors of national life are included. This must imply an apportioning out of the responsibility among Party committees at different levels, according to the importance and type of the appointment to be made.

Thus, the degree of central control over appointments would depend on the degree of central control over the Party committee making them, and this depends in part on the degree of control of central appointees to Party committees once they had been appointed—that is, the extent to which the center could afford to dismiss them if they championed local interests, or whether such dismissal would generate ill will between center and provinces which the center would be unwilling to risk. We cannot speak with any certainty on this topic until more study has been done on the turnover rate and mobility between provinces of members of provincial Party secretariats. Even with this knowledge, assessment of its significance would be difficult. We know, for example, of certain cases where the central authorities have dismissed such officials. We do not know how often the center may have wished to order dismissals but refrained because of reasons cited above. (Michael Oksenberg, who is studying career patterns and channels of upward mobility in China, and to whom I am grateful for a discussion of the topics, would give greater weight to central power than I have done here.)

In any case the extent of decentralization must not be exaggerated. The centripetal factors mentioned earlier make possible a greater degree of unification and of control by the central government than has ever existed in China before. In any large country or organization, centripetal and centrifugal trends are liable to alternate. This is natural and need cause no surprise. However, the "norm" around which these oscillations take place must vary with the size, nature, and traditions of the units in question. All these factors point to a greater degree of decentralization from the national government to the next lower level in China than in most other countries. Thus we may judge the degree of centralization attempted in the First Five-Year Plan period to have been abnormal. The corollary is that the decentralization that subsequently occurred in China is less likely to be reversed than the decentralization in the Soviet Union, to which it bore many resemblances and by which the Chinese decrees were no doubt influenced.

The provincial level authorities were the primary beneficiaries of the devolution of authority from the center. (In the northeast, formerly known as *Manchuria,* historic and economic ties lessen the force of provincialism and make the whole region more of a unit in itself.) The overwhelming advantage possessed by these authorities as against the national government in the task of economic control and development is that of size. Averaging 20 to 30 million population each (30 to 40 million if only the provinces of China proper are taken into account), their administrations are better placed than the ministries at Peking for making decisions on policies and priorities for most types of industrial growth and agricultural improvement. The province has become the main unit for the promotion of agricultural mechanization. Powered irrigation and electrically motivated processing industries have been based on transmission lines radiating mainly from provincial capitals. These power systems rarely span provincial boundaries, unlike the regional electric grids. For many agricultural functions even the province is too large a unit; this explains the leadership of the *hsien* in such activities as demonstration farms. But for the promotion of industry, except on the very largest and the very smallest scales, the provincial level is now the most significant.

The Province: The Locality

When we consider relations between the province and its subordinate units—the special administrative districts, the *hsien,* and the municipalities—we know much less than we do with regard to central-provincial dealings. The latter are the subject of national directives, many of which are accessible in the volumes of *Collected Laws and Regulations*. These directives also have something to say about the provincial level's relations with lower units as, for example, when maximum permitted rates of agricultural tax are specified. However, a large degree of latitude is given by the directives to the major local authorities in the manner and extent of their control of the affairs of subordinate authorities. This presumably means that in different provinces and autonomous regions the amount of power exercised by these subordinate authorities may differ considerably. However, we hazard the opinion that political and economic factors combine to make the province and its equivalents the key units for economic development in China today.

These provincial level authorities vary in resources (even after making allowance for the greater levies made by the center on the wealthier ones) and in efficiency. For example, in 1958 certain coal mines in Yunnan, Kweichow, and Ninghsia were to remain for the time being under the management of the central Ministry of Coal on the grounds that these authorities were not administratively capable of managing them.[27] Differences in policy are manifest in matters such as interprovincial variations in size of communes not always accounted for by differing circumstances; as in the formation of communes among the Yi national minority in Yunnan but not among the Yi in neighboring Szechuan, among whom the unit or organization is reported still to be the agricultural producers' cooperative;[28] and in the pioneering of linear programming, especially in transport, by Shantung, and the use of special features, notably the multi-branched Labor University, which in Kiangsi characterizes the movement for "sending down" youths to remote mountainous areas of the province.

The position of the provinces might be thought to be threatened by the campaign waged from 1962 onward to restore commerce to its former channels and directions according to economic regions instead of according to administrative units, as had tended to be the case since the growth of local self-sufficiency in 1958. However, the deliberate restoration by administrative means of old trading patterns, as by the resituating of state commercial organs, has been slow and cumbersome, especially compared with the apparently spontaneous revival of two other instruments of the traditional channels of trade: rural markets and trade warehouses. The trade warehouse is a traditional wholesaling unit where, in the old days, traders not only stored goods but also did business and were boarded. The managers would also provide them with commercial contacts. (The fluctuations in the fortunes of the trade warehouses in recent years will be treated in the author's forthcoming book.) In 1965 the change was still far from complete;[29] perhaps local Party committees were far from enthusiastic. It may be wondered how far the reaction can go against the organization of trade according to administrative units without causing wide repercussions, not only in the economy but also in the political structure.

Since 1957–58 almost all activities occurring within a province, except those concerning the army and the most important economic enterprises, have come under the surveillance of the provincial Party committee and more especially of its first secretary. Beneath the provincial level, the Party committees and secretaries of lower local authorities have enjoyed a similar sway. If commerce is no longer to be based on the administrative units of province, district, and *hsien,* transport and production are likely to follow suit. The planning and fiscal jurisdictions of the units of local government will then be difficult to maintain in their present form. The real professionals in the commercial systems probably hope that by basing their activities on nonpolitical units, they may lessen the hold of the political men on them. Whether the local politicians, especially the provincial first secretaries, will accept this situation remains to be seen. Awareness of the political implications involved may perhaps be shown by the leading role taken in encouraging the change by the regional bureaus of the Party, which each control several provinces,[30] and which may see in the movement a way of limiting the power of provincial and other local Party secretaries. If political and economical ad-

169

ministration were disjoined at the provincial level, it might assuage the anxiety of the center about waxing provincial autonomy, but it would leave in its place the problem which decentralization was designed to solve—the administrative impossibility of far-reaching direct control throughout the country from Peking. The choice before the central government, if it has one, may therefore be between seeing provinces develop on increasingly autonomous lines, or permitting a considerable relaxation of political control over the economy. Perhaps a measure of each will be unavoidable.

Provincial Autonomy

In any case the strengthening of autonomy at the provincial level is unlikely to be quickly reversed. In the short and medium term, we may conclude, the future of China lies in great measure with the provinces. Our present ignorance of what is happening at the provincial level, in both political and economic matters, is profound. Presumably in some provinces strong administrations are being built up. Negotiations between provinces and the central government are likely to be tough on the matter of transfer balances—the net transfers of revenue, of grain and other major commodities; the allocation among provinces of raw materials, of central budgetary investment and of banks' loanable funds. The permitted total wage payments within a province may also be the subject of hard bargaining and even harder struggle in enforcement. The onus for enforcing this must fall largely on the provincial branches of the People's Bank, for it is their duty to refuse to release cash for unauthorized wage payments. A number of press references indicate that overspending the wage fund has been difficult to prevent. However, it has not occurred on a scale to undermine the value of the currency, and for this the People's Bank must have been kept under firm central control on all vital matters, and have been able to stand up to pressure from organs of the provincial authorities. Indeed, it may be that the Bank has succeeded in this respect where the

170

Party has failed, in that it has kept its identity as an organ of central control while local Party branches have tended to be assimilated with their corresponding local authorities. In the past, weakness in organizing the large impersonal undertakings of modern economic life has characterized the Chinese scene. Without an opportunity for close study on the spot at the present time we must speak with caution, but it seems at least probable that the People's Bank has, to a large extent, overcome this weakness. This is relevant to the question of central control of the army, for the Bank presumably is the channel for paying the army. It will be remembered that during the period of war-lord rule in China, control of local military units was determined by who paid them.

When linked with the question of provincial-central relations, China's imports of grain take on an additional significance. While 5 to 6 million tons a year (the approximate rate at which these imports were running in the early 1960s) represents only some 3 per cent of China's total grain output, it is the equivalent of around 20 per cent of total grain procurement, and probably a good deal more of total interprovincial transfers. Hence the imports of grain serve to ease relations between the center and the provinces, as otherwise Peking would be forced to try to squeeze larger grain transfers out of grain-surplus provinces. Thus this supply of imported grain, which is under its direct control, strengthens the central government by making it to that extent less dependent on provincial compliance with its levies. Foreign trade in this way fulfills the same role as the "key economic areas" which in days past gave the imperial government of China much of the grain supplies for its own needs.[31] As well as importing grain, the present government of China is also fostering "key economic areas" for the same purpose in the form of "areas of high and stable yield." These areas receive priority for central government investment funds for agriculture, which presumably gives the center a greater hold on their surpluses of grain and cotton.

171

A Cellular Society

China is not a monolithic society or economy, but a cellular one. This is the burden of the evidence. Repeatedly, economic discussions in the Chinese press refer to the "responsibility (or guarantee) system" (*paokan chihtu*). According to this traditional and deeply rooted concept, a unit guarantees performance in a certain sphere to the authorities of the level immediately above it, in return for which it is allowed a very wide latitude in the conduct of its internal affairs, including its relations with its lower units, without interference from superior authority. Thus, so long as a province, localized lineage, village, or other group fulfilled its obligations to the outside world, it would be left alone in peace to deal with its members or subordinates. This satisfied the Chinese attachment to the notion of harmonious self-sufficient groups. At the same time, it was an eminently practical arrangement in a society where direct administration down to the grass roots was impossible. This "responsibility system" is so taken for granted in China that it is seldom explicitly set forth, but is something that the observer must always bear in mind. The concentration of center-provincial relations on marginal transfers, and not on total production, revenue, or expenditure within provinces is fully consonant with the "responsibility system." Practical considerations contributed, in 1958 and the subsequent years of disaster, to the trend toward autonomous self-sufficiency implied in this concept. At a deeper level, the process may have been hastened by the instinctive return in times of crisis to familiar patterns of doing things.

We must indicate certain consequences which flow from this organizational pattern of the Chinese economy. Any direct revenue or expenditure by the central government—for example, on the nuclear program, other military expenditure, foreign aid, etc.—should, to determine its relative internal significance, be calculated as a percentage of *direct central government* revenue or expenditure and not only as a percentage of total

172

budgetary revenue or expenditure; similarly with the quantities of grain and other commodities at the disposal of the central authorities. In other words, the central government cannot draw directly on the total taxable capacity of the country. The center can always, of course, call on the major local authorities to increase their contributions of cash or commodities. Even when a definite period of years is stipulated before changes can be made in any regulations, there are always loopholes, and in any case plenty of examples can be quoted of the free way in which law is interpreted, or ignored. The real limit on the expansion of central revenues lies in the relations between the center and the major local authorities. The center depends on the cooperation of these authorities, and only in an extreme situation could it afford openly to use crude force—i.e., its control over the armed forces—to secure increased levies of revenue or commodities. The tension between center and provinces with respect to transfers in cash and kind must be seen in the context of their mutual dependence.

While stressing the cellular nature of the present-day Chinese economy, a word of warning is necessary. As the economy becomes modernized, the tendency will be for its cellular nature to evolve into more complex systems of relationships. Even now the economy is less cellular than in the past, as exemplified in particular by the countrywide operations of the People's Bank and also in the changes taking place in the more modernized parts of the country. The latter is brought out in the study of Tangshan, Hopeh, being undertaken by Professor John W. Lewis, to whom I am indebted for a discussion of this point.

Another point must be emphasized. Given the size and circumstances of China, the surprising thing is not the amount of provincial autonomy, but the extent of central control; not any fissiparous strains we may have noted, but the degree of underlying and persisting unity which binds this quarter of the human family, and which must claim our tribute of admiration.

Apart from the growth of local autonomy, other basic causes weaken the control both of the center and also of local authorities over the economy. Deficiencies in statistical work and accountancy figure prominently in this list. These weaknesses set very severe limits to the possibility of any kind of control. The same result follows from the shortage of competent administrators and managers. In discussing the difference between developed and underdeveloped economics, too much prominence is usually given to technological matters and not enough to management and to financial and statistical know-how. Administrative failures may have been one reason for the frequent choppings and changings of policy which have marked the economic scene in Communist China.

The concentration of central control on marginal transfer balances is due in good measure to the virtual impossibility, given the deficiencies just mentioned, of trying to ascertain— much less to control—output and revenue totals; transfers are easier to check. A similar importance has come to devolve on profits as a success indicator for enterprises.[32] Whether a given amount of profits has or has not been remitted to the state by an enterprise is less liable to uncertainty or abuse than is the use of output, quality, cost of production or labor productivity as success indicators. This is apart from the economic superiority of the profit index over the alternatives.

To return to the limitations placed on economic control by administrative and accountancy weaknesses in China, a major example is the inability to prevent the illicit use of extra-budgetary funds. These were originally those items of revenue at the disposal of local authorities of different grades, or of economic enterprises and of institutions of various kinds and their controlling ministries, which were not entered in the budget and which might be used without higher authorization. Large sums from this source have been diverted to unplanned investment, thus making nonsense of state investment plans. Also this unplanned investment has often led to the diversion of state-allocated raw materials from their planned use. Apparently the People's Bank was not able to prevent all this, possibly because the transactions involved were settled in cash, contrary to regulations.

174

Public Face and Private Face

The Chinese have a sophisticated attitude to outward expression of opinion, which renders government control simultaneously easier and more difficult. Words are regarded as symbolic counters, to be moved about the chessboard of life in order to produce the desired effect. This results in reservations and subtleties of expression and action which need to be interpreted within the framework of the Chinese environment, and which a stranger might not understand. The effect is that outward compliance is easily obtained; but an individual's or a group's "public face" must not be taken as an indication of their "private face." Thus conformity, although easily won, is apt to remain superficial. Alongside this, however, is an implicit understanding by both government and people of the limits to which both can go, an understanding which was ruptured during the Great Leap but which may now have been restored. It is relatively simple in these circumstances for a government to see that stipulated formulae are repeated throughout the country or that demonstrations are held when ordered, but quite another thing for it to ensure that its writ should run in enforcing against local interests. In this case there may be little in the way of outward protest, but a sabotage need be none the less effective for being done in silence. Indeed, the more contrary to central orders local cadres may be acting, the more loudly they may give verbal support to those orders.

Connected with this trait is another, the strong tradition in China of not discussing family difficulties and dissensions with outsiders. This holds not only for families but also for larger groups and for the nation itself. Thus the Chinese are apt to present a seemingly monolithic front to foreigners. Added to this, foreigners at present are restricted mainly to those places and sectors of Chinese life which are directly controlled by the central government: the capital and other large cities and their environs, diplomacy, international trade, and institutions of higher education. In consequence, the picture given to the

175

outside world is of a gigantic slab of humanity under tight centralized control, whose actions are based on certain highly simplified slogans. An impression so untrue, so dull, and so terrifying may be thought to serve the purposes of prestige: certainly it ill serves the cause of international understanding, of world peace, or even of China's national safety.

NOTES

1. On the decentralization movement in general, see Donnithorne, "Background to the People's Communes: Changes in China's Economic Organization in 1958," *Pacific Affairs*, XXXII, 4, December 1959.
2. *Collected Laws and Regulations of the Chinese People's Republic* (in Chinese), VI, p. 392; Siao Liu, "The Problem of Building Industrial Bases and of the Balanced Development of Local Economies," *Planned Economy*, VII, July 1958, p. 8.
3. *People's Daily*, June 25, 1958, p. 1; *Collected Laws and Regulations*, VII, p. 331.
4. Wang Kuei-wu, "An Important Change in the Method of Drawing Up Annual Plans," *Planned Economy*, IX, September 1958, p. 14.
5. *Collected Laws and Regulations*, IV, p. 376.
6. *Ibid.*, VII, pp. 281–82.
7. *Ibid.*, VIII, p. 101; She Yi-san, "A Discussion on the System for Distributing Commodities," *Planned Economy*, X, October 1958, p. 34.
8. Hsu Fei-ch'ing, "Unified Leadership and Delegated Management Is the Correct Policy for Budgetary Control," *Finance*, XIX, October 9, 1959, p. 13.
9. *Collected Laws and Regulations*, VIII, pp. 168–69.
10. *People's Handbook*, 1958, p. 214; 1959, pp. 226–27; 1960, pp. 182 and 184; also *Collected Laws and Regulations*, IX, pp. 63–64.
11. "The Agricultural Bank of China: Review of the Work in 1964 and Arrangements for the Work in 1965," Minutes of the Third National Conference of Branch Managers, *Rural Finance*, IV and V, February 28, 1965 (SCMM 468).
12. Fan Yeh-chun, Li Te-sheng, and Chang Chih-tao, "The Problem of Centralization and Unification in Financial Work," *Ta Kung Daily (Dagong Bao)*, Peking, June 25, 1962, p. 3.
13. *Kweichow Daily*, August 30, 1959 (SCMP 2142).

176

14. See Jung Tze-ho, Vice Minister of Finance, "Some Problems in the Reform of the System of Financial Management," where expenditure on organizing conscription is included in the "regular annual expenditure" of provinces, *Finance*, January 1958, p. 1.
15. Yang Chao-ch'iao, "Financial Work Must Serve the Party's General Line," *Finance*, October 1958, p. 1.
16. Kao Yu-huang, "The Need for Vigorous Organization of Rational Transport in the Economic Activities of the Nation," *Economic Research*, VII, July 1959, p. 5.
17. See, for example, the case of Pan Fu-sheng from 1953–58, First Secretary of the Honan CCP Provincial Committee, *Honan Daily*, July 4, 1958 (CB 515, pp. 7 and 10); Wu Chih-p'u, First Secretary, Honan CCP Provincial Committee, "Rightist Opportunism Is the Principal Danger in the Party Now," *Honan Daily* (CB 515, pp. 20–21); Editorial, *Honan Daily*, July 15, 1958 (CB 515, p. 41).
18. Huang Chih-kang, "Strengthen Leadership over Basic Level Rural Cadres' Study," *Red Flag*, XIX, October 10, 1961, p. 28.
19. *Liberation*, June 5, 1961 (SCMM 312).
20. Yu Shu-fang, "Political and Mass Organization Cadres in Enterprises Who Are not Engaged in Production Should not Receive Bonuses," *Labor*, November 11, 1957, p. 17. Yu argues the case against these cadres receiving bonuses, but assumes it is still an open question. He writes, "At present bonuses for Party and mass organization cadres not engaged in production are decided by the director of the enterprise, or even by the wages department, or some are not even assessed by anyone. Thus the work of such cadres is not judged by higher levels of the Party, Youth League, or trade union."
21. *Ta Kung Daily (Dagong Bao)*, June 16, 1965, p. 1, editorial and news item. See also *China News Analysis*, No. 581.
22. Chang Feng-lin, "The Appropriate Distribution of Enterprises' Bonus Funds," *Labor*, August 8, 1964, p. 27.
23. *Ta Kung Daily (Dagong Bao)*, June 16, 1965, p. 1.
24. *Collected Laws and Regulations*, I, pp. 103, 109, 122.
25. *Ibid.*, VI, p. 394.
26. Report by Chang Chung-liang, First Secretary of the Kansu Provincial CCP Committee, *Kansu Daily*, August 16, 1958 (CB 528).
27. *People's Daily*, June 25, 1958.
28. NCNA Kunming, July 26, 1965; NCNA Chengtu, July 19, 1965; whether this difference is merely verbal or more substantial is admittedly uncertain.

29. *Ta Kung Daily* (*Dagong Bao*), August 9, 1965, p. 1.
30. *Ibid.*
31. Chi Ch'ao-ting, *Key Economic Areas of Chinese History*, New York, 1963.
32. This topic will be developed in the author's forthcoming book on the economic organization of China, to be published by Allen & Unwin. This article is based upon that study. See also F. Schurmann, "Economic Policy and Political Power in Communist China," *Annals of the American Academy of Political and Social Science*, CCCXLIX, September 1963, p. 63.

178

CHINA'S ECONOMIC PROSPECTS
Dick Wilson

C HINA INAUGURATED her long-awaited Third Five-Year Plan
at the beginning of 1966. It arrived without publicity,
and no information about it has yet been published. It followed a three-year hiatus in China's economic planning, the
abortive Second Plan having theoretically ended in 1962 (in
practice it was abandoned from the start in favor of the unplanned Great Leap Forward of 1958–59). The Third Plan
inauguration thus marks China's rediscovery of self-confidence
after the failure of the Leap, the natural disasters and famine
of 1959–61, and the suspension of Soviet aid in 1960. After five
painful years of readjustment, the Chinese leaders now hope
to swing back into a pattern of steady annual growth, but on
the basis of "self-reliance" and without benefit of foreign aid.

It was rumored in Peking in 1965 that Chen Yun, the ailing
Politburo economist whose criticism of the Leap caused his
relegation to the sidelines eight years ago, was involved in
drafting the new Plan. If so, this would strengthen the view
that Chinese economic policy has settled into a more pragmatic
mood after the excesses of the Leap and the subsequent setbacks. What little has been said officially of the Plan suggests
that it broadly continues the policies forged in the recovery

179

period of the past five years. This means giving first priority to agriculture and second priority to those industries which supply agriculture, notably the chemical fertilizer industry.

The only important shift in emphasis apparent now is a renewed interest in heavy industry, which was over-invested during the Communists' first decade and then allowed to mark time during the past five years. The State Capital Construction Commission, an important instrument of investment in heavy industry until its abolition in 1961, was revived in 1965. Two new Ministries of Machine-building were created at about the same time; this makes a total of seven Ministries of Machine-building, and the majority of these are believed to be under military guidance. This leads to a second observation about the Third Plan, that it is likely to favor defense-oriented industries. China now depends on her own weapons and military hardware and feels herself increasingly likely to come into conflict with the United States.

The Vietnam conflict is probably the main cause of the tentativeness of the Third Plan and of the secrecy surrounding it. China faces a virtually open-ended commitment to supply foodstuffs, consumer goods, and military equipment to North Vietnam, and these represent a considerable drain on her meager surpluses. The Plan is therefore likely to be full of contingency provisions and may be implemented for the time being only on a year-to-year basis. It is in any case doubtful that the Chinese Third Plan is anywhere near as detailed and sophisticated as the current Indian Fourth Five-Year Plan.

Any discussion of the Chinese economy and its prospects must begin with agriculture, still more important than Chinese industry and now officially recognized by the Communists as the "foundation" of their economy. Their postwar experience has been strikingly similar to that of the Indians; in the first decade of economic planning (roughly the 1950s), substantial increases, ranging from 50 per cent to 100 per cent, were obtained in food production. The government hoped that this tempo could be maintained or even quickened, but instead the curve has flattened out since 1958. The early investments gave high returns which were, in part, simply the effect of restored law and order after decades of fighting (in the civil war as well as against the Japanese). But the limits of easy, cheap agricultural expansion have now been reached, and in the future each increase will have to be paid for by costly inputs of chemical fertilizer, electrification schemes, and the like.

The Chinese are also much chastened by their failure to win independence from the freaks of weather: this year they again faced a spring drought of the kind which can cut 10 million tons off their wheat harvest. The 1965 rice crop, unofficially estimated at 85 millions tons, was the best since the bumper years 1957–58. But the northern drought caused a fall in the wheat harvest, and total food grain output was unofficially estimated (no official statistics have been issued since 1960) at 160 million tons, or 180 million tons if potatoes are included, as is the statisticians' custom in China. This level of output is the same as seven or eight years ago, and over the entire seventeen years of Communist rule the average annual increase in food production appears to work out at only 3½ per cent.

There are reasons to believe, however, that agricultural growth can be resumed. Work is continuing again on water conservation and irrigation, and indeed the winter of 1964–65 saw the biggest mass drive in this area since the Great Leap. Investment is now concentrated on high-yielding areas which are relatively free from flooding or drought because of good dikes and water storage facilities in the locality. In the past, investment tended to be evenly spread over rich and poor areas alike out of a concern for egalitarianism and justice. Another 3 million hectares were allocated to demonstration farms last year, and these institutions have been made more appealing to the ordinary peasant, who in the past tended to regard them as academic, bookish, and highfaluting. Yields on demonstration farms are said to show 30 per cent improvement over the local average. Most important of all, the supply of chemical fertilizer, which was neglected until 1960, is now being expanded rapidly. Last year China probably produced 5 million tons and imported a smaller amount to make a total supply of some 7 million tons. This is still a mere one-tenth of the per-acre supply in Japan or Britain, but it is very much more than was formerly available in China. Two chemical fertilizer plants, a British and a Dutch, have recently been bought and erected in Szechuan province. But these things are costly. In 1964 I visited one of the first Chinese-designed and Chinese-manufactured chemical fertilizer factories, at Wuching near Shanghai. It produces only 1 per cent of China's needs, and yet it cost $25 million to construct.

It is difficult to judge the adequacy of incentives for production in the People's Communes. Despite murmurings from the ideological fanatics in the Communist Party, the "private sector" in agriculture has survived and is estimated to be responsible for about 10 per cent of national production. The three pillars of this "private sector" in what is at bottom a thoroughly collectivized rural economy are the production team, the private plot, and the private pig. The commune is usually a vast organization comprising some 50,000 people in about a hundred villages. It remains the basic unit of local government and economy, running the increasingly important native-style rural industries, organizing large-scale public works in the off-seasons, collecting taxes; and supervising commerce, law courts, social services, and public security. But the tactics of cultivation, and the *usus* (though not the *dominium*) of draft animals, plows, and tools, are in the hands of the production team (the third tier of the commune, below the production brigade, and often roughly equivalent to the old village community). The team is given its goals by the commune, but is largely left to itself in deciding how to achieve them.

This small community has, therefore, an incentive to work hard, since its remuneration at the end of the crop year depends on its own success and diligence. In addition, each household has its own small private plot for growing vegetables and domestic products. These can even be marketed at the rural fairs, as can the pigs (80 per cent of which are

182

privately raised, apparently because the Party acknowledges that a household looks after livestock better than would a larger collective group in which responsibility is diffused). The Communists are trying to prevent the villages from polarizing once again into dynamic, potentially exploitive, rich peasants on the one hand, and unenterprising, potentially exploitable poor peasants on the other. They have set up Poor and Middle Peasant Associations everywhere. But they refrain from policy changes which, while promoting a more egalitarian society, might also cause the enterprising peasants to reduce production. As a Canton newspaper admitted candidly a year or two ago, "Commune members' domestic production is an essential supplement to the socialist economy and cannot possibly be replaced by the public economy for a long period of time to come." (*Nan Fang Jih Pao,* October 9, 1964) Agricultural prospects, for all these reasons, do not appear too gloomy in the short term.

The same can be said for industry. Prime Minister Chou En-lai set for last year the modest target of an 11 per cent increase in production, and later it was claimed that capital construction in 1965 had been 20 per cent greater than in 1964. The work of refurbishing mines and transportation, the two weakest links in the industrial economy, came to a head in 1965, on the eve of the Third Plan. Many new mines and pits were opened. Coal production probably reached 240 million tons, and the US Bureau of Mines has estimated China's 1964 mineral output at $4 billion (1965 production was almost certainly in excess of that). Electricity generation in 1965 was unofficially estimated at over 40,000 kilowatt hours and crude oil output at 9 million tons or more. Refining capacity can probably only cater to this amount of crude oil, and imports of oil products have been reduced to a mere 1 million tons or so. China still enjoys a mere 5 gallons of oil per head per year (against Japan's 150 and America's 900 plus), but the nation's total supply has more than tripled in the past eight years.

All this should enable the steel, machine-building, and chemical industries to stride ahead after the pause of the past

183

few years. Steel production in 1965 was unofficially estimated at 10 million tons. New industrial investment in the past two or three years included the purchase of a score or so of complete plants from Japanese and west European manufacturers, mostly in the chemical and related fields (petroleum chemicals, oil, synthetic fibers, plastics, fertilizer) but including one or two in metallurgy. Some of these are now under construction or actually in operation. Much of the excess capacity put up during the Leap is now being utilized for the first time, thanks to the reorganization of raw material supply.

Light industry is also in the news. The manufacture of plastic household goods has mushroomed, and the textile industry is undergoing expansion. Forty mills were due to be expanded last year, and 700,000 new spindles were installed in the first six months, according to official claims. China's first home-made vinylon plant went into production in 1965, and the domestic cloth ration was raised at the end of the year to 6½ square yards per person per year in Shanghai (probably less elsewhere). But the cottonfields are still lagging behind the mills' needs, and large raw cotton imports are made from East Africa, Pakistan, and Mexico. Transistor radios have been made since 1963, and there is an infant television industry; a refrigerator was displayed at the principal export fair last year.

The great slogan in industry now is self-reliance. Factories are encouraged to improvise solutions to their production problems without recourse to expensive equipment from outside. Official reports sing the praises of the Shanghai engineers who recently built a 12,000-ton hydraulic forging press, and of the serial production of 2,000-horsepower diesel locomotives. Last year's claimed achievements included the manufacture of a large electron microscope with a magnifying power of 200,000, and an electronic computer "which solves differential equations to the twenty-fourth order." The Taiyüan Heavy Machine Plant claims to have constructed a 102-foot high traveling crane lifting 350 tons; other factories have produced 72-megawatt water-driven turbines; and visitors to

184

Peking report that Chinese-made light motorcycles are now to be seen in the streets of the capital. Doubtless none of these things are being produced in the numbers really needed, but it is something of a revolution for them to have been made at all in China. It is a good start.

Industrial development still depends on a financially modest but technologically crucial import of foreign machinery and know-how, and this in turn depends (under "self-reliance") on how much China can earn from her export trade. In the earlier years of Mao's rule the exchange of Chinese primary and light industrial products against foreign equipment and industrial raw materials was predominantly conducted with the Soviet Union. But Peking's foreign trade has been completely reoriented since the split with Russia in 1960. The new pattern is for China to conduct two-thirds of her trade outside the Soviet bloc. Her commercial exchanges with the USSR have declined steadily since 1960, although they may now have stabilized at some $450 million annually. In 1964, the last year for which published Soviet statistics are available, China sold $310 million worth of goods (half of them textiles and garments) to the USSR and bought only $135 million worth (mainly oil products, machinery, special steels, timber, and aircraft) in return. An additional four Russian aircraft and five helicopters were contracted for 1965 delivery to China. At the end of 1964 China completed the last installment of her $2.25 billion debt to Moscow (incurred by the extension of commercial and military credits during the 1950s), and the annual export surplus in her trade with Russia can now be used to buy more from the USSR. Probably the Chinese will continue to try to market their consumer goods in the Soviet Union as a means of acquiring a corresponding amount of Soviet spare parts and raw materials needed by China's industry, assuming that political relations between the two countries allow trade to continue on this scale.

China's total trade is still remarkably small. Last year it apparently rose by about 15 per cent to reach $3.8 billion (see Table II). This represents only a quarter of Japan's trade

185

turnover and is even smaller than India's (about $4 billion). The whole of China's foreign trade is only half again as big as that of the tiny British Colony of Hong Kong ($2.6 billion). But this partially reflects the incipient self-sufficiency of the Chinese economy.

At the moment China appears to be devoting some two-fifths of her overseas spending to farm products, importing some $700 million worth of these items annually—mostly cereals from Australia and Canada, but also raw cotton. This fact alone explains the new (and strictly un-Marxist) priority given to domestic agriculture. There is much speculation over the future of China's wheat imports, which began in 1961 as emergency famine relief. That need has now passed, but the imports continue at the level of 5 to 6 million tons a year. One reason is the need to build up and maintain good stocks against future disasters; another is Peking's need for bargaining power *vis-à-vis* its restless food-surplus provinces (Mrs. Indira Gandhi faces an identical problem); a third is the fact that wheat is cheap on the world market—$70 a ton, against $115 a ton for the rice which the Chinese export to Hong Kong, Ceylon, and southeast Asia. As might have been expected, China was a net agricultural importer during the famine years, but in 1965 she emerged once again as a net agricultural exporter, selling high-priced soybeans, rice, preserved or processed vegetables, and meat to the tune of some $800 million. In April, 1966, the Chinese government signed another long-term contract with the Canadian wheat farmers for a minimum delivery of 1.5 million tons a year over the next three years with the option of going up to 4 million a year (and possibly for a longer period of years). But it seems likely that China will gradually reduce her dependence on wheat imports in the future.

As for the rest of China's current overseas purchases, these are mostly industrial goods—materials, machinery, and vehicles. The main exception is chemical fertilizer, on which Peking spent $140 million in 1965.

This import bill of $1.75 billion in 1965 was more than

186

balanced by China's export proceeds of roughly $2.05 billion. Farm products were still the most important earner, at $800 million, with textiles second at $525 million. The Chinese are naturally making every effort to expand their export earnings, especially in Hong Kong (which is now China's biggest single customer, surpassing even Russia and buying more than $400 million worth in 1965) and in southeast Asia. Textile sales to these areas have risen recently. Malaysia banned Chinese steel, paper, and textiles at the end of 1965, and the recent changes of government in Ceylon and Indonesia have adversely affected Peking's trade with those countries. But China will probably recover her trading base in newly independent Singapore, where she resumed rubber purchases at the end of 1965; and her trade with Japan is booming in spite of political tensions. With better cotton crops, high cotton imports, and the development of synthetic fibers, there is every chance of another Chinese textile export offensive. Food processing is another burgeoning export industry, and such lines as watches and radios are at last beginning to make a serious impact on foreign markets. The possibility of crude oil exports to Japan has been rumored. But the difficulty remains that China's traditional export lines are extremely limited in scope (furs, bristles, feathers, tea, essential oils), while the new, manufactured products which she will be able to offer in increasing quantities face stiff barriers in all the industrialized markets and are totally banned in the United States. As Japan and Hong Kong have already discovered, it is in these rich markets, rather than those of the developing countries, that worthwhile pickings are to be made.

China's export surplus in 1965 was thus on the order of $300 million, but this was probably offset by foreign aid disbursements of perhaps $60 million and invisible imports such as ship charters, insurance, and diplomatic expenditures. Peking does not keep much foreign currency idle, although there was some switch in 1965 from sterling to Swiss francs, gold, and platinum. The foreign aid program, essential to China's image as a serious world power and ideological leader, was being expanded until last year, especially in Africa and in neutralist Asian countries; but there are indications of increasing disillusionment in Peking with its results, and it may decrease in the future. China has disbursed some $1.25 billion in aid since 1949, mostly in Chinese goods and services, and is committed to another $1 billion promised. Incredibly enough, this means that China has given away far more than she ever received in aid from the Soviet Union. Other small sources of foreign exchange which are being encouraged are remittances from overseas Chinese, which run at almost $100 million annually, and tourism (apparently 4,000 west Europeans were booked for summer tours in China in 1965, something of a record).

What about the longer-term prospects? It is becoming apparent that China does not lack the material natural resources for industrial development. The earlier image of a poorly provided China was based on the restricted surveying and prospecting which had been done by foreigners near the seaboard. In fact, the interior uplands of western China are more likely to be rich in minerals, and this is what the Communists now claim. Since they no longer allow foreigners to be associated with their prospecting, there is no way of checking their claims definitively. Emotional factors enter into their propaganda in these matters, as witness the *People's Daily* (Peking) editorial of January 2, 1966, proclaiming that the pioneers who had been developing the new Taching oilfield in northern China since 1960 had "blown the theory of oil scarcity in China sky high." Western analysts now estimate China's oil reserves at between 2 billion and 5 billion tons (plus very considerable shale reserves), and the Chinese give every appearance of confidence in their eventual self-sufficiency in oil. Some minerals (notably tin, manganese, tungsten, antimony, and mercury) have been exported by China in recent years, but in decreasing quantities, a fact which may suggest that the development of industry is providing a bigger domestic demand for these ores. The three key minerals of which there is an obvious shortage are copper, chromite, and

188

nickel. The shortage is met by imports and by the improvisation of substitutes and alternative techniques. Gold and uranium are among the ores now claimed by Peking to be present in satisfactory quantities in Tibet, Sinkiang, and other parts of western China.

The finances of development present more difficulty. The Peking government can raise about $15 to $20 billion a year for its annual budget, all drawn from the profits of state-owned enterprises and taxation. Since this represents a rate of capital accumulation approaching 25 per cent, it seems obvious that the screws cannot be tightened any further. This level of public spending can presumably, in a reasonable year, yield an economic growth rate of about 5 per cent a year (in the absence of any data from which the growth rate can be scientifically calculated, one has to rely on informed guesses). The Peking regime probably achieved an average rate of growth of about 5 per cent a year in the 1950–57 period, and this probably doubled to 10 per cent during the Leap, only to decline sadly in the following five years. If a 5 per cent growth rate can be maintained over the next fourteen years, then the Chinese economy could double in real value; over thirty-three years (say one generation) it could quintuple. But there are three major handicaps to be considered.

The first is technology. Soviet aid to China in the 1950s was marginal to the financing of Chinese development, and the loans have all been repaid with interest. But Russian technical assistance was indispensable, and it must be questioned whether the Chinese can achieve the fast industrialization on which they have set their hearts if they insist on doing without a comprehensive across-the-board inflow of know-how from a rich and highly industrialized country—such as Russia or Japan. The Soviet walk-out in 1960 was helpful in forcing Chinese managers and technicians at all levels to develop their own knowledge and imagination, and in some matters it is probably true that the Chinese, faced with the challenge of going it alone, have in the course of several years come up with something better than the Russians had originally prom-

189

ised. But in many areas the short cuts which full access to foreign techniques can bring are denied to the Chinese. I was told at the Anshan steelworks in 1964 that they had still not overcome the difficulties brought about by the sudden withdrawal of the resident Soviet technicians four years before. In special steels, in high-grade petroleum products, in precision instruments and giant machinery, the Chinese will continue to feel the pinch of technological poverty.

The second handicap is politics. Political idealism and economic pragmatism make uneasy bedfellows, and it cannot be assumed that during the next decade or two the theorists in the Chinese Communist Party will not insist on doctrinaire policies inimical to economic growth. This is particularly worrisome in the field of science. Most of the scientists in China are from bourgeois backgrounds and are not trusted by the Party. Again, in the communes, it is always possible that the Party will at some point begin to insist on another dose of collectivism. The present leadership sets more store on ideological purity than on material wealth, and even its successors may conceivably be prisoners of their ideological training.

The third handicap is the population explosion. The current population is probably about 740 million, increasing at the rate of about 2 per cent a year. This means an extra 15 million mouths to feed each year. It also means that the national economic growth of 5 per cent a year will have to be shared by more people, and that the per-capita increase in income or wealth will be only 3 per cent. The Party was reluctant to promote a birth control program because of its intellectual anti-Malthusian bias, but it now seems to have been convinced by the demographic evidence. A big drive has been developed to make people delay marriage, postpone childbearing, and adopt contraceptive techniques. There is evidence that this program is showing results among the educated elite and in the cities, but it remains to be seen how soon the less enlightened peasantry can be made to give up its traditional yearning for large families.

During the euphoric days of the Great Leap, one slogan

190

said that China would surpass Britain in major industrial production in ten years and would draw level with the United States in fifteen. Today, eight years afterwards, China's steel and electricity output are only one-third of Britain's (and even if they were equal to Britain's, this would still be little to boast of because China has fifteen times the population of Britain). China's national budget is roughly comparable to that of France and is able to afford an atomic weapons program costing some $250 million or so a year. But her citizens enjoy a material standard of life only one-tenth that of the average Frenchman. Chairman Mao said in the summer of 1965 that it would take twenty to thirty years for China to become a powerful nation; and most Chinese estimates of the time it will take to modernize, and to reach the current levels of industrialization and prosperity of western Europe, are longer than that. Fifty to eighty years will be needed to catch up with the West in terms of bridging the moving, and not merely the static, gap. The long-term challenge of economic development is daunting in China just as it is in India. But the short-term outlook is less grave, especially when viewed against the background of the disasters of 1960–62. The mood is one of confidence and purposeful dedication.

TABLE I

China's Economic Place

The following are rough figures for 1964 comparing China's economic situation with that of her two main rivals in Asia and of Britain. China has published no statistics since 1960, and the figures given here are unofficial estimates.

	China	India	Japan	Britain
A. *Vital Statistics*				
Population (millions, year-end)	725 ?	460	97	54

191

Population growth per annum

	+2½% ?	+2½%	+1%	+½%

Area in thousand square miles

	4,300	1,175	183	93

B. *Wealth*

Gross national product (in millions of dollars)

	60,000 ?	40,500	70,000	81,200

Per capita income (dollars per annum)

	85 ?	88	570	1,500

Growth rate	+5% ?	+4%	+14%	+6%

Budget (in millions of dollars)

	17,000 ?	7,750	9,110	19,600

C. *Production*

Electricity (in billions of kilowatt hours)

	40 ?	28	154	143

Steel (in millions of tons)

	9 ?	7	40	26

Coal (in millions of tons)

	230 ?	65	51	194

Food grains* (in millions of tons)

	160 ?	70	15	11

D. *Trade and Payments* (in millions of dollars)

Exports	1,780 ?	1,760	6,675	17,545
Imports	1,475 ?	2,575	7,940	18,305
Total Trade	3,255 ?	4,335	14,615	35,850
Trade Balance	+305 ?	−815	−1,265	−960
Invisible Balance	−250 ?	−300	−460	−2,400
Foreign Aid	−50 ?	+1,000	−244	−532

* Rice, wheat, barley, oats, and miscellaneous grains; not potatoes

TABLE II

China's Main Trading Partners in 1964

	In Millions of Dollars		
	Total Trade	China's Exports	China's Imports
USSR	450	314	135
Hong Kong	355	345	10
Japan	311	158	153
Cuba	188	106	81
Australia	176	23	153
Canada	135	9	126
Britain	119	69	50
Malaysia	104	104	–
Indonesia	104	40	64
Argentina	92	–	92
France	80	31	50
West Germany	77	52	25
Others	1,064	529	536
Total	3,255	1,780	1,475

China's Over-all Trade, 1963–65

In Millions of Dollars

	1963	1964	1965
China's Exports	1,555	1,780	2,050
China's Imports	1,200	1,475	1,750
Total Trade	2,755	3,255	3,800

All trade figures are calculated from partner country statistics and should be treated with caution.

‖ Agriculture

*H*istory records many famines in prerevolutionary China which sacrificed millions and millions of lives. It is generally acknowledged that the Communist regime has been able to survive three successive years of disastrous harvest failure without a similar famine. How this was accomplished is a subject of debate. Some suggest that the system of communes kept communities together; others, that the centrally controlled distribution of food removed inequities which had characterized prerevolutionary China. Still others point to the massive importation of food which the government had undertaken. In any case, comparison with the harvest failures that previously swept China is not unimportant.

The transformation of agriculture has meant to the Chinese leaders the transformation of the traditional patterns of village life—a problem shared by all developing nations. One of the Conference panelists commented that no other nation has tackled this problem with as much energy—and often brutality —with as many mistakes, or with as much success, as Communist China. The programs adopted to bring about reforms in agriculture are known by name to most Americans but little

197

understood in the Chinese context—cooperatives, collectives, communes, and the workpoint.

The following two articles are descriptive and detailed and have been contributed by two British scholars who have had the opportunity to observe Chinese agriculture at first hand. Jack Gray is Lecturer in Far Eastern History at the University of Glasgow, and Joan Robinson is Professor of Economics at Cambridge University.

SOME ASPECTS
OF THE DEVELOPMENT
OF CHINESE AGRARIAN POLICIES
Jack Gray

THE CHINESE COMMUNIST PARTY, originating as an urban-based group mainly composed of very young intellectuals, began with orthodox, doctrinaire, and extreme views of how the rural revolution should be conducted. Their aim—the collective organization of agriculture on the largest possible scale—has never varied, but their methods have undergone progressive modification.

Three main factors were involved in this. The first was the nature of Chinese rural society, which stood in contrast to that of Russia. Briefly, the Russian village consisted of a group of farmers whose serf background had left them substantially equal in economic status and with a strong egalitarian ethic. The small minority of rich peasants who had risen above this mass had done so only recently—most of them within living memory; they were regarded with considerable jealousy; and many of them, established in their *hutors* (isolated steadings) apart from the village, were conspicuously cut off physically as well as socially from their fellow villagers. They were politically vulnerable. Moreover, the evidence suggests that a large proportion (80 per cent in some regions) of the marketed surplus of agriculture came from this small group

199

of rich peasants. It was thus possible to believe that much of the surplus Russian agriculture produced could be put at the disposal of the Party, and the main source of resistance to the collectivization of agriculture destroyed, by the liquidation and expropriation of this small and isolated group.

Peasant Status

In China the Communist Party very quickly discovered that the Chinese village was different. There were, of course, enormous local variations, but in general the marketed surplus of Chinese agriculture did not come predominantly from any one stratum of the population. There were very few wholly subsistence farmers in China. Poor peasants, middle peasants, and rich peasants all sold a substantial proportion of their produce. The surplus of the poor peasant was certainly partly an artificial one, for two reasons: first, because it was common for poor farmers to grow a high-value crop for sale and to buy low-value foods for family consumption; and second, because at their low level of income, it was to be expected that rising incomes would reduce rather than increase the proportion of crops which they sold—in some parts of China subsistence farming was a luxury which only the most prosperous farmers could enjoy. Land reform could thus be expected to reduce the surplus sold by the poor peasants rather than to increase it. If land reform involved expropriation of the rich peasants, their part in the production of a surplus would also virtually end, and the surplus of the middle peasants would be of crucial importance; even if the rich peasants were protected from land reform, the middle peasants' surplus was still indispensable.

The middle peasants formed about 25 to 30 per cent of the population in most villages. They were an integral and respected part of the village community, bound to other members of the village by ties of kinship. They could not be subjected to coercion as the Russian *kulaks* had been. In most

200

villages they owned, on the average, more than the average landholding of the village, and were therefore as a group hostile to egalitarian land reform. Reasonably well endowed with land and equipment as a group, they could not be expected to give ready support to the cooperativization of farming.

On the other hand, although always referred to as a coherent group, an examination of their characteristics in a number of villages shows that they were by no means such. As far as their incomes were concerned, judged by the size of their farms, they represent merely the middle section of a smooth concave distribution-curve, a curve on which most middle peasants were nearer to being poor than rich, even though they were a part of the prosperous minority of the village. As far as their social position was concerned, although they were in theory all independent proprietors, and indeed represented to Chinese social thinkers the ideal peasant of tradition, in fact a minority of them in most areas (and a majority in some) were at least part-tenants and therefore had something to gain from a land reform based upon the abolition of tenancy. As for the question of indebtedness, it is probable that as a group they were more deeply in debt than the poor peasants, many of whom had become poor because they could borrow no more or had lost the land on which their debts were secured. The middle peasant group was therefore one which, although not amenable to coercion, was open to manipulation by compromise policies designed to split its members.

Land Policies

The second factor in the development of Chinese Communist agrarian policies, and one which very largely determined their response to the situation described above, was the fact that from early in the Party's history, it ruled over a territorial base. Its first base was established not much more than five years after the foundation of the Party, and its

201

leadership has been continuously involved in responsibility for government ever since. The Chinese Communist Party enjoyed only for a very short time the opportunity for purely destructive and irresponsible activities in a hostile state; its first concern since 1927 has been the survival of its own growing territories.

The first important modification of its rural policies came within months of the foundation of the Chinkangshan Soviet, when egalitarian redistribution of land and terrorist tactics were repudiated by Mao Tse-tung in defiance of the orders of the Central Committee. By 1953 the land of middle peasants was wholly excluded from the redistribution, and even the possibility of protecting the productive capacity of the rich peasants had become a matter for agonizing consideration. When land reform was recommenced in 1946 after the end of the Second United Front, there seems to have been considerable uncertainty—or considerable local variation—in policy. At one extreme, a plan for the mere limitation of estates at a quite generous level was implemented. Then later, when the reform had entered a new area, there was a brief return to full egalitarianism, tempting in north China where there were relatively few landlords and when recruitment to the People's Liberation Army was at its peak. This was firmly squashed by Mao Tse-tung, but in some areas, for example in Honan, the local cadres were beyond control. The reform involved middle peasants and went to extremes of egalitarianism; it had to be brought to a halt and reorganized firmly on the lines which Mao laid down. As a consequence, Mao insisted on the organization of an elected village government with full representation of the middle peasants prior to the redistribution of land, and on the inclusion of middle peasants in the Peasants' Associations. The reform continued along these lines; but when conquest spread south to the lower Yangtze and the much more commercialized and complex rural society of that area, the Party decided that it was necessary to protect not only the middle peasants but the rich peasants, who were thereafter deprived only of the land they had rented out, or in other words were attacked only insofar as they were landlords. This line, written into the final Agrarian Reform Law of June 1950, at last recognized the fact that the rich peasants of China as a group were no longer (if they ever had been) seriously involved in exploitation. They certainly employed labor—one or two full-time laborers on average—but they rented out little land and in some areas rented *in* much more than they rented *out*, and by the 1930s they seem to have ceased to play a large part in money-lending, having been overtaken by the banks in this role. But the Party was never in full control of its lower levels. Cadres were so scarce that land reform was often carried out by local peasants hurriedly briefed at county headquarters, and the crude methods used by the Party to discredit the landlord class—there were still a million Kuomintang troops fighting in the hills—were in themselves such as to make the maintenance of moderation difficult in the face of the passionately egalitarian convictions of the village cadres. Nevertheless, in spite of widespread and often irreversible excesses in the redistribution of land, the result as a whole was to keep intact the farms operated by middle and rich peasants.

The third factor in the formation of Communist agrarian policies was that, after 1927, increasing study of Chinese rural society and increasing despair at the Nationalist government's inability to enforce even the most moderate reforms brought Chinese public opinion to a view superficially not very different in principle from that espoused by the Communist Party leadership. "Land to the tiller" was a slogan almost universally accepted; and in addition there was a widespread acceptance of the idea that the association of China's dwarf farms in some sort of cooperative system was a necessary preliminary to increased agricultural production and rural prosperity. Moreover the patent failure of the Kuomintang political apparatus to make any impression on those who ruled the villages had prepared Chinese opinion for a more or less ruthless village-by-village struggle before any significant changes could be brought about in rural life.

In short, the high value attached by the Communist Party as experienced administrators to the need to avoid disruption and loss of production while revolutionary changes were carried through, their knowledge of the limits which Chinese village society set to their power, and the trend of Chinese opinion generally, produced a sort of consensus concerning the rural revolution. Like any other consensus, it depended upon tactful vagueness on both sides, and although this was easy enough in the honeymoon days after liberation, the progressive revelation of what communist policies meant in practice soon tended to erode away the first solidarity. As far as land reform is concerned, however, although there was much disagreement over whether there should be any land reform at all in southern Kiangsu (which, the dissidents argued, was a capitalist and not a feudal society), armed resistance to the reform seems to have been confined very largely to Chekiang, the heartland of the Kuomintang. There was much alarm and bitterness over local excesses, however, and in the extreme south the movement ran full tilt into the loyalties and interests involved in the corporately owned clan estates, said to amount to one-third of the total arable land, a situation out of which the Party emerged with its reputation for justice and moderation much impaired.

These ill effects of land reform, however, were more than offset by the satisfaction of having completed a long-desired revolution in land tenure, and also by the rising prosperity which the maintenance of order, the rationalization of taxation, and the restoration and rapid growth of urban markets brought about. Thus, in conditions of relative peace and prosperity, the first campaign for the cooperativization of agriculture was begun at the end of 1951.

The campaign was explicitly experimental. It was launched by a Party directive which was not then published, although the gist of it appeared in government policy statements. The directive was finally published in February, 1953, marking the end of the experimental period. There had already been some progress towards the establishment of mutual aid teams,

204

but this had been prejudiced once more (and in the same areas as in the case of land reform) by the egalitarian predilections of local cadres; progress had apparently come to a halt, with about 20 per cent of the farmers in mutual aid teams. In any case, most were temporary teams, merely representing a new name for traditional practices.

Villager Attitudes

Two new factors were involved in the attitude of villagers to the prospect of cooperativism. First, the rather limited nature of the redistribution of land had left many of the recipients in a position where, because of the smallness of their holdings and their lack of tools, animals, and capital, they could not hope to make an independent living. Moreover the distribution of animals and tools along with the land had in many cases been to groups, not individuals—each family might, for example, find itself with a fifth share in a mule— so that some degree of cooperative working was dictated from the start.

This situation perhaps offers another contrast with Russia. There seems to be a general assumption that the redistribution of land and the expropriation of the *kulaks* had left the Russian peasant in a position where he could carry on as an independent proprietor, and so he had no incentive to accept collectivization. In China, however, it is obvious that many peasants, in spite of land reform, could not hope to farm effectively unless they could get access to the land and capital of the middle peasants, either through further redistribution, which was not to be considered, or through cooperative working. There was thus a motive force in the village for the development of cooperative agriculture.

On the other hand prosperity had strengthened the already prosperous. Few middle peasants would now see an advantage in cooperative working, and in particular many Party members who had taken seriously the Party's advice on how to achieve greater production found themselves embarrassingly prosperous. Some quietly forgot their former radicalism; some sold to avoid the dilemma of having to employ labor if they were to expand production further; and a few used their new wealth to found mutual aid teams. There was a danger of the demoralization of the Party in the rural areas, as there had been in Russia. The new cooperative campaign had to be preceded by a rectification of the rural Party machine to bring home to Party members their duty to participate in the campaign; there is no evidence, however, that there were widespread dismissals of Party members, or any attempts to flood the local branches with new and more activist elements.

The attitude of the middle peasants was crucial in the development of organized agriculture as it was in land reform. But they could not be excluded from the process of co-operativization as they had been from land redistribution, even temporarily. Poor-peasant cooperatives to which, at some future date when the farms had sufficiently raised production and incomes, the middle peasants could be brought in, were not viable; the inclusion of some middle peasants was economically necessary from the beginning, and they had to be attracted into, and attached to, the cooperatives by solid advantages.

Conditions for Development

In these circumstances, Party documents associated with the campaign of 1952 stressed five conditions for successful development. These were that:

1. Adherence to Agricultural Producers' Cooperatives (APCs) must be voluntary.

2. Arrangements for the distribution of income, etc., must adhere to the principle of mutual benefit.

3. Development must be gradual, by a series of "firm steps."

4. Development must not outrun "collectivist consciousness."

5. The basic conditions of success are increased production and increased personal income.

Examination of documents which gave practical instructions and recommendations to the cadres involved in APC work—

as opposed to general policy statements to which perhaps no great credence can be attached—strongly suggest that these principles were taken seriously. Indeed, they are never listed explicitly in this way, but emerge from practical discussion of the conditions of local work. The sanction for failure to take them seriously was the breakdown of APCs or the resignation of members; both these results are widely attested to. Local instructions, moreover, describe in detail what these principles implied and how they were to be achieved. In 1952 particularly, alternative methods of implementation were usually given, and the nature of these alternatives strongly suggests that most APCs were set up on the basis of a consensus achieved by a process of bargaining: the range of issues left to the discussion of the founding members of the APC is quite impressively wide. There appears to have been a substantial degree of "democracy" in the process of formation of the first cooperative farms. Space will not permit the exposition of the full evidence upon which this opinion is based; it is possible here only to give examples.

The extreme point of the voluntary principle was reached in one county in north China early in 1953; there, before an APC was formed, the cadres had to have the "voluntary agreement in full consciousness [of the implications] of every member of every family involved." County cadres elsewhere were warned that they must not mistake the enthusiasm of a few Party members and activists for the opinions of the masses, but must in every case check for themselves the state of local opinion. The stress upon the necessity of voluntary adherence to the APCs continued until at least late 1955. For example, in a case in the Sian suburbs in which the cadres were singled out for praise on account of their political methods, only two points in their work were criticized. They had used the argument to the middle peasants that gratitude to the Party for their prosperity in the preceding years should make them feel obliged to support the APC movement; this was condemned as a form of pressure. They had also taken subscriptions to the APCs in a full meeting of the village; this was condemned

207

as a form of pressure because many of those present felt obliged to conform to the attitude of the majority, and it was stressed that in the future subscriptions should be made individually.

The principle of "mutual benefit" was of crucial importance; without positive steps to ensure that this principle was upheld, APCs might either become a means of exploiting the labor of poorer members for the benefit of the more prosperous, who provided more land and most of the tools and animals, or alternatively they could become a means of further redistribution of income in favor of the poor. As one poor peasant member of an APC said, "Land reform isn't complete: but the APCs will fix that!" Perhaps more was written about the arrangements necessary to ensure mutual benefit than about any other aspect of the cooperatives. The practical problems involved included the proportion of the society's income to be paid to land shares, the purchase or leasing of tools and working animals, and the system of remuneration of labor. Not least was the question of the rational use of labor, because it was very easy for the poor peasants to "live off" the middle peasants by the creation of remunerative, but relatively unproductive, employment. In some parts of the north in 1952 the Party settled for a distribution system by which 60 per cent of the society's income went to land shares—an extraordinary concession made explicitly to encourage the middle peasants to join.

Functioning Gradualism

Gradualism meant several things. It meant, first of all, growth "from a point to a plane," with successful individual APCs assisting the mutual aid teams around them to develop in the direction of fully cooperative work. It also meant that the internal development of the APC would be gradual. This does not simply mean the three well-known stages of development, from mutual aid teams to lower APCs to higher APCs (collectives); the transition from stage to stage was to be

208

softened by development within each stage. Mutual aid teams, starting from the mere regularization of existing local mutual help practices, would become permanent; they would then be encouraged to undertake ventures which would establish common property (land reclamation, the planting of an orchard, the purchase of an oil-press, and so on), and to arrive at unified working of the land by the rationalization of the use of labor and by a modicum of joint planning—for crop specialization, for example. In time, they would not be too far from the cooperation level of development. Within the APCs great stress was also put upon the accumulation of joint property, which would give members a stake in the society, and upon gradual rationalization of land use which would wean the farmers from their own plots and submerge these under a new cropping pattern. But for the APCs, the most important form of gradualism was the step-by-step reduction of the proportion of society income paid to land, or the fixing of the reward to land shares in the form of a low fixed rent, as productivity and income rose. In this way it was hoped that the final transition to the collective, in which no reward went to land, would be painless in the sense that even those with much land and little labor power would receive a slight increase of income every year in spite of the falling proportion of the product paid to them as landowners.

This vital form of gradualism depended wholly upon the possibility of steadily increasing the income of the APC members; it is therefore important to estimate whether the increases in productivity and in incomes in the APCs are likely to have been sufficient to lubricate the process of change in this way. The figures quoted for various individual, and usually exemplary, APCs in *The High Tide of Socialism in the Chinese Countryside* (Peking, January, 1956) give average increases of 23 per cent per annum for agricultural productivity over the short periods involved. In most APCs existing at that time, three sets of circumstances must be taken into consideration: (1) middle peasants were in receipt of substantial extra income in the form of leasing charges or installment payments for animals and tools put at the disposal of the APC; (2) labor-intensive methods used to increase agricultural productivity involved only very small amounts of capital, so that in most cases costs form a higher proportion of the higher gross incomes; and finally (3) income from cooperative auxiliary occupations seems, on the whole, to have risen in these years much more than agricultural income. It is therefore probable that the transition could have been made painlessly in most cases at this level of increase of agricultural productivity in two or three years. This is, of course, a selected group of cooperatives.

The question is whether the recorded increases, averaging 23 per cent, but ranging from 10 to 110 per cent, are plausible, especially in view of the fact that in these years the increase on a national average was estimated at only about 4 per cent per annum. There is no reason to suppose that they are not. The *High Tide* collection inspires confidence by its frankness in other respects, for example in the readiness with which it is admitted that local successes in the APC campaign were due to especially favorable local conditions. This suggests that production claims may also have been honest. In addition, it was an essential part of the propaganda process that members of local mutual aid teams should participate in the estimates of APC crops, and this must have limited the tendency to over-report. And finally, in most cases, perfectly adequate technical reasons were given for the increases. The accounts and figures, in fact, merely tend to confirm what is probably generally accepted—that at existing yields and with existing practices, there were few *technical* obstacles to substantial and rapid increases in China's yields, and that the obstacles were social and psychological rather than natural. In other words, startling and immediate increases could be expected in particular places where technical expertise, political zeal, and economic assistance could be concentrated for the purpose of experiment or demonstration.

The Final Campaign

By early 1955, about 14 per cent of China's farmers were in lower-level APCs. The number in collectives proper was negligible. By the end of 1955, the proportion in lower-level APCs was 60 per cent. In early 1956, it was virtually 100 per cent, and by the end of 1956, almost 90 per cent were in collectives proper. These were drastic changes, which seem to fly in the face of the gradualist policy which had until then been emphasized. In one sense, they were even more drastic than they seem, in that the national averages conceal the very great disparity between the north (much of it Old Liberated Area), where development had been rapid, and the center and south where it had been much slower.

Before accepting this as a dramatic and unscrupulous reversal of policy, let us in all fairness try to make the best case that can be made for the Chinese Communist Party in the circumstances. Let us take first of all the *High Tide* jump from 14 per cent to 60 per cent.

The first question to ask is: How much potential support for cooperative farming could be expected in the average Chinese village? It is reasonable to suppose that the poor peasants, left after land reform with insufficient land and without the means to work it efficiently, were potential supporters. Among the middle peasants it must first of all be reiterated that, on the assumption that their incomes were generally in proportion to the size of their farms, most of them were nearer to poor peasants than to prosperous middle peasants; increases of income demonstrated upon existing APCs would not have to be very large in order to excite the interest of two-thirds of those classed as middle peasants. Another factor is that the lower-middle peasants, many of them risen recently from the ranks of poor peasants, were probably more closely associated with the Party than any other class; they were especially numerous on the rural Party committees, and many of them were therefore politically committed to co-

211

operativization. Among the middle peasants as a whole, in-dividual economic circumstances varied, quite apart from the level of their incomes; some had more labor than they could employ and might welcome the increased employment opportunities offered by the APCs, while some had more land than they could work, especially when there was political discouragement of the private employment of labor, and so might find it an advantage to invest their land, equipment, and beasts in a successful APC. Economic considerations apart, the Party could expect in the early fifties the solid support of the 25 per cent or so of the village population in adolescence or early youth, as well as the support of many women who saw a means to emancipation in the employment which the APC would offer them. There were also individuals among the more prosperous who were politically committed to the communist program in spite of their short-term economic in-terests. Kinship ties were constantly used; in particular the relatives of cadres would tend to support Party policy, as a matter of principle and ancient custom. In sum, providing that the existing APCs were able to demonstrate their effi-ciency, the Party might expect about 75 per cent support in the village for cooperative agriculture. By mid-1955, the vast majority of villages in China had at least one APC with a history of one or two years of operation, after some mutual aid training, open to inspection. In addition, virtually all the farmers of the village, excluding rich peasants, were in mutual aid teams with an average three-year history, more or less closely associated with the APC itself through help and advice given on agricultural methods, accountancy, the organization of labor, and the planning of production. It is therefore not beyond belief that a determined campaign in a year of bumper harvests might induce most of the mutual aid teams to accept the change to APC status.

Although further investigation is necessary on this point, one significant change in Party policy at this time may have materially assisted the APC movement. It is clear from the record that many middle peasants, although willing to invest

212

their land in the APCs and hire or sell their animals and tools to them, balked at the prospect of being asked to invest their savings in them as well. This was to put all their eggs in one basket with a vengeance; it caused more strain within the early APCs than any other issue, and it was an obstacle to the adherence of the more prosperous, who felt that the poor peasants in this sense brought nothing, or at least risked nothing, except a paltry entrance fee. At the same time, recruitment of poor peasants lagged because many of them could not raise even the entrance fee and, more important, many cadres were worried about the economic viability of an APC composed very largely of the poor, and so kept them out. Sometime in 1955 the habit seems to have grown up of raising the entrance fee to a level which would represent a real investment and of lending the necessary sum out of agricultural credit funds to those peasants who could not raise the sum for themselves. If this was in fact general, it represents a major change in the hitherto very niggardly use of agricultural credit funds, and a very good reason why there should have been a sudden breakthrough in recruitment to the APCs.

The next question is that of the completion of cooperativization: the rise from 60 per cent to 100 per cent. The significance of this depends upon who was still outside. The rich peasants and former landlords (10 per cent of the rural population), it may be assumed, were not in a position to refuse when their time came; they were essentially an enemy class. It cannot, however, be assumed that the remainder was composed mainly of the middle peasants. In the first place, as we have seen, the APCs could not be built up from cooperatives of poor peasants, as these would not have been economically viable. Almost all APCs included middle peasants from the beginning, and a large minority of them were even formed with the adherence of one or two of the most prosperous peasants. The necessity of forming the APC on a relatively compact area of land also made it difficult to form APCs entirely based upon a single class. Some figures for individual villages show that successively formed APCs differed little in class composition. In early 1956 some areas reported that the new recruits were composed 80 per cent of poor peasants; these were clearly areas where, rightly or wrongly, the mass of the farmers had been excluded for economic reasons at the earlier stages of the movement. There had been complaints in 1955 and earlier that the APCs had failed to absorb *both* the poorest and the most prosperous. The last stage of cooperativization did not consist, as is very readily assumed, of dragooning the prosperous minority of the village into cooperatives of the poor. The situation is rather obscure, but it was certainly more complicated than that. What is certain, given the Party's bias in favor of large-scale cooperatives, is that when virtually 100 per cent cooperation was achieved, it would be normally in the form of cooperatives each embracing the whole population of a single natural village. Since the original demonstration cooperatives had been spread as widely as possible, and since by early 1955 they averaged well over one per village, it can be assumed that most villages had a well-established cooperative by that date. Examples of villages wholly cooperatized before the end of 1955 suggest that the normal process was the merging of the more experienced mutual aid teams with this existing APC. Presumably this is what brought the total cooperatives up to 60 per cent. The pattern of progress suggests that in the north the regional average at this stage would be considerably higher, perhaps very nearly 90 per cent. The increase to a national average of over 90 per cent probably took place as a result of increased recruitment in central and south China. The main point, however, is that the spread of cooperativization was not a spread from class to class, but a spread from one area of the village to others whose inhabitants had much the same class structure as the first. The exception to this, of course, is the rich peasant group, which was excluded until the very end of the whole movement.

The rapid collectivization of the cooperatives during 1956 seems to have been an even more striking departure from gradualist policy. By February, 1956, only four months (and

214

they were the idle months for farming) after the recruitment of almost 50 per cent more of the population into cooperatives, the same total were in collectives, mainly in north China. Most of these, therefore, went virtually straight into collectivism, for in early 1955 only 14 per cent of the population were in cooperatives, and consequently most of the recruits to the cooperatives of late 1955 had been only formally members of the societies, having taken part in virtually no farming operations. At the end of 1956 after the autumn harvest, the other half of China's farmers were also collectivized, mainly in central and south China, where the much slighter development of cooperative farming—demonstration farms with a shorter history and swamped by an even larger number of new recruits than in the north—made an additional year's experience of farming necessary before the change.

Mao Tse-tung might argue (and did) that China in mid-1955 had reached the point where mass adherence to the cooperatives was feasible, and the main problems—political, administrative, and technical—had all been solved in some places and could be solved everywhere; but this argument could not be used, and never was, to justify immediate and rapid collectivization. Virtually all of the few collectives existing in China at the end of 1955 had been formed in exceptional circumstances. Apart from a few established on state-owned land, they were all formed where for one reason or another labor was scarce in relation to the demands made on it. This might occur on farms devoted to specialized production of cotton or other labor-intensive crops, or in areas of resettlement such as the Huai River area; but most often it occurred on farms organized for vegetable production in the rural suburbs of the cities.

A Decisive Difference?

How drastic was the change to collectivization? As opposed to cooperativization, it made little or no difference to the organization of the farm; it was merely a change in the distri-

215

bution of the product by abolishing the payment of dividends to land. This assumed, however, that the change was made after the cooperative had solved all the problems of large-scale management; implemented, against the usual opposition, a strict system of piecework and contracts; imposed on this basis a degree of labor discipline wholly unfamiliar to independent peasant farmers; and put through the tricky business of equalizing the productive resources of the brigades. These developments had probably already taken place on the old APCs which became the nuclei of the new collectives. But to extend them to the vast new membership was a formidable task, depending on the ability of the society to cover the loss of income which the most prosperous 20 to 30 per cent of their new members faced, by successfully maintaining on the enlarged farm the increases of production and income which *at their best* they had won on the old. Furthermore, they must make this good in one agricultural season. The loss to which the more prosperous new recruits were liable was, of course, partly offset by their reduced liability to land tax and by the installment payments made to them for their tools and animals; the data are too scanty to make any judgment of the importance of this possibility, but it is not likely to have made a decisive difference.

The 1955 harvests had been very good. This, combined perhaps with a growing confidence that the Party's taxation and procurement levels were stable, produced a mood of confidence and buoyancy, of which the writer was a witness at the end of 1955. Added to this, the local reports, upon which Mao Tse-tung had based the *High Tide* speed-up of the cooperative movement, must have strongly suggested to him that the productive potentialities of organized agriculture were such as would obviate the possibility that, at the end of the season when the produce was distributed, the middle peasants would find themselves with reduced incomes. The increases of production achieved on the best cooperatives suggested this. The means by which they had been won also suggested, first, that the essential condition of such increases was a very

216

great intensification of labor and that the abolition of dividends on land would help by making all members of the societies largely dependent on labor income; and second, that the investment of large amounts of labor in the collection of organic fertilizers, increased tillage, extended irrigation, and marginal land reclamation could pay off *in a single season.* The farmers were assured that 90 per cent of them would have increased incomes in the first year; and the state planned for a 10 per cent increase in agricultural productivity in 1956. Even this increase in production could not have given 90 per cent of the farmers higher incomes, but it is to the hopes of a 100 per cent increase in productivity by 1957, expressed in Mao's *High Tide* preface, that we must look perhaps for the justification of his optimistic assurances.

The actual increase was 4.4 per cent. This failure, however, does not seem to have changed the Party's assumptions about the lessons to be drawn from the cooperative movement: that intensified labor, working with the little local capital available, could produce substantial increases in production; that these increases could be largely immediate; that the larger the scale on which labor could be organized, capital mobilized, and planning done, the greater the increases in productivity would be. Other lessons, which were remembered when the time was ripe, were the important part played in the creation of local capital by cooperativized auxiliary occupations, and the importance in this respect of freedom for local initiative. These lessons formed the basis of the Great Leap Forward and of the commune movement. They tended to reinforce Mao's belief that, in this as in other matters, human resources are what count; the key is to find the organization within which human resources can be employed to the best effect. The problem of production is essentially a political, not an economic one. Hence the communes, which carried labor-intensive, large-scale, leap-forward, quick-return policies to the limit.

The Communes

The communes in their original form were a failure. Labor was over-extended when the country faced the extreme natural disasters which occurred from 1959 to 1961; the communes defeated the weather, but at an unrepeatable cost of social dislocation and exhausting labor. The Leap Forward put planning in chaos. The results of the attempt to substitute labor for capital were disappointing—large, long-term investment was needed too. Finally, economies of scale were got at the cost of a departure from normal Party leadership techniques, which were based in the countryside upon natural social groupings and personal relationships.

The "retreat" from the communes was, however, far from a mere withdrawal. Their difficulties appear to have led to a reconsideration of the problems of determining the most appropriate scale for different purposes—problems which every type of community development faces. The solution gradually arrived at put local leadership back on the basis of as small and personal groups as was practical. The history of the organization of Chinese farming made this relatively easy. It had been built up on small units associated in larger bodies in successive layers, and the constituent bodies could easily be revitalized. Their existence had been, from the point of view of their membership, continuous. This mutual aid team was a group of neighbors who were already associated in traditional forms of seasonal cooperation. It remained as the basic unit of work allocation. The mutual aid teams had been merged in the first small APCs of about twenty neighboring families; these remained as the production teams. The larger APCs upon which collectivization had been based usually covered the natural village and were the seat of the Party branch, composed of village farmers and from whom the village and APC administration leaders were drawn; these became the brigades within the communes.

In the new dispensation, the conduct of farming reverted

218

from the commune to the production team; the former small APC now became the unit of production management and of distribution of profits. The brigades (the village) became the contracting unit *vis-à-vis* the state trading and procurement organs, with the duty of coordinating the farming of the village—but with little authority to enforce its policies, if the recorded complaints of brigade cadres are to be taken seriously. The commune confined itself to the tasks for which its larger scale fitted it and in which the impersonality arising from its scale was not too great a disadvantage—planning and carrying out, with investment funds derived from its constituent teams and brigades, the establishment of small factories, the coordination of water-conservancy plans, and in general the provision of the social overheads of the local economy. In principle, this is an excellent device worth the attention of community development authorities elsewhere. From the point of view of communist political methods, it sought to restore the face-to-face relationship of groups of neighbors led by neighbors (often indeed relatives rather than mere neighbors), while at the same time leaving the Party as free as political conditions permitted to renew the emphasis upon increased scale.

But for all its increased sophistication and flexibility, it is interesting that the system is still based upon natural social groupings; the Communist Party has not yet succeeded in shaking the Chinese rural population free from its intensely personal and local loyalties and imposing an impersonal labor-discipline upon them.

ORGANIZATION OF AGRICULTURE
Joan Robinson

T HE MOST URGENT ECONOMIC PROBLEM facing the Chinese Republic in 1949 was to raise agricultural output so as to improve the standard of life of the rural population, to increase the surplus available for the cities, and to permit a growth of industry. With the example of USSR before their eyes, the authorities were determined to find a means of extracting the surplus without alienating the peasants.

The Land Reform

The first step was a comprehensive land reform. In each village of Han people, excluding national minorities at the first stage, the classification of families according to their land-labor ratio was agreed to by general consent. The criteria were that the landlord family lived from rent and other exactions; the rich peasant family worked but also hired labor; the middle peasant neither hired labor nor rented land; the poor peasant and landless family was obliged to work for others. On the basis of this classification, in each village separately, the land of the landlords was distributed—so much per head, man, woman, and child—among the landless families, which, by

221

typical Chinese logic, now included the families of landlords. (Some landlords were executed, but the proportion seems to have been very small—only those convicted of an exceptional number of murders. The great majority were absorbed into the labor force.) Rent is said to have taken formerly about half of gross produce. Tax in kind was now about 15 per cent. The thrifty peasants took advantage of this rise in income to buy fertilizers and so forth, to increase production. The incentive to work and save was sharply increased. A network of supply and marketing cooperatives was instituted to promote trade between town and country, and Technique Popularization Stations assisted in improving methods of cultivation. Mutual aid teams were encouraged, and "lower-form cooperatives" began to be set up.

In the lower-form cooperative a number of families pooled their land, animals, etc., and worked together on an agreed plan. The distributable proceeds were divided, with 30 per cent in respect to property put into the pool, and 70 per cent in respect to work days earned.

In 1953, when I first visited China, the bulk of all production was still in the hands of individual peasants. There had been an upsurge of output, but its growth was not fast enough. Moreover, since the rich peasants had not been disturbed by the land reform, holdings were very uneven; the natural course of births, deaths, and marriages was upsetting the labor-land ratios established by the land reform. At that time, the authorities seemed to have been bemused by the Soviet doctrine that the purpose of agricultural collectivization was to facilitate mechanization, and that, since mechanization would have to await the development of industry, the time was not ripe for establishing cooperative farms.

Cooperatives to Communes

Weighing and analyzing experience, the authorities realized that the Soviet doctrine was the reverse of the truth in their conditions. Collectivization was not a means to mechanization, but a substitute for it. The only hope was to organize labor in such a way as to raise productivity ahead of the provision of sophisticated equipment.

In 1956, in the "high tide of socialization," the whole of the Han countryside was brought into "higher-form cooperatives." In these, land contributed did not rank for a share in produce, but holdings were registered, and every member had the right to withdraw. (This right still exists and was exercised in some cases during the bad years 1959–61). The system ran for only two years. In the Great Leap of 1958 the cooperatives were amalgamated into communes.

Economies of Scale

The change from the cooperatives of 1956 to the communes of 1958 was connected with the problems of scale of management. The choice of the scale of organization is an important matter and by no means a simple one.

For the deployment of labor, a rather small scale is required. Workers are spread out over space so that discipline is hard to enforce; an incentive wage system is not easy to arrange or to administer; there has to be a great diffusion of managerial responsibility; every field is different, every day is different, and quick decisions have to be taken. For getting work out of the workers, a peasant family is hard to beat. Discipline and responsibility are imposed by the pressing incentive to secure the family livelihood. But for the deployment of land, the family unit is much too small. Transport and marketing are costly; specialized production is worthwhile only for valuable cash crops. The bulk of consumption is provided for on the spot. The various products required must be raised on whatever land the family happens to command. There are obvious advantages in a number of families pooling their land and allocating each crop to the area best suited to it.

The deployment of knowledge requires still larger units. A team of experts can service a wide area, but generalized science has to be digested and adapted to local conditions and its results demonstrated convincingly. The peasant cannot afford to risk his daily bread in experiments. Investments in water control and land reclamation require a larger scale again.

The cooperatives of 1956 proved to be too large from one point of view and too small from another. When a thousand or more workers are sharing their joint proceeds, the relationship between individual effort and individual earnings is much too diluted to be a strong incentive for conscientious work. The personal and technical problems of control and accounting were a strain on available managerial capacity, especially where the cooperative comprised a number of separate villages. On the other hand, an area of a few hundred acres was often insufficient for the best deployment of land, while both the labor force and the area were much too small to exploit the possibilities of improvements through irrigation, drainage, forestation, and so forth. The communes, which were inaugurated in a burst of enthusiasm in 1958 and hammered into shape in the three bad years that followed, have evolved into an ingenious system for reconciling the requirements of large and small scale.

The organization is in three tiers. The team is a smaller unit than the cooperative of 1956. In some cases it corresponds to the preceding "lower-form cooperative." Where villages are large, there are several teams in one village. The brigade, usually between five and ten teams, covering a single village in plains where the villages are large, is often a continuation of a "higher-form cooperative" formed in 1956. A commune may comprise five brigades or thirty, covering as much as fifty thousand acres, or, for intensive cultivation, as little as one thousand acres. Broadly speaking, the team is the unit for labor management; the brigade for the crop program; the commune for the external relations of the group, for investment projects, and for industrial enterprises ancillary to agriculture.

The Team

In the standard case (with many variations) the team is the basic accounting unit for production and distribution. It consists of the labor force of some thirty families; it controls a particular block of land, with working animals and implements (tools are individually owned). Sometimes its fields are the very ones that these families formerly owned or received at the land reform twelve years ago; sometimes they have been regrouped for convenience in cultivation. The team, provided with the appropriate seed, fertilizers, etc., accepts responsibility for a particular plan of production over the crop year; and for a particular quota of sales, at fixed prices, to the government procurement agency. It may also contract with neighboring city cooperatives for sales of vegetables, meat, and so forth. Planned sales are calculated so as to leave the team members a reasonable livelihood. Poor teams may be asked to supply no more than 5 or 7 per cent of gross produce.

From the annual income of the team, in kind and cash, is deducted:

The Agricultural Tax

The tax was assessed on the national productivity of each piece of land and is guaranteed not be changed for at least the next three years. The nominal rate is 11 to 13 per cent of gross produce; since productivity has generally been increasing, the actual rate is less; 4 or 5 per cent is common. I came upon one case, where land had been turned over to highly profitable market gardening since the assessment was made, in which the tax was less than 1 per cent. On the other hand, a team which fails to achieve the assessed productivity is penalized by a higher burden of tax. An effective rate of 14 per cent or more may occur but is said to be rare. When failure is due to "natural disasters"—drought, flood, typhoon, unsea-

225

sonable frost—the tax is forgiven. The tax is collected simply as part of the deliveries to the state procurement agency.

Costs of Production

Fodder, seed, etc., are replaced in kind. Fertilizers, fees for tractor ploughing, electric power, and so forth are paid for out of cash income.

Contribution to Accumulation

This varies according to the margin above the needs of subsistence and according to the keenness of the team on socialist construction.

Contribution to the Welfare Fund

This is generally 1 or 2 per cent of gross income. It is used to secure for member families who are in difficulties the five guarantees: food, clothing, shelter, medical care, and funeral expenses. Poor teams provide them at a pretty meager level. Prosperous teams support schools and provide free medical care and other amenities to all member families.

A Management Fee

Usually 1 per cent of team income is paid to the commune for this purpose.

The remainder, usually about 60 per cent of the team's gross income, is distributed to the members. There is an elaborate system of job evaluation, acceptable to public opinion among the workers, in terms of workpoints. Points given for organizational work, attending meetings, and so forth must not exceed 2 per cent of the team's total points earned in the field. Forward estimates of the value of a workpoint are made, and members of the team are partially paid in advance, out of the proceeds of the last harvest, in three or four installments.

226

Then, after the autumn harvest, there is a grand reckoning and the balances are paid out.

The leader, deputy, and accountant are elected by the team members, and a meeting is called from time to time to discuss any personal or technical problems that may arise.

A team may choose to sell more than its quota of grain to the state (thus having so much the more cash to distribute); it may have some side activities such as pig-breeding for the market or for the benefit of members; it may operate small enterprises such as a brick kiln, but this is more common at the brigade level.

The Brigade

The teams forming a brigade elect a management committee and appoint a leader, deputy, and accountant. The brigade, in consultation with its teams on the one side and the commune management on the other, controls the allocation of land to special uses, such as planting orchards, and works out the annual crop program. It may operate enterprises employing wage workers and provide conveniences such as grinding flour and making noodles for member households. It breeds draft animals and may own a truck. Profits from its activities may provide an independent accumulation fund, or it may take a levy from the accumulation funds of its member teams to finance investment, for instance, in electrification of pumps, chaff-cutters, etc. A family depends upon the team to which it belongs for daily bread, but something like regimental morale attaches to the brigade; rivalry stimulates production.

The Commune

The director of the commune, with his staff of ten or twenty "cadres," is from one point of view the representative of the cooperative, from another of the administration. The commune has absorbed the lowest level of local government (the *hsiang*) and in that capacity is responsible for registration of births, deaths, and marriages, taxation, controlling the militia (police and law courts are at county level), and gearing the commune's contribution to education and health services into the county's.

It is the point of contact between the cooperative and the administration for purposes of framing the annual plan and looking after its implementation, for receiving loans, for organizing procurement in the broad (actual contracts are made with the respective accounting units), and for digesting and disseminating technical progress.

It may operate enterprises such as manufacture and repair of tools—some of the famous miniature blast furnaces have found a useful function here. In some cases, it owns a park of tractors. (Elsewhere a county tractor station or a state farm will plough for neighboring communes on contract.)

As well as such positive functions, the communes have the no less vital task of coping with the effects of natural disasters. They can claim credit for preventing the breakdown of the economy in the "bitter years," 1959–61, and they are still called upon, in the smaller misfortunes that every season brings in one district or another, to mobilize labor, distribute relief, and organize reconstruction as may be required.

Creating Land

The original nucleus of the commune system was the pooling of resources by a number of cooperatives to organize schemes, too large to be undertaken individually, of land reclamation, irrigation, drainage, and communications—investments which in effect create land. This remains a continuing function of the communes, and the work goes on from year to year. Where the terrain requires a plan covering an area larger than a single commune, it is easy for two or three to work together and to arrange to share the benefit, which would have been impossible for dozens of cooperatives, let alone thousands of peasant households.

One of the regulations laid down in the 1960s is that the

228

labor time devoted to capital works must not exceed 3 per cent of the annual total. This, presumably, was to defend the peasants against overenthusiastic pressure from the Party. The limit seems to be frequently disregarded, by general consent, the only rule being that capital works must not interfere with regular agricultural production.

Some communes have a considerable accumulation fund derived from profits of industries; others depend upon levies from the accumulation of brigades or teams. In a typical case, for a large scheme such as cutting a canal, the outside expenses for such things as cement or pumps are met by a levy on the teams allocated in proportion to the area of land that will be benefitted, while the work is allocated according to the labor force available. Work days are earned by the team members employed on the scheme and entitle them to a share in the produce of their team. Thus the value of a work day is diluted by employment in the investment scheme. The team as a whole benefits from the investment since their land will be more productive in the future and easier to work. During the year that the work is carried out, an unchanged total income of the team is distributed among the members. The "opportunity cost" of the work contributed to the scheme was mere idleness in the slack season. The peasants are getting something for nothing. In this way the strong personal incentive of the peasant family to preserve and improve property is harnessed to a small collective unit, fitted into the larger unit, and provided with expert technical assistance. At the same time, massive investments are carried out in a way which avoids inflationary consequences.

The Household

The average size of households ranges, between one commune and another, from three to five. (A vigorous campaign for late marriage and birth control is expected to lower this sharply in the future.) Normally three generations live together in a house that they have always had, or received at the land reform, or have newly built. Standards vary. In one province, a miserable dark hovel, shared with the chickens, is typical; in another, a little mud-walled homestead, with a vegetable garden, a pigsty in the corner, the courtyard shaded by grape vines, and clean, airy, well-roofed rooms.

The system of distributing rations irrespective of workpoints earned, which was introduced in the first, utopian, phase of the commune system, had to be abandoned in the bad years. Family income now depends primarily on the earnings of its members on the team. Besides this, the household has the use of a private plot. The team (which retains property in the land) allocates to its member households so much per head. The plots are very small; a family of six may have one-tenth or one-fifth of an acre of dry land, or perhaps one-tenth of a *mou* (.15 acre) of irrigated land. Vegetables, pigs, and chickens around the house and handicraft production for use or sale further supplement the family income. Subsidiary production is important to the family, but it is reckoned to contribute less than 10 per cent to marketed supplies for the nation.

The rearing of pigs is especially encouraged as a source of manure. It is also an economical way of turning all sorts of scraps to good account. A common pattern is for a team or brigade to run a breeding station and to give out piglets to individual households to be fed and disposed of as they please —a combination of private and collective activity beneficial to all parties. Similarly, the private plot provides a productive use for scraps of time and energy that cannot be organized for team work. It has an economic function, as well as the political function of a stepping stone between peasant property and collectivization.

Where the household is too small an economic unit for its own activities, spontaneous cooperation develops. For instance, individually owned goats and sheep are herded in common. Team dining rooms have gone out of fashion, but groups of unmarried workers sometimes organize a common kitchen for themselves.

Variations

The general scheme of organization is adjusted to local conditions with great flexibility. Different treatment is required for a poor grain-growing district, where 90 per cent of produce is consumed on the farm, for a cash-crop area where income in money accrues from sales to the state procurement agency and grain for food has to be bought in, and for suburban market gardens supplying city distributors on contract. History also creates local differences; the old liberated areas have proud traditions and even in the last six years experience has molded policy in many ways. There are considerable variations upon the standard pattern of relations between team, brigade, and commune. Among a casual sample of a dozen communes in four provinces which I was able to visit in the summer of 1963, there were three where one of the brigades was different from the rest. In each case it was the continuation of a higher-form cooperative that had taken root and chose to continue as a basic accounting unit. Control of land and equipment then inheres in the brigade, and teams are merely convenient subdivisions of the labor force. The peasants have formed and tested their own leaders, and a strong collective spirit makes them less dependent upon individual incentive. This promotes efficiency in a number of ways and is rewarded by material success. In these brigades average earnings are markedly above—in one case double—those of the other teams in the commune.

Quite a different pattern was found in a commune where the teams were old lower-form cooperatives which seem to have been very little affected by the subsequent stages of collectivization.

In some of the prosperous, sophisticated market gardens near Peking, the brigades are accounting units; it is said that in a few cases the whole commune is the accounting unit.

There are considerable variations in methods of forming the annual plan, in details of the distribution system, in the management of subsidiary enterprises, and so forth. There are also differences in the level of morale. In some, revolutionary *élan* has been maintained through the difficult years. In others, slackness and even corruption crept in. The general mass, between the brilliant and the bad, are more or less satisfactory and steadily improving.

Social Services

There are also great variations in the organization of medical and educational services. There is no cut-and-dried system of rights and obligations; the communes do what they can, and the county fills in the gaps. One way or another there is a complete network of schools, hospitals, and clinics covering the rural areas. Generally, brigades—sometimes teams—are responsible for primary schools and communes for secondary schools. The buildings—often an old landlord's house or a temple—are usually provided, teachers' salaries (not much above a laborer's wage) are sometimes paid partly or wholly from the welfare fund. Parents sometimes have to pay for books and sometimes not. In the poorest communes the county authorities carry all the costs.

Similarly a hospital is usually provided by the commune, and clinics by brigades. Sometimes everything including drugs is provided free from the welfare fund; at the other extreme a doctor is merely invited to come in and collect what he can from fees. Fees for indigent patients must be paid from the welfare fund, according to the five guarantees.

Public entertainment is provided by loudspeakers for those who have no radio of their own, and a film projection unit gives a show in each village about once a month. There are occasional visits from theatrical companies, dance troupes, etc. The schools provide adult literacy classes.

232

Marketing

Like production, sales are organized in three tiers. At the lowest level there are periodic fairs at which housholds can sell eggs, fruit, and so forth in small quantities. A team may send in a cartload of vegetables. Prices are freely formed under the pressures of supply and demand.

At the next level, individual teams and brigades can sell such products as noodles, sauce, and wine to the supply and marketing cooperative, to be retailed in the village or supplied to the town; and such products as hog bristles to be passed on to industry. Here prices are fixed in what is considered to be a reasonable relation to costs.

The main outlet for agricultural produce is the state procurement agency, which has the sole right to handle the main crops. Deliveries are agreed on in advance in the annual plan, and prices have been held substantially unchanged since the currency stabilization of 1950. Retail prices are also fixed. In some cases the margin is not sufficient to cover transport and handling charges, so that the urban population is partly getting its food below cost. Where a team is allotted some specialized work and has to buy its grain, purchases must be made through the state organization, although the actual grain may come from next door.

The vegetable market for the cities is highly organized. Plans are framed in the broad between the city authority and the commune. Within that framework, state retailers contract directly with teams and receive daily deliveries straight from the field. In the summer flush, procurement prices are lowered so as to keep earnings fairly stable, while selling prices are pushed down to clear the market. The consequent loss to the city authorities is made good out of the profits on early spring crops. Winter prices are reckoned to cover hothouse and storage costs.

Fruit and vegetable production is far and away more profitable than grain, though it involves more continuous work.

233

Chinese economists are discussing the problem of "socialist rent," and ways to siphon it off for the benefit of the nation without upsetting the system of incentives in agriculture. For the time being, it lies where it falls.

The procurement system for cash crops, surplus grain, and market-garden products, which guarantees to the producer a stable market for fixed quantities of output at fixed prices, is the basis of the whole system and makes all the rest possible.

‖ Population

*A*bout one-fourth of the world's population is Chinese, and the proportion is not likely to grow any smaller. Demographers have estimated China's population as between 700 and 750 million; if the present trend continues, it could be 800 million to 1 billion by 1980. If, in addition, the mortality rate continues to decline at its present pace, and the birthrate is not reduced drastically, China could have a population of up to 2 billion by the year 2000. The same demographers caution, however, that population growth estimates are a complex phenomenon. Even in the United States and western Europe where so much more intensive data are available, the predictions cannot be considered accurate.

These estimates of the present and anticipated population increase have implications for economic development. For example, in most advanced countries about one-quarter of the population is under the age of 15; in China, children under 15 constitute about 40 percent of the population. Thus China, in comparison with the United States, will have a relatively greater proportion of nonproducing people to be fed than productive people to work.

The Chinese government had initiated a population control

campaign before the Great Leap Forward, but abandoned it, presumably because the campaign had failed. Analysts report that the New Five-Year Plan outlines a birth control campaign advocating not only late marriages but use of the cheap and effective intrauterine device.

According to Leo A. Orleans of the National Science Foundation, these efforts may be modestly successful. However, as yet no state with a large, poor, rural population has achieved a decreased birth rate. The present efforts of the Chinese government will be watched with considerable interest by many other countries—can a government with state controls so extensive achieve influence over this most personal area of human existence?

CHINA'S POPULATION:
REFLECTIONS AND SPECULATIONS
Leo A. Orleans

IT IS, of course, well known that the study of Communist China is seriously hampered by the paucity and questionable validity of the published data. Nevertheless, an economist, although lacking the detailed statistics, can pick up enough bits and pieces from the mainland newspapers and other publications to assume certain activities and developments and to support his estimates. A specialist in foreign affairs can screen the daily flow of propaganda from Peking, follow China's exchanges with the Soviet Union, and observe her activities in the developing countries of Asia, Africa, and Latin America.

A demographer, however, is at a particular disadvantage, not only because during the past half-dozen or more years there has been virtually no mention of the subject of population, but also because most of the population data published during the early and middle 1950s were insufficient in quantity and inadequate in quality. Furthermore, there is no pre-1950 base for population analysis—no reliable benchmark that would permit meaningful projections and analogies. The few population statistics that have been published have been thoroughly and repeatedly analyzed, digested, and debated.

239

This paper will not attempt to come up with yet another estimate of the size and rate of growth of China's population, but rather, will examine three major premises:

1. The government in Peking knows neither the size nor the rate of growth of China's population.

2. The size and rate of growth of the population have been of continuous concern to the regime, despite vacillating population policies.

3. Given the desire to reduce fertility and a willingness to expend the necessary resources and effort, there is reason to believe that the Communists may now be able to achieve a measurable drop in the Chinese birth rate.

Estimates of Size

Virtually all population estimates for China move forward and backward from the mid-1953 figure of 582.6 million—a product of a year-long intensive effort to count and register the country's population. Although frequently maligned, the figure is nevertheless generally accepted as the best available and the most usable approximation of China's population. The enumerators and registrars received training courses, while the general population was informed about the importance of co-operation and accuracy. There is every reason to believe that the 1953 effort was genuine and that there was no politically motivated tampering with the figures once they reached Peking.

Theoretically, the registers established by the Communists should have provided the regime both with a total population count and with the necessary data to calculate the nation's birth and death rates. Current registers were to contain basic information on the number of permanent residents, as well as on births and deaths.

It was, presumably, on the basis of these registers that in 1957 Peking published the official year-end estimates for the country's population for 1954, 1955, and 1956, and followed them up with a series of population totals by province as of

240

the end of 1957. The question, of course, is whether the registers and special surveys conducted during these years were capable of providing the government with accurate and acceptable population statistics.

Although population registers for China go back hundreds of years, neither the *pao chia* records of the Ch'ing dynasty, nor the various population counts of the Republic of China, were established for the purpose of deriving demographic data. In all cases the major intention was political control, as much as the need for taxation, military draft, or labor conscription. The motivation for population registers of the present regime, since 1956 under the Ministry of Public Security, continues to be political control, as explicitly stated in the 1958 regulations governing population registers: "These regulations are enacted to maintain social order, to protect the rights and interests of the citizens, and to serve socialist construction." This alone would be a major handicap to the collection of data for population analysis. The post-1953 population figures may be legitimately challenged simply because they are a product of the registration system. They may also be questioned on the basis of demographic considerations, since the reported high rates of population growth imply death rates that are inconsistent with the medical, social, political, and economic conditions of the country. Whatever their defects, however, the figures are accepted and used, and for all practical purposes constitute the most recent population data of any consequence.

Since 1957 there have been virtually no population statistics emanating from Communist China. The reason for this may well be the fact that the already weak statistical system received two grave setbacks. First, as part of the Great Leap, much of the statistical responsibility was taken away from experienced personnel and given to Party leaders, who were instructed to produce only figures that would be politically acceptable. Many of the standard statistical principles were termed capitalistic and were discredited and discarded, while literally millions of people with no formal training were reported to be participating in "statistical work," with predictable results. The second setback to statistics resulted from the economic crisis that came on the heels of the Great Leap, when survival, rather than accurate statistical reporting, was uppermost in the minds of the Chinese leaders. Since 1961, along with the gradual improvement in China's economy, there has been an apparent return of some of the statistical responsibilities to the statisticians. Much of their effort, however, has been devoted to reconstituting the demolished system; there has been no evidence of sufficient progress to produce current population statistics.

A good example of the flagrant and unsophisticated use and abuse of population figures was provided by a series of recently published figures for Tibet. The report stated that between 1960 and 1965 the population of Tibet Autonomous Region increased at a rate of 2 per cent each year and grew from 1,197,000 to 1,321,500. Is this reasonable? Not entirely. In the first place, considering the years of complete absence of population data, remote and sparsely settled Tibet would seem to be the most unlikely region to produce any precise population figures. In the second place, considering the economic and medical backwardness of the area, the lasting consequences of the 1959 uprising, and the still unstable political situation, the reported 2 per cent rate of growth between 1960 and 1965 seems excessive. Finally, if the 2 per cent growth rate is applied to the reported 1960 base population for five consecutive years, the exact 1965 figure is obtained. Unfortunately, real populations, particularly those undergoing the type of change implied by the reports, simply do not grow in this orderly fashion. It would have been much more realistic to show an ascending trend.

Why, then, would the Communists report a 2 per cent rate of growth for Tibet's population? Because this rate has come to represent an acceptable minimum for a developing country. A lower rate would imply that perhaps the regime has not been able to introduce the necessary reforms, improve the standard of living, and thus reduce mortality. The figures were obviously designed to make a point and to impress.

242

Population: Reflections and Speculations

Is it possible that the Chinese actually do have population figures for the country, but do not publish them because of security considerations? This is a most unlikely premise. They published national totals for some ten years, and there is no reason to believe they would cease publication if the data were available for the following years. Provincial population distributions were released for 1953, 1954, and 1957, and individual *hsien* populations were reported in various dispatches. The fact that so few data have been published on population characteristics such as age and sex composition, for example, may well be an admission that the system has been unable to produce such information.

On the other hand, because in the past the basic population figures were reported when available does not necessarily ensure publication of any future figures, should the registration system again begin to function. It is quite possible that the regime would have difficulty in rationalizing the past with the present and in explaining any contradictions and implications inherent in the new figures. The new total population for the mainland may reveal the full intensity of the food crisis of the early 1960s, for example. It may also be difficult to make the new total fit the growth rates of the middle fifties, if the latter were as unrealistically high as suspected. Another deterrent to the publication of the new figures would arise if the implied natural increase were lower than that reported for 1954 and 1955. The reported natural increase for 1954 was 23.4 per 1,000 total population, while for 1952 and 1957 the Ministry of Health reported incredibly low death rates of 13 and 11 respectively. It is most improbable, under the best of circumstances, that China will be able to achieve this low level of mortality in the near future.

But since statistics in Communist China must always show progress, it would be most surprising if Peking reported any figures that would imply a higher mortality.

The Continuing Concern

Although the Chinese Communists do not know the size and rate of growth of the country's population, they do know that the enormous obstacles facing the country would be easier to tackle if the annual population increment were 5 or 8 million, rather than 10 or 15 million. Ignorance of whether there are 500 or 600 million peasants in the country may not basically affect China's overall plans and policies, but the absence of precise information has not clouded the leadership's recognition of the problems associated with a large population. For example, according to Edgar Snow, "China's leaders are clearly aware that a substantial gain in living standards can only come about through a reduction in birth rates." (*The Washington Post*, February 20, 1964.)

Thus China's leaders were never oblivious to the immediate and potential consequences of the 25 million or more births that occur annually. Their minds did not fluctuate along with vacillations of the prescribed policies; the problem of numbers was too great and too pervasive.

It is to the credit of the regime that, despite the limitations of resources, China has been able to give almost all children at least a four-year primary education, to provide them with at least the minimum medical facilities, and, of course, to feed and clothe this unproductive multitude.

But after a child is reared and educated, he must be put to work in such a way as to assure the maximum benefit to the state from his activities, be he peasant, worker, or professor. How well has Communist China been able to utilize her manpower in the past and what are these policies at present?

The ability of Communist China to utilize effectively the hundreds of millions of persons of working age depends directly on the well-being of the country's economy and on a balanced growth of both its industrial and its agricultural sectors.

To examine the problems of labor absorption, let us consider separately the urban and rural sectors of the economy.

244

The 1953 urban population of China was reported at 77 million, or just over 13 per cent of the total population. A few years later, when the State Statistical Bureau published China's total population, it also included an urban population series covering the years 1949 through 1956. These figures, ranging from 57.6 to 89.2 million, indicate an average annual growth of 4.5 million, but with significant fluctuations from year to year. The rapid growth of the urban population was the result of two major forces: (1) the push applied by the ruthlessly enforced collectivization of agriculture, and (2) the pull exerted by rapid industrial development. The migration of some 20 million peasants into the cities between 1949 and 1957 resulted in serious problems of housing, feeding, and employment of rural migrants. Throughout this period, efforts were made to return peasants to their villages and to restrict the continuous flow of "nonproductive elements" into the cities. Yet, despite new and stringent regulations, the unplanned rural-to-urban flow of migrants was never entirely halted and, in fact, received new impetus with the introduction of the Leap Forward in 1958.

Past experience, and reason, make it obvious that the cities of China could not possibly absorb the reported 20 million persons in less than a year. Apparently the figure was related to the almost overnight increase in the reported number of workers and employees in the productive sector of the economy, which, in turn, was actually the result of a reclassification of millions of persons, both urban and rural, to the category of the labor force that receives wages and salaries from the state.

Because the definition of "urban" is partly based on the occupational composition of the labor force in a particular locality, such a reclassification could have shifted many communities into the "urban" category, without any major shifts of population. There was also, however, an actual acceleration of migration into the cities during this period.

In 1959, the Minister of Building stated that the urban population had grown to "about 100 million," probably a fairly reasonable estimate. At any rate, within the context of the present discussion, the important factor is that even during this period of most rapid industrialization, China's cities have not been able to accommodate the surplus rural manpower.

The serious internal crisis that developed on the heels of the Leap, and ensuing natural calamities, forced a complete re-evaluation of China's economic policies.

The accent on agriculture instead of industry went hand in hand with renewed efforts to control and reduce the urban population. Many of the industrial enterprises in urban areas were forced out of operation by the shortage of raw materials, particularly the food-processing and textile industries. Other enterprises were designated as uneconomic and closed down, and the excess labor was sent back to the rural areas. Every extra person in the city was considered a burden on agriculture.

Although the authorities were probably unable to transfer all the surplus urban manpower to the rural areas, "the urban population was appropriately reduced." Despite reports that the 1963 grain output in Communist China had returned to approximately the 1957 level and has continued to increase gradually, urban growth is still restricted. This is not only the result of the continued emphasis on agriculture and a shortage of industrial crops effected by the diversion of acreage to food production, but also because many thousands of young urban "intellectuals" are still being evacuated to the countryside.

There are indications that, at least for the time being, the Communists may be willing to limit urban growth to little more than its own natural increase, which would amount annually to perhaps 2 million persons.

The purpose of this discussion is not to arrive at a specific estimate of the urban population, but simply to indicate that during the foreseeable future, the expansion of the industrial sector of the economy cannot be relied on to accommodate even the annual increment into the labor force. Rural China has had to find a place for them in the past, and will have to do so in the future.

The Communists made no secret of their awareness of the

problems posed by disguised underemployment and seasonal unemployment in rural China. As with everything else, the drastic change came in 1958 with the introduction of the People's Communes and the Great Leap: Peking abandoned its propaganda for birth control, "liberated" the women from domestic chores to work in the field and factory, and proclaimed a severe manpower shortage throughout China.

The manpower shortage was real, but artificially created. A nationwide campaign was initiated to mobilize every available pair of hands for some form of productive labor.

Most significant was the diversion of millions of male peasants from farming to irrigation projects, manure collection, and various other water and soil conservation activities, as well as to the much-publicized production of steel in back-yard furnaces. Whereas it was reported that in 1957 about 90 per cent of the peasant's time was devoted to agricultural and subsidiary production, by 1960 it was stated that "only a little over 50 per cent of the manpower is actually engaged in agricultural production." Natural calamities, held to be solely responsible for the crisis, were actually superimposed on already critical rural conditions resulting from the inefficient utilization of available manpower, attempts to do too much in too short a time, and general mismanagement. The consequences were disastrous and, according to some, brought China to the brink of collapse.

It is important to note here that, despite the economic crisis, the Communist approach to labor utilization during the late 1950s was economically sound. There was a reasonable effort to reallocate individuals who were not fully active economically into alternative employment, where they could make a positive contribution, no matter how slight. The problem was that reclamation projects—irrigation, drainage, desalinization, and other mass programs—became the primary purpose, rather than a bonus, and millions of people spent their time in marginal labor at the expense of agriculture. Similarly, the idea of introducing some basic, handicraft-type industries into rural areas was a sensible attempt at utilizing excess manpower;

247

it was the emphasis on industrial production, suitable neither to manpower nor resources, that was so harmful to the effort. There are indications, however, that China is now taking a much more reasonable approach toward effective utilization of excess labor forces.

During the last few years many of the Leap Forward schemes for utilizing surplus manpower have been reintroduced in a different wrapping and with a more rational approach. The emphasis is on developing "multiple operations" and striving for general improvement and expansion of "subsidiary occupations," by "fully developing the human personality, fully utilizing the natural resources, and opening up ways for multiple operations." Translated, this means that when people can be spared from basic agricultural production, they should be utilized in reclamation projects, in expanding arable land, in developing mountain lands, in planting subsidiary crops, and in providing special care for domestic animals.

It is quite apparent to China's leaders that high population growth tends to perpetuate the labor surplus characteristics of the economy, that the growth of rural population increases agriculture's own consumption requirements, and that the implementation of the prescribed measures would be facilitated by reducing numbers. They are also aware that as increasing numbers of women reach child-bearing age themselves, there will be secondary waves of even larger birth cohorts to cope with.

There were three main reasons why efforts to control the birth rate in the middle fifties did not meet with the success of some of the other campaigns: (1) there was no receptivity or motivation on the part of millions of largely illiterate or poorly educated peasants; (2) the government was unable to provide the population with effective, acceptable, and inexpensive means of birth control; and (3) given the absence of both means and motivation, the pervasive channels of Communist control dissipated at the threshold of the commune bedrooms. Now there are reasons to believe that the government may be able to overcome these obstacles. If Communist China assigns the program the necessary priorities, there is a possibility that some progress can be made in reducing the country's fertility.

First, the question of receptivity. In 1965, people under thirty constituted approximately two-thirds of China's total population. They have few memories that predate 1950. If the current campaign can reach just this group, its success is assured. They comprise the most thoroughly indoctrinated and, coincidentally, the most fertile group. They have been saturated with propaganda against the family, against cultural traditions, and against domesticity; but for socialist conformity, for service, and for sacrifice to the motherland. They are also better educated—most of them have at least a four-year primary school education. It is quite conceivable that they would be willing both to postpone marriage and, within the marriage relationship, to practice birth control, provided the means were readily available.

This introduces the second requirement. Although in China there are no cultural obstacles to the use of contraceptives or, for that matter, to induced abortions or sterilization, in the earlier campaign contraceptive devices were apparently inadequate and too expensive. The supply and distribution of all contraceptives have now probably increased, but the most promising aspect of the current effort lies in the discovery by China of the intrauterine contraceptive device (IUCD), so widely publicized in the West in recent years.

The IUCD has all the characteristics necessary for a successful contraceptive under the conditions prevailing in China: (1) Consisting of a small plastic coil, it is easy to produce at a very small cost. IUCDs are known to be manufactured in China and presumably are also imported from Hong Kong. (2) Although some women cannot use the IUCD, the device is well over 90 percent effective for those who can. This level is more than adequate for China, especially because of the increasing availability of induced abortion. (3) Whereas in the United States the insertion of the IUCD requires the services of a medical doctor, this is not the case in China. The process is relatively simple and, after a short course of instruction, may be performed by a rural medical assistant, by a midwife, or by other specially trained personnel. (4) The man, who is usually less receptive to troublesome precautionary measures, is not involved in any way. (5) Finally, one of the most important advantages of the intrauterine device is that effective limitation to impregnation can be achieved by a single decision and action on the part of the woman. She does not have to remember to take a pill, she does not have to count days, and she does not have to go through any pre-intercourse or post-intercourse procedures.

In addition to the requirements of receptivity and means, there is the problem of organization and implementation of any full-scale, centrally directed endeavor aimed at birth control. The natural channel for any such effort is the expanded public health service, whose organization parallels the general administrative structure of the country, reaching down from Peking and the provincial capitals, to the lowest level of the communes: the production team. Reportedly, all cities and *hsien* centers have medical bureaus, which, in turn, control all the hospitals, clinics, and other medical facilities under their jurisdiction. All production brigades are supposed to have at least one health center, while health services in the production units are provided by part-time workers, midwives, and nurses working under the direction of brigade health centers.

Adequate sources confirm that the health system permeates down to the lowest rural administrative unit. But of what quality and quantity are the medical personnel? As in the case of other statistics from China, quantitative information on public health is inadequate and lacks uniform definitions. In 1958, the last year for which integrated health statistics are available, there were 75,000 doctors trained in Western medicine, 131,000 medical assistants, 138,000 nurses, 35,000 midwives, and 1,781,-000 others. For the most part, practitioners of traditional medicine, midwives, and paramedical personnel with little formal training were responsible for the health care of the peasants.

250

Based on scattered data, it may be estimated that by 1965 there were perhaps 135,000 persons with higher medical education and some 350,000 graduates of secondary medical education on the mainland. These staff most of the urban health facilities and probably represent the leadership in the *hsien* medical bureaus and some of the rural facilities. The number of health workers in the rural areas is, of course, even more difficult to obtain, but based on descriptions of health organizations in specific communes, they may now number in the vicinity of 8 million—most of them engaged in public health work on a part-time basis.

Only the graduates of the formal medical schools, both higher and middle level, can be said to have adequate medical training. Most of the part-time rural health workers have only a rudimentary knowledge of human anatomy. But for the present discussion, the number of people with some medical responsibilities is more important than their overall competence. Presumably, their number has reached significant proportions, they are widely dispersed, they operate within a chain of control, and they are accessible and trainable. A large proportion of the health personnel are women. Not only have many medical personnel been transferred to rural health centers, but the much publicized mobile medical teams apparently reach the most isolated areas of the country. The lines of control go down through government agencies and Party channels, as well as through the public health system.

It is important to remember that to a certain extent this discussion is speculative. There is some evidence in the Chinese press and elsewhere that the birth control campaign now in progress has considerable impetus and is, in fact, operating through the public health system, but there is no indication that the regime has assigned to it the high priority necessary for effective fertility control. It is impossible to determine whether the intrauterine devices have become an integral part of the program, and there is no sign that a training program —essential if intrauterine devices are to be made available in rural China on a mass scale—is in progress. And yet, despite the absence of direct evidence, it is quite conceivable that the investment in financial and human resources necessary for an all-out effort to reduce the birth rate is contemplated in the near future. The ingredients for success appear to be present.

Science and
Education

*S*cience has no national boundaries, and occasional attempts at secrecy in science have had little success—the spread of nuclear weapons and reactor technology is a case in point. What is relevant in the case of China, however, is the degree to which her present isolation may be slowing down the growth of science and technology; whether she will find a substitute for the Soviet Union to train her science and engineering students and provide them contacts with advanced technologies. Recently Chinese graduate students have gone to France and Great Britain and informal scientific contacts have been initiated with other countries.

With respect to general education, the Chinese government has accomplished a great deal. Official sources report that illiteracy has been substantially removed and that at present one out of every four persons is engaged in formal education either in the spare-time, part-time, or full-time schools. Great gaps in our knowledge of education in China exist, since our data depend upon official Chinese reports, speeches, and impressions offered by foreign visitors.

Theodore Hsi-en Chen, Director of the Asian-Slavic Center at the University of Southern California, is concerned here *with the role of education in a communist society and its special organization in China.*

C. H. G. Oldham, geophysicist and presently with the Unit for the Study of Science Policy, University of Sussex, has visited China twice during the past two years. His first-hand report of visits with scientists and scholars and his evaluation of the universities and institutes cast a much needed light on the system of higher education and investment in research.

EDUCATION IN COMMUNIST CHINA: AIMS, TRENDS, AND PROBLEMS

Theodore Hsi-en Chen

The Importance of Education in Communist Society

Education plays a direct and prominent role in consolidating communist rule and establishing a communist society. Education, indoctrination, and propaganda are forms of persuasion which the communists deem more important and effective in the long run than coercion or force. As Mao Tsetung clearly stated,[1] the communist "democratic dictatorship" uses both dictatorial and democratic methods. The former, consisting of suppression, punishment, and the use of force, are applied to reactionaries, counterrevolutionaries, and "enemies of the people"; while the latter, consisting of education and persuasion, are applicable to the people. Whenever possible, persuasion is preferred to coercion. To be sure, there are times when persuasion becomes virtually coercive, but as long as they stop short of direct force, the communists claim that they are only educating the people and teaching them to become good citizens of the new society.

This reliance on education is not only justified by theory, but also necessitated by the nature of the communist program. The communists are not satisfied with the absence of opposition; they demand wholehearted compliance and active support. They do not tolerate indifference or passivity. They realize that it is relatively easy to stamp out opposition by force, but the support of the masses must be won by the "milder" methods of persuasion and education.

Moreover, the communists want something more than compliance in overt behavior. Believing that action issues from thought, they want to delve into the minds of the people to examine ideas and convictions. They demand that thought and action be accompanied and reinforced by the proper attitudes and emotions. The remolding of mind and heart, as well as of behavior, is a task so great that only education in its broadest sense can perform it.

It may be said that there is no phase of the communist program that does not require the support of education. For example, the abolition of private ownership and the liquidation of private enterprise are not only economic measures. They are accompanied by an extensive program of "socialist education," in which the people are taught the superiority of the socialist system and the evils of capitalism. It is not enough that merchants and industrialists surrender their assets to the state for "collective" management; they must attend classes and institutes to study Marxism-Leninism and the theories of socialism. They must be re-educated to see the advantages of the socialist economy and to accept their new role in the collectivized enterprises willingly. Furthermore, they are asked to proselytize their fellow merchants and industrialists.

Education in communist society, then, goes far beyond schooling. The worker and the peasant must be taught basic skills and knowledge for production; the street cleaner and fertilizer carrier must learn to take pride in the dignity of labor; the housewife or the old grandmother must understand the new responsibilities of women; the barber and the dressmaker must be taught to avoid the outlandish fashions of bourgeois society and guide their customers in the appreciation of the "simplicity and dignity" of proletarian aesthetics; and so on. At the same time, the entire population—young and

258

old, male and female—must be given the proper information about internal and foreign affairs and government policies, so that they may actively support whatever is planned by the Party and the state.

There is no line of demarcation between formal and informal education, no distinction between education and propaganda or indoctrination. To shout slogans or carry banners in an anti-American parade is a practical lesson in politics, just as attendance at a mass trial for reactionary landlords or recalcitrant capitalists is an educational experience in the class struggle. Education, or "study," goes on in the government office, the farm, the factory, the mines, and business enterprises. Motion pictures, drama, story-tellers, circus entertainers —all have educational functions and are governed by the same objective—molding a new socialist man with proletarian tastes, loyalties, and convictions.

The Nature of Communist Education

One of the most noteworthy features of Chinese Communist education is the systematic schooling given to adults in their after-work hours without interference with their employment. This instruction does not take place in the regular schools: classes are held aboard ship for crews, as well as on farms and in factories.

"Spare-time" education is a major form of education for workers and peasants and the most important means of combatting illiteracy. It provides in-service training for teachers, some of whom have had little more education than their pupils. The variety of spare-time schools and their growth may be seen from the figures in Table I on page 260, published by the State Statistical Bureau.

In addition to spare-time schools, there are part-time schools in which young students spend some time in productive labor. Full-time schools, therefore, constitute only a fraction of the educational facilities available to the population. Taking into consideration spare-time schools, part-time schools, and full-

TABLE I.

Number of People Attending Spare-Time Schools

	Spare-time institutes of higher learning	Spare-time technical middle schools	Spare-time middle schools	Spare-time primary schools
1949	100	100	...	...
1950	400	100	...	...
1951	1,600	300	...	...
1952	4,100	700	249.000	1,375.000
1953	9,700	1.100	404.000	1,523.000
1954	13,200	186.000	760.000	2,088.000
1955	15,900	195.000	1,167.000	4,538.000
1956	63,800	563.000	2,236.000	5,195.000
1957	75,900	588.000	2,714.000	6,267.000
1958	150,000	...	5,000.000	26,000.000

time schools, as well as numerous short-term institutes, correspondence courses, and indoctrination classes, one can see some justification for the Communist claim that one out of every four persons in China is receiving some kind of schooling. At any rate, there exists a vast network of educational and indoctrinational agencies which aim to produce an impact on the minds of the people.

All education is governed by three cardinal principles: (1) it must serve *politics*, (2) it must be combined with *production*, and (3) it must be directed by the Communist *Party*. These are what the writer has called the "Three P's" of Chinese Communist education.

Education for politics demands the study of politics and Marxist-Leninist-Maoist ideology as the core of any kind of education, be it a literacy class, a technical school, or the university. Political education means more than imparting knowledge; it calls for translating knowledge into political

260

action. Participation in political activities, from killing flies in the anti-pest campaign to anti-imperialism parades and demonstrations, is considered an essential part of educational experience.

Politics, furthermore, must permeate the whole school. The slogan, "Let politics take command," guides education as it does every other phase of life. Teachers and students are commended or demoted on the criteria of their political fervor and ideological correctness. "Thought reform" makes sure that the Party line is understood and followed. Since the class struggle is central to the approved ideology, "class education" is of major importance.

Besides molding political activists, education must make every person a better producer. Mao Tse-tung once said that there are two basic fields of knowledge: knowledge of the class struggle and knowledge of the production struggle. This means not only the provision of both in the school schedule, but their integration, so that the problems of production may be studied in the classroom, and the knowledge gained in study may be applied to improving production. Participation in productive labor is required of teachers as well as students. Even those in full-time schools must take time off to work on farms, in factories, or in other productive enterprises.

Finally, all education must be under the direction and control of the Communist Party. In every school a "Party leadership," represented by a branch organization of the Communist Party, sees that Party guidelines are followed. The Party leaders keep a watchful eye on thought reform, the labor record, and the "ideological consciousness" of students and teachers. The Party sponsors the youth organizations, which exercise a powerful influence on school life.

Education for a Proletarian Society

Education is directly and immediately involved in building the kind of society visualized by the communist planners. In any plan for economic construction or political action, education is expected to play an active role to implement the plan and ensure its success. The critical observer may criticize communist education as a political weathervane without stability or continuity, but from a different point of view, it may also be observed that there is no gap between education and society, no "ivory tower."

It is easy to see how education is essential to the Five-Year Plans: it must produce the various types of personnel needed by the Plans. Just as direct is the role of education in bringing about the class revolution. Take, for example, the emphasis on worker-peasant education. Besides special schools for workers and peasants, regular schools give priority to students of "worker-peasant origin" who seek admission despite their inadequate academic preparation. Schools of all levels have been urged to increase the percentage of worker-peasant students. As a result of this drive, it is claimed that worker-peasant students now constitute over 90 per cent of the elementary school population, 75 per cent of the enrollment in secondary schools, and more than 50 per cent in the higher institutions. This change in the "class composition" of the school population is heralded as an important step in the establishment of a proletarian society.

To the same end intellectuals and all students are required to engage in labor. It is hoped that after working on the farms and in the factories and living with peasants and workers, the intellectuals and the youth of bourgeois background will learn the proletarian viewpoint and overcome their "white collar" limitations. Thus, by transforming bourgeois intellectuals into proletarian workers and by producing a new "proletarian intelligentsia" from the ranks of workers and peasants, education is expected to hasten the arrival of the classless society envisaged by Karl Marx and his followers.

A further implication of combining education with productive labor may be noted. To facilitate student labor, the schools maintain farms, factories, and other productive enterprises as a part of their regular operations. Thus they serve as "centers of production." At the same time, the productive enterprises providing "spare-time" schooling for their workers assume the simultaneous role of "centers of learning." This development not only entails new concepts of "learning" and "education," but also, in the communist view, leads to the gradual elimination of the differences between mental and manual labor.

Perplexing Problems

Judging by statistics, one cannot but be impressed by the growth and expansion of education on the Chinese mainland under Communist rule. Substantial progress has been made in reducing illiteracy. Education has been made available to the entire population on an unprecedented scale, and there has been a marked increase in enrollment at all levels.

This educational expansion is accompanied by a number of serious problems that perplex communist planners. Some of the problems arise from the political and economic scene, while others are dilemmas which admit of no easy solution, because they are inherent in the nature of communist education or communist society. A few may be briefly examined.

The New Emphasis on Class Education

Since 1960, the Communists have stepped up the campaign for "class education." The purpose is to heighten ideological fervor and to generate more enthusiasm for the Maoist style of revolution. An essential method is to remind people of the hideous evils of precommunist society and to develop an "intense hatred of the past and a passionate love for the present."

The study of "histories" has been adopted as a most effective form of class education. Students study the history of their school and the history of their families; school history contrasts the inequality of educational opportunity in the past with today's education of the masses, while family history would bring out the bourgeois background of some parents

263

or the extreme hardships suffered by worker-peasant parents under the oppression of landlords and capitalists. Workers gather to study the history of their factory, again contrasting the ruthless exploitation of the past with the new position of the working class in socialist society. Commune members study the history of their commune, and residents of a neighborhood study the history of their street or their village. The "teaching materials" are furnished by "old workers, old cadres, old peasants, and old army veterans" who relate their "bitter experiences" of oppression and exploitation in precommunist society.

What are the reasons for this new campaign to generate "class consciousness"? First, the program of socialization has met with resistance and opposition. The existence of opposition was frankly admitted by T'ao Chu, member of the Central Committee of the Communist Party, First Secretary of the Central-South Bureau of the Party's Central Committee, and Vice-Premier of the State Council. He said:[2]

> After the socialist transformation of ownership is basically completed, the class enemy who opposes socialism tries his utmost to restore capitalism by means of "peaceful evolution." That is why we must sharpen our vigilance, always hold class struggle as the key, adopt correct lines and policies and wage a protracted and unremitting struggle to shatter the "peaceful evolution" intrigues of the class enemy.

The overthrown reactionary classes conspire to stage a comeback; embezzlers, grafters, and degenerates also launch wanton attacks on socialist positions. Evidently there is no small number of reactionaries and degenerates, and consequently it becomes imperative to launch "a movement to re-educate the people."

Second, the economic difficulties following the big socialist push of 1958 caused much public discontent. To counteract it the Communists launched an intensive campaign. People are told that class enemies still abound, that the class struggle must continue for a long time, and that every one must be

264

ready for more hardship and sacrifice. It is wrong to think too much of better livelihood; comfort and enjoyment must be postponed until the success of the revolution is assured.

Third, the new "vigilance" has been stimulated by the Sino-Soviet dispute. The anti-revisionist campaign is directed not only against the Soviet leaders, but also against people within the country who hold similar views. An anti-revisionist campaign attacked historians, philosophers, playwrights, novelists, and other intellectuals who seemed to have deviated from the Party line.[3] "Revisionists" were found even among Party members. T'ao Chu spoke of "Right opportunists in the Party" who stood "on the side of the bourgeoisie" and "did their best to find pretexts to oppose the agricultural cooperation movement led by the Party."[4] Among the revisionists subjected to concerted attack in 1964 was Yang Hsien-chen, a veteran Communist who, until recently, was so highly esteemed as a Party intellectual that he was made president of the Higher Party School, where he was an authoritative lecturer on Marxist doctrines. Now he was accused of spreading "bourgeois and revisionist views."[5]

Fourth, there is the constant fear of "the rebirth of capitalism" and the revival of "bourgeois thinking." Just as many of China's intellectuals who are enthusiastic about the communist promise of change and reform are reluctant to accept the communist program of a bitter and ferocious class struggle, so the masses of China are far more interested in the practical benefits of agrarian reform and in tangible improvement of their livelihood than in Marxist ideology. To the communists, however, advocacy of reform without Marxist ideological underpinning, or the desire to settle down on a small farm and enjoy more food and better housing are expressions of bourgeois thinking which endanger the socialist revolution. Hence the need to drive home to the masses and the intellectuals alike the indisputable Marxist "truth" that the class struggle is essential to progress and a determined war must be waged against all class enemies—revisionists, purveyors of bourgeois thinking, and all reactionary elements.

265

Fifth, the Communist leaders have been worried about the problem of "successors." Realizing that those who have guided their revolution through the past difficult decades are now advancing in age, they ask if the younger generation of Communists will be ready to take over. They fear that the younger generation, without personal experience of the life-and-death struggle that deepened the dedication of the veterans, may not fully realize the need for ideological vigilance and continued class struggle. Lacking depth and firmness of conviction, they may be easily influenced by bourgeois infiltrators. Thus, they must relive the revolutionary past and make the long and arduous struggle of earlier years a part of their own experience. They have to learn from the "old" veterans and hear their moving stories. The large number of articles in magazines and newspapers dealing with the question of "successors" is evidence of the deep concern of the Communist leaders over the transfer of leadership to persons whose ideological fervor may be questionable.

Quality Versus Quantity

Another perplexing problem is that of educational standards. To overcome illiteracy in a predominantly illiterate population, the Communists want to teach as many people as possible in the shortest possible time. To produce the technical personnel and cadres needed for the multitudinous tasks of construction under the Five-Year Plans, they are also under pressure to turn out large numbers of trained persons quickly. Consequently there is a demand for speeded-up programs and educational short-cuts. Abbreviated courses, short-term institutes, and *ad hoc* special classes are devised to meet the need. Education is reduced to concentrated doses and minimum essentials, taught without the encumbrance of materials not directly related to the immediate purpose. The inevitable result is superficiality and low educational standards.

Educational quality has also suffered because of the priority given to political education. This takes so much time that there is not enough left for academic learning. In addition, all students must engage in labor. Moreover, knowing that they are more likely to be judged according to their political record than their academic performance, teachers and students tend to pay less attention to scholarship. Another obstacle to high quality is the policy of admitting into schools poorly prepared students of worker-peasant origin who are allowed to advance to higher levels after brief attendance at short-term or part-time schools.

The Communists are not altogether unaware of this situation. They know that some students enter technical schools and higher institutions without the basic fundamentals which they were supposed to have mastered in the lower schools. Impressive statistical reports of large numbers of new literates have proved misleading, because many new literates or semi-literates quickly forget what they have learned hurriedly, and soon slide back into the ranks of the illiterate. In the industries and construction enterprises, the graduates of speeded-up training programs have not proved adequate to the tasks assigned them. Some of the economic difficulties which became conspicuous after 1958 may be attributed to the incompetence of "leading cadres" in industry and business who had been hastily trained for their positions: they were strong in ideological and political qualifications, but weak in their knowledge and understanding of the practical problems of production or economic development.[6]

Some efforts have been made to upgrade educational quality. The schools have been told that political instruction and political activities, essential as they are, must be kept within reasonable limits. Short-term institutes and abbreviated courses still exist, but they do not play so prominent a role as formerly. College courses have been extended to five or six years, and academic learning has been accorded more attention and respect.

Emphasis on quality, however, is not a firm, consistently enforced policy. It has had its ups and downs according to shifts in the Party line, which itself reflects a serious dilemma arising from the opposing demands of doctrinairism and realism. In between proclamations of academic emphasis, the demands for more politics and labor are often so loud and persistent that the academic voice becomes very faint, if heard at all.

Frequent shifts of position reflect an inability to find an adequate solution. Take for example the problem of political education. When the Communists came to power in 1949, they lost no time in launching a campaign for political education and political activities in the schools. Political instruction became the core of the curriculum, and regular classes were often dismissed to make room for indoctrination sessions or participation in political campaigns. Not only was academic learning neglected, but the pressures of a crowded schedule affected the physical and mental health of students. By 1953, the situation had become so serious that orders were issued to curtail political activities to provide more continuity of academic learning, and schools were asked to take measures to safeguard the health of the students. For a while such remedial measures brought a much-needed relief, but gradually politics reasserted its dominance, and academic learning was again overshadowed.

By 1956, a new spate of articles and speeches appeared in Communist newspapers and periodicals, again drawing attention to excessive political activities. Realism was asserted once more, but again it was short-lived. In 1958, the Party laid down the principle that education must be combined with productive labor. Now, whole days and weeks were taken off the school calendar for full-time labor in productive enterprises. Schools and universities were to become "centers of production."

The failure of the Great Leap Forward, however, brought the ideological enthusiasts to their senses. As high an authority as Liu Shao-ch'i[7] declared that the main business of the school is study, and that labor and production must be considered secondary.[8] "More study and less labor" became the new cry of academicians, who had felt that way all the time

268

but had discreetly kept quiet until the Communists themselves spoke out against inordinate stress on labor and production. A wave of economic realism, reinforced by the need for well-trained and well-educated personnel after the withdrawal of Soviet advisers, brought about a new awareness of the importance of systematic study and mastery of subject. Voices were heard urging "more quality, less quantity." A professor of Tsinghua University related in 1962 that in the craze for speed and quantity, a mathematics teacher allowed only ninety minutes to explain six geometrical curves, with fifteen minutes for each curve, and timed himself with a watch.[9] Taking advantage of the change in mood of the authorities, he and his colleagues now proposed "quality even at the expense of quantity."

There are two aspects of communist dogma which tend to militate against educational quality. One is the insistence on the practical value of knowledge. Mao Tse-tung decried "book knowledge" and ridiculed pedants who knew nothing about farming, labor, war, or practical affairs.[10] This view tends to breed a scornful attitude toward the study of fundamental subjects and of knowledge that does not have immediate practical value. In 1961, one of the periods of relative realism, the well-known scientist Ch'ien Hsueh-sen[11] assailed the tendency to neglect the study of fundamental science and to despise the teaching of science not directly related to production. He criticized the prevalent policy of promoting technology and neglecting the patient, painstaking study of fundamental science without which there would be no technology.[12]

The communist "mass line" also tends to stress quantity over quality in education. For example, the communists have always stressed science. But in their enthusiasm for the mass line and their haste to bring up a new generation of "proletarian intelligentsia," they decided to promote science among the masses, to "strip science of its mystery." Bourgeois scientists were accused of deliberately making science appear difficult to keep it away from the masses, and workers and peasants were asked to "storm the gates of science." Peasants with practical experience in seed selection and workers who devised new tools were hailed as the scientists of the new age. Their "research" was given recognition by awards and citations. "With Communist Party guidance and state assistance," it was said, "farmers in all parts of the country are entering the once remote field of research by the thousands." [13] Not until the serious decline of food production shook the ideological zealots out of their trance did they acknowledge that scientists could not be produced overnight, that there was still a need for "old-style scientists."

During the period of the "popularization of science," there was a rush to recognize "new-type" scientists among the students as well as peasants and workers. Students and young instructors were encouraged to prepare outlines for study, and their textbooks were heralded as superior to those prepared by the old-style scientists. A writer for the authoritative ideological journal *Red Flag* said of these young scientists:

> The accomplishments of these young people prove that science is not so mysterious. By keeping firm the correct direction, by daring to think and to act, and by hard work, they have been able to pierce through the heavy layers of fog which the bourgeois scholars have tried to wrap around science . . . In the social sciences using Marxist theories, even though for the present lacking experience and deficient in knowledge, they are more apt to arrive at the truth than the bourgeois scholars confined by their erroneous viewpoints.

Redness Versus Expertness

The slogan in China is that students and scholars must be "both red and expert." The practical question is: What is the best way to achieve the twin objectives? Which is more important, redness or expertness?

Educational literature abounds in the discussion of these

questions. No one dare question the importance of redness, of course. But academicians have debated whether the schools should not consider it their first duty to produce competent experts and then to see that the experts are also given political and ideological training. They have also asked whether the development of expertise does not require longer and more sustained study than political and ideological education.

Until 1959, the position of the Communist Party was very clear: redness and expertness were inseparable. To advocate "expertness first and redness later" was a negation of the supremacy of politics, a cardinal principle of education. If one should have to be sacrificed, expertise requirements might be reduced, but never political and ideological qualifications. The rectification campaign of 1956–58 demanded that old-style intellectuals and experts purge themselves of bourgeois influences and become thoroughly red by labor and thought reform.

As noted, there was a reversal of official view on this question during the short reign of realism in intermittent periods from 1959 to 1961. "Do Not Disregard Book Knowledge, Do Not Disregard the Role of Experts" was the title of an article in the authoritative *Peking People's Daily*.[14] Another writer reflected the shift in emphasis as follows:[15]

> Should we learn from those experts who hold the viewpoint of bourgeois scholarship? As long as these experts are distinguished in their fields of scholarship, we can learn from them. Naturally, we do not want to learn their bourgeois viewpoint; what we need to learn is their mastery of the valuable heritage accumulated in the past. Generally speaking, learning from the old teachers and the old experts is an indispensable phase of our program of scientific and cultural development.

This new realism was threatened by the anti-rightist and anti-revisionist campaigns of 1960, but was reaffirmed when Foreign Minister and Deputy Premier Ch'en Yi declared in an address to an audience of college students that even "white

271

experts" were worthy of respect.[16] This was again a welcome reprieve for the "old scholars" and "old teachers," but how long would it last? The pendulum was bound to swing again.

The Problem of the Intellectuals

In January, 1956, the Chinese Communist Party called a conference to discuss "the question of intellectuals." It was not a new question. From the early years of their movement, the communists had been troubled by China's intellectuals: how to win them over, how to reform them, and how to mold them to the communist pattern. Six years after they came to power, they were still unable to solve the question. Today, after sixteen years, Communist policy toward China's intellectuals still vacillates between rigid and liberal.

The problem admits of no easy solution because it involves a serious dilemma. Aware of the prestige and influence of intellectuals in Chinese society, and the crucial need for the services of every educated person in the "socialist" construction, the Communists have always wanted to win over the intellectuals. At the same time, they distrust them as products of the "old society" and carriers of "bourgeois ideology." The process of winning them over, therefore, is inseparable from "reforming" and converting them. To win them, it behooves the Party to treat the intellectuals with respect and consideration; but to reform them, it is often necessary to adopt severe repressive measures.

As early as 1939, the Communist Party had adopted a resolution on "the absorption of intellectual elements" which stated that "without the participation of the intellectuals, victory in the revolution will be impossible." The same resolution cautioned that the intellectuals who joined the Communists should be "trained adequately and led gradually to correct their weaknesses." [17] After the Communists came to power, they tried to "absorb and reform" the intellectuals of the entire nation. Since the whole country was now under one rule and the intellectuals had no other place to go to, the task of "absorption" became less pressing than that of "reforming." Reform measures ranged from the milder forms of political "study," to participation in the class struggle against the landlords and urban bourgeoisie, to the more severe and heart-rending processes of ideological remolding by means of attacks, excruciating self-examination and self-criticism, and incriminating confessions. The intellectuals were reviled, humiliated, and downgraded. Many succumbed to pressure, at least overtly; others withdrew into a shell of inactivity, passivity, and pessimistic resignation.

Meanwhile the First Five-Year Plan (1953–57) was making headway. The transitional stage of the "New Democracy" was terminated to clear the way for a big push toward socialism, and grandiose plans were made for the Second Five-Year Plan and the Great Leap Forward, to start in 1958. The need for the active service of all available intellectuals became imperative. In the conference on intellectuals, Chou En-lai admitted mistakes in the policy toward intellectuals and promised remedial measures.

A period of liberalization, though brief, was ushered in. The intellectuals were given better housing, more food rations, higher salaries, more favorable conditions of work, and special privileges. The overbearing dominance of cadres over intellectuals was mitigated, political requirements were eased, new rewards and incentives were offered. Scholars were given more reference books and laboratory equipment and permission to order books and journals from capitalist countries. A drive was launched to admit the more "progressive" intellectuals into Party membership.

The climax of this period was reached in the "Hundred Flowers campaign" of 1957, when, in the name of allowing "A Hundred Schools to Contend, A Hundred Flowers to Blossom," the Communists encouraged free speech, open criticism, and the airing of views beyond the confines of the Marxist straitjacket. How the criticism went out of control, and how the Communists abruptly shut off free discussion is now a familiar story. The anti-rightist and rectification campaigns that followed brought back repressive measures, and doctrinairism became once more the guide of official policy. Intellectuals had to sign "Heart Surrender" vows, pledging complete obeisance to the Communist Party and surrendering to it their "whole heart," unconditionally and without reservations.

The downgrading of the "old-time intellectuals" was evident in Liu Shao-ch'i's address commemorating the fortieth anniversary of the October Revolution. He said:

> To build socialism, the working class must have its own army of scientific and technological cadres; it must have its own professors, teachers, scientists, journalists, artists and writers, or legalists, and Marxist theoreticians . . .

Beleaguered and defenseless, the intellectuals sought avenues of escape. Some withdrew into a study of China's past, taking up subject matter without political implications. They avoided the contemporary scene. They took refuge in such research as whether the famous concubine Yang Kwei-fei was a virgin when she was taken into the court of Emperor Ming Huang of the T'ang dynasty! To combat this subterfuge, the Communist Party directed its attack against the trend of "emphasis on the past, neglect of the present," and urged instead "emphasis on the present, less study of the past."

And so the see-saw has gone. In 1960–62, there was talk of reviving the "Hundred Flowers" policy; but, at the same time, a nation-wide call was issued for an intensive study of the thought and writings of Mao Tse-tung. "Socialist education" and "class education" merged with the anti-revisionist campaign, until intellectuals became once more targets of concerted attack.

In the sixteen years of the regime, the intellectuals have been reviled, cajoled, chastised, praised, scorned, respected, downgraded, and exalted. The alternate shifts of repression and liberalization may reflect a policy of using the stick and the carrot at the same time. Or, they may be the expression of a fundamental dilemma with no easy way out.

274

What To Educate For

The intellectuals are not the only sector of the population that has caused concern to Communist leaders. The youth of the nation constitutes another problem. Many young people have been successfully indoctrinated and support the regime with enthusiasm and devotion, but others are skeptical, un-enthusiastic, even disillusioned and hostile. At the time of the "Hundred Flowers" free discussion of 1957, some students openly voiced their opposition to the Communist Party, and the current polemics about "successors" to the revolution[18] betray a fear on the part of Communist leaders that the ideological convictions of the young generation leave much to be desired.

In a country where schooling and scholarship have traditionally commanded social esteem and prestige, the new opportunities for education are welcomed and eagerly sought by young people. Yet young people seem to have been besieged by doubts in regard to the purpose of education. Such doubts have been expressed in the correspondence section of publications like *China Youth*. Young people ask many questions. Do they go to school for academic learning, for productive labor, or for political training? If one is judged by his labor and political record, is it necessary to put effort into academic learning, or to be in school at all?

Communist educational literature has discussed two problems of very different nature. One is the problem of students who drop out before the completion of a designated course. Many young people give up schooling because they conclude that schooling is of no significance, that only political and ideological qualifications really count. The other problem is that of students who, after the completion of a designated course, clamor for the opportunity to go to a higher school instead of going to work.

"Work" means accepting jobs assigned by the Party or the state. The Party-state wants young people to complete the

275

course of study they have been accepted for and has a plan for them to work on designated jobs at the completion of study. Continuation of study on a higher level is granted when additional education is necessary in order to meet specific needs of the Party-state. Every year, students of graduating classes in lower and higher schools are pressured to sign pledges promising to accept any job assigned by the Party-state, no matter how far away from home or how unrelated to personal interests.

From the practical point of view, continuation of study is not possible for most people because there are not enough schools to accommodate them. Consequently, the government has spent much time and effort to convince young people that it is not always desirable to think of further study. For most students completing their course in lower schools, the "glorious" path is to answer the call of the Party-state for service in the interest of the revolution and socialist construction. When amidst proud reports of expanded educational opportunity, one reads in Chinese Communist publications of an officially sponsored campaign to discourage continued schooling, one wonders if this phenomenon is not another of the contradictions in communist society. And is it one of many inherent in communist ideology?

Young people in China also ask whether there is any other purpose of education than service to the Party-state. They wish that their personal interests and preferences could be given more consideration. For a young couple to be separated by assignment to jobs in different cities may be accepted as temporarily necessary, but prolonged separation inevitably raises questions and doubts, if not resentment.

Much of what the communists attack as "bourgeois ideas" would be recognized as no more than human nature in a noncommunist society. People are willing to work hard, but they feel they are entitled to the fruits of hard work—improved living conditions, more food, better clothing, etc. In the communist view, these are bourgeois ideas: the true revolutionary must always sacrifice his own comfort, enjoy-

276

ment, and personal interests. But, after sixteen years of "ideological remolding," the communists find that the people still care for personal matters. Communist education combats such unproletarian thoughts and desires, but they are tenacious and seem to have deep roots in human nature.

The communists believe that the human mind and heart are as subject to conditioning as human behavior, and that thought, attitudes, desires, and ambitions can be "remolded" as easily as overt action. But they have had a few surprises. In the brief "Hundred Flowers" period of 1957, the intellectuals showed little evidence of proletarian thinking, despite six years of thought reform and ideological remolding. And the Communists must have been puzzled when in the short period of thaw in 1961–62, recognizing the need of "more study" and "more respect for expert knowledge," students took up academic study with astonishing enthusiasm, far beyond the expectation of the authorities. One observer reported as follows.[19]

> There are no vacant chairs to be found in the libraries, either by day or in the evening. In some schools the students line up waiting for a seat. Everybody wants to study . . .
> . . . With the concession of this new freedom, freedom to study, the students have dashed to their books with the same eagerness as students elsewhere dash to illicit pleasures, or to the playing fields.

It was reported that students in Tsinghua University were so interested in foreign languages that, in addition to the one language they were supposed to study, they audited classes to learn a second or even a third foreign language. Many students even exceeded the weekly number of hours provided in the pedagogical plan. The desire for learning seemed insatiable, and the authorities had to step in to advise against over-eagerness and trying to accomplish too much in too short a time.[20]

The Communist leaders might have wished that students would take up labor and political tasks with equal zeal and initiative. But after more than a decade of the new education, young people evidently have not yet fully developed proletarian tastes and desires. What the Communists may not realize is that in education one deals with the mind and with ideas, and these have a way of getting out of hand. Just as the intellectuals seized the freedom of criticism and went beyond prescribed limits, so students in their demand for more education and in their spontaneous enthusiasm for study (rather than labor and politics) threatened to upset the neatly calculated planning of the Party-state. Moreover, when communist propaganda tells the people that life for the masses is infinitely better than in the past, the people begin to expect tangible evidence: they ask for more food and more comfort. In their education and propaganda, the communists raise more hopes than they can fulfill and arouse more desires than they can satisfy. Then they find it necessary to reverse their propaganda line and launch a campaign to curb the aroused hopes and desires.

The communists launch campaigns and call them off to suit their purpose. Today, the nation is "mobilized" to take Taiwan by force; tomorrow the propaganda line is changed and the aroused emotions are supposed to subside. Yesterday, "learning from the Soviet Union" was the guide for the entire nation, and schools followed the Soviet "model" in curriculum and methods and taught Russian instead of English; today, the Russians are revisionists and traitors to the revolution, and the schools are teaching English once more. Yesterday, the "old intellectuals" were to be replaced by new "proletarian intelligentsia" and "red experts"; today, young people are asked to respect the "old teachers" and learn from the "old experts." The communists seem to believe that the mind of the people can be wiped clean at any moment—clean not only of bourgeois ideas, but also of discarded Party lines—to make room for any new thoughts and ideas the manipulators of "public opinion" may choose to implant.

But the human mind has a way of breaking through the walls that confine it. A person exposed to education—although

278

no more than indoctrination and propaganda—is likely to think beyond what he is asked to think. An illiterate person hitherto taking no interest in affairs outside his home and village, who learns to read and write and participate in political affairs, may become interested in things other than those prescribed by the rulers. Less than ten years ago, a massive nation-wide campaign was teaching the whole nation to adore the Soviet Union; now a new indoctrination campaign is launched to reverse their thinking about the erstwhile "Big Brother." It is no surprise some people raise questions in regard to the veracity of the "truths" that make up the content of communist education and propaganda.

Education, aspirations for better livelihood, dissatisfaction with the past, and expectation of change and reform: these are powerful forces that have a way of gaining momentum. This momentum may accelerate and become irresistible. If and when that happens, the communists may find themselves engulfed by the very forces they have helped to release. By extending educational opportunity, by inciting rebellion against exploitation and oppression (of feudal and bourgeois society), by occasional relaxing rigid control, by making such concessions as the private lot of the peasant or "free discussion" in academic circles, the communists may start what they cannot easily stop at will.

NOTES

1. *On People's Democratic Dictatorship,* 1949.
2. T'ao Chu, "A Guide for 500 Million Peasants Advancing Along the Socialist Road," *Peking Review,* September 10, 1965, p. 22.
3. Among these attacked in 1964–65 are Feng Ting, Chou Ku-Ch'eng, Shao Ch'uan-lin, Ou-yang Shan, Hsia Yen, Yang Han-sheng, Li Ling, and others.
4. *Peking Review,* August 20, 1965, p. 7.
5. See Chou En-lai's report to the Third National People's Congress. *Peking Review,* January 1, 1965, p. 13.
6. For further details, see the author's article "Education and Economic Failures in Communist China," *The Educational Record,* October 1963, pp. 348–53.

279

7. Communist China's chief of state since 1959.

8. *Chinese News Analysis*, April 24, 1959.

9. Union Research Institute, *Communist China*, 1962, Vol. I, (Hong Kong, 1963), p. 186.

10. See his 1942 address on "Correcting the Tendencies in Education, Party, and Literature and Art." (Also translated as "Rectify the Party's Style in Work.)

11. Formerly at the California Institute of Technology.

12. Ch'ien's article appeared in *Kuang Ming Jih Pao*, June 10, 1961.

13. *Peking Review*, September 27, 1960, p. 4. Also story of a "peasant-scientist" in *Peking Review*, March 6, 1961.

14. *Jen Min Jih Pao*, April 25, 1959.

15. *Hung Ch'i*, March 1, 1959, p. 31.

16. *Kuang Ming Jih Pao*, September 3, 1961.

17. See Chapter I of the author's *Thought Reform of the Chinese Intellectuals* (Hong Kong University Press, 1960).

18. See above section on class education.

19. *China News Analysis* (Hong Kong), February 9, 1962.

20. *Kuang Ming Jih Pao*, January 1, 1962.

SCIENCE AND EDUCATION IN CHINA
C. H. G. Oldham

INFORMATION AND IMPRESSIONS gained during two visits I made to China in October-November, 1964, and May, 1965 form the basis of this article. These are supplemented by the impressions of other Western scientists and educators who have recently visited China, together with the opinions of Chinese friends now living in Hong Kong who had previously been students and scientists in China. Also, a number of recent publications on Chinese science and education have been used to help set the scene into which these facts and impressions can be more meaningfully put.

Thus, to a certain extent this article is impressionistic and interpretive; it is *not* a survey of the field.

A general discussion of almost any activity in China needs to be prefaced by a number of points. In the first place, it must be realized that all activities in China are given an ideological coating. To the Chinese leaders this coating is an essential ingredient, which in fact provides the *raison d'être* for all their actions.

The pharmaceutical analogy can be carried a stage further. The Chinese leaders' ultimate aim is to generate a new society where, like a chemical compound, the two ingredients

281

will combine to form a new entity. As an intermediate stage, "political ideology" and "other activities" would be changed from the state of "coating" and "core" into a homogeneous mix—with the ideology as the basic framework to which all other activities are attached.

It is a temptation to Western observers to try and separate "ideology" from "the rest" and to consider the two separately. For a real understanding of China, however, it is necessary to consider them together—applied as Chinese remedies to a Chinese situation.

Reports about China which attempt to draw conclusions need another *caveat*. No matter what the sources of information, the available facts are still very few. This should always be borne in mind when assessing the reliability of answers to the different types of questions that can be asked about China. In general, questions about science and education can be grouped under four headings: (1) What are the official objectives or policy goals? (2) What are the ways and means of implementing these policies? (3) To what extent are these ways and means effective in achieving the stated objectives? (4) In the Chinese situation, are these policies good, bad, right, or wrong?

The first group of questions is the easiest to answer. The Chinese press publishes many policy objectives, and the foreign visitor is usually given a policy statement when he visits an institute or organization. The second group of questions is a little more difficult to answer, especially since statistical information is either poor or lacking. Attempts to formulate answers at this stage are usually recognized as educated guesswork. Answers to the fourth, and in many ways the most interesting, set of questions are the most difficult to provide. At present, they represent only the personal opinions of the respondents.

One further explanation. I have here separated science and education and written two separate pieces. The connections between the two, however, are very close. Not only is this true at the advanced level, but also at the peasant and worker

282

level, where science and education are combined to provide the basis for a new Chinese society.

EDUCATION IN CHINA

The Objectives

When the Chinese Communists came to power in 1949, 80 per cent of the Chinese population was illiterate, and there was only one college student for every 10,000 persons of the population. During the past sixteen years a major effort has been made to change this situation, and although the illiteracy rate is still high among the older peasants, most Chinese children now go to primary school; by the end of 1962 there were twelve college students for every 10,000 population.

Most of the problems faced by Chinese educators in bringing about these changes are those confronting any large developing country once it realizes the enormous economic significance of education. In the case of China, however, there are two complicating factors. One is the legacy from the past; the other is the Chinese government's hope for the future.

One of the legacies is the traditional Confucian emphasis on classical education, with a corresponding disdain for things practical. It resulted, in China, in a great reluctance on the part of the scholar to engage in any form of manual work. Another legacy stems from the tradition of close family unity, where allegiances were primarily to the family, and only secondarily to the city or state. This resulted in a lack of civic consciousness among many Chinese.

The Chinese government's hope for the future is the communist millennium in which, I was told, "There is no exploitation, no dichotomy between the rural village and the urban township, and no division between physical and mental labor." The Chinese leaders view education as one of the principal ways of achieving this goal.

As a consequence, two major objectives, explicitly stated at almost every educational institution I visited, have been

283

given to education. They are: (1) to change the traditional attitudes of the past to the communist attitudes of the future; and (2) to give appropriate training so that the needs of the state can be fully met. These objectives are aptly summed up by one of the commonest of the ubiquitous Chinese slogans: "Both red and expert."

The short-range goals related to the second objective are to provide a universal primary education of a general character, followed by a more varied secondary education for a limited number of students. Higher education is to provide the specialist personnel needed by the state.

Much longer-range goals are for universal primary and secondary education condensed into ten years, but reaching a level equal in quality to present first-year university standards. Then, in addition to the existing full-time higher education institutions, it is expected that each of the 1,700 counties will run full-time or half-day institutions of higher learning.

The policies to achieve these objectives have changed, sometimes radically, over the sixteen and a half years of Communist rule. Sometimes redness has been emphasized, other times expertise. It seems to have been a problem for the Chinese educators to find an optimum balance. At the time of my visits in 1964 and 1965 the "expert" aspect which had been emphasized since 1961 was still predominant, although there were indications that "redness" was rapidly catching up.

Education System in Outline

These are three distinct types of education: full-time; part-work, part-study; and spare-time.

Full-time primary education normally begins at age seven and continues for six years. The policy to provide universal primary education seems to have been achieved in the cities. The number of rural children of primary school age at full-time school is estimated to be between 80 and 90 per cent.

There are three kinds of full-time secondary education: middle schools, which are in two parts, upper and lower, each

284

of three years duration; normal schools for training primary school teachers; and professional schools which give specialized training. The number of full-time secondary students is difficult to determine, but it would seem that only about one in ten primary school graduates go on for full-time secondary education.

Full-time higher education takes place in about 400 institutes. About twenty of these are comprehensive universities—that is, they provide education in both arts and sciences—and about fifteen are polytechnic universities. The rest are mostly either medical universities and colleges, agricultural universities and colleges, or specialized engineering colleges. There are approximately 900,000 students in full-time higher educational institutes. This represents a further selection of about one in every ten middle school graduates.

Part-work, part-study education is carried on at both secondary and higher levels. It was started in rural areas in 1958 and has been tried experimentally in the cities on a large scale since late 1964. The system is exactly what the name implies—with students spending half their time in school and half at work. It is claimed that this type of education has considerable merit. First, it provides a continuation of education for some of the many students who failed to get into full-time schools, and helps to offset the frustrations and disappointments of this failure. Second, it is an economically sound proposition for a country as poor as China, since it means more workers to help with production. It also means that the student's formal education is supplemented by practical experience. It seems likely that this type of school will become increasingly important.

Spare-time education is distinct from part-time education and provides a continuing education for peasants and workers who have left school. It is most common in the urban areas where the spare-time schools are run by the trade unions. In fact, the National Trade Union law stipulates that management of enterprises should allocate to their trade unions 2 per cent of total wages, of which 25 to 37.5 per cent is to be used for spare-time education.

285

Classes are held after work and provide instruction ranging from literacy classes to university-level courses. Between 1958 and 1962, 9 million workers learned to read and write at such schools, more than a million finished the equivalent of primary education, 600,000 finished the equivalent of secondary education, and 15,000 finished higher education. I found that at those factories which I visited about one-third to one-half of all the employees were making use of the spare-time education provided.

In order to flesh out this skeletal outline of Chinese education, I shall single out three different topics, one at each educational level, and discuss these in more detail. The first will be a very specific example of a primary school in Soochow. Second is a summary of my observations of science education in several secondary schools. Third are observations about higher education.

A Soochow Primary School

The following is an account, reproduced from detailed notes, of the visit I made to a Soochow primary school. The statement made by the director, Miss P'an, was typical of that given at many schools. Her words, better than any summary account, convey the atmosphere pervading much of Chinese education today. This and other quotations of statements made to me by Chinese officials are translations made by the interpreters at the time of the interview; the possibility of misinterpretation must be borne in mind.

Miss P'an was extremely self-confident and precise. She was, I am sure, a dedicated Communist. Whenever she spoke of "the Party" her eyes shone, and her references to Mao were in the *tones* of an ardent evangelist speaking of Christ. After a brief welcome she said:

This school, has a history of fifty-nine years. Before Liberation the school served capitalist exploitation, but now it serves the workers and peasants. We carry out the

286

policy of the Communist Party and educate the students morally, physically, and intellectually. . . .

We know that it is the workers and peasants who will construct our country. Our socialist revolution must be carried on incessantly, and we must educate our children to have a social consciousness.

Our students are educated with internationalism, and are taught to love all the people in the world. The children listen to the words of Chairman Mao, and learn the internationalism of the Canadian, Dr. Bethune. They are also taught that they must strive for the liberation of all the people in the world, and they know that our enemies are the United States imperialists.

Our children love their country, love Mao, and love the Communist Party. Last Friday [October 16, 1964] when the children heard about the atomic bomb they were very happy and cheered. The teachers themselves study politics for half a day each week. This week, we have been studying the ninth comment on revisionism. Also, one evening a week, the teachers meet to discuss teaching methods.

The students know that by studying hard now, they will be better able to work for the construction of the country when they grow up. The students themselves use mutual aid whereby the good students help the backward ones. They love their group achievements and also love to do manual labor.

At question time, I asked about the number of characters taught and the use of romanized script. In the first half year, the children learn 337 characters. By the end of the first year they are expected to know 850 and by the end of primary school they should know 3,000. Romanized script is used for the first two years as an aid to teaching characters.

I had found elsewhere in China that most people had heard of Norman Bethune. In fact, after Lenin, Marx, Engels, and Stalin, he is probably the best known foreigner in China. I therefore asked for an elaboration of what the children were taught about this enigmatic Canadian. Miss P'an explained that although there were no formal classes in politics at primary school, many of the Chinese language lessons had a high political content. The story of Bethune, for example, occurred in the second-year student's Chinese language textbook. I translated the passage and made notes:

> Bethune was a member of the Progressive Labor Party of Canada. He was also a famous doctor. In 1937, the Anti-Japanese War broke out. Bethune led a medical brigade through mountains and rivers in order to help the Chinese people resist Japan. . . .
>
> He gave aid to the wounded. He was not afraid of difficulties, and sometimes walked more than 10 li in one hour. When in Hopeh in the middle of the front line, bullets fell before him. He still calmly carried out operations on the wounded. . . . Sometimes, he even gave away his own blood to the wounded. He frequently said, "The wounded are more my relatives than my own brothers because they are comrades."
>
> In 1939, when he was giving treatment to the wounded, he himself was poisoned and died. . . . In order to remember this great international friend . . . Military District Public Hygiene School changed its name to Bethune School.
>
> *Questions*
> 1. Why is Bethune a great international friend?
> 2. Listen to, and write down the following words. Write two separate sentences using the two words with asterisks.
>
> | *help | lead | international |
> | *survivors | famous | |
>
> 3. Learn this essay by heart.

Science Education in Some Chinese Secondary Schools

I found it particularly interesting that the children spoke fluently the Mandarin dialect, which has been made the lingua franca of China. At home, the children would speak Soochow dialect.

The following observations are based on visits to six middle schools, three in cities and three in communes.

1. In all six middle schools, science and mathematics accounted for about 50 per cent of the student's time.

2. Physics and chemistry are usually given greater stress than biology in both time allocated and equipment provided.

3. The physics laboratories in both city and commune schools were all equipped with what seemed to be a basic set of demonstration apparatus, at least a part of which I had seen manufactured in Nanking. Also, all the schools have sufficient sets of simple apparatus—such as ammeters, volt-meters, and batteries—to enable students to carry out their own experiments. The city schools were undoubtedly better equipped than the commune schools, and the physics laboratory at the Shanghai school was very good. There seemed to be an emphasis on electricity; the children at the Shanghai school had made quite elaborate radio sets.

4. The chemistry laboratory at the Shanghai school was well equipped, but those at the commune schools were quite rudimentary.

5. Biology seemed to be stressed much more at some schools than at others. For example, at the Peking school I saw a class of forty-eight fifteen-year-old students studying the cell structure of various plants. There was one microscope for every two students, and each student had his own textbook. The commune near Nanking also had quite a good collection of specimens and models, although there was little such material at the other schools.

It is, of course, impossible from these observations to generalize about the quality of science teaching in Chinese schools. What is significant, however, is that the importance of science is recognized and a beginning has been made in giving children in both city and countryside a solid grounding in the basic sciences.

Observations on Higher Education

Visits to the Universities of Nanking, Fu Tan in Shanghai, Hangchow Agricultural, Sun Yat-sen in Canton, Wuhan, and

289

the College of Geology in Peking provide the basis for the following general observations about higher education.

Academic Work

In the early 1950s higher education was remodeled, largely along Soviet lines. Technical education was emphasized, and only a few of the comprehensive universities were retained. The courses at the latter are usually for five years, the first three and a half being general, and the last one and a half specialized.

At the time of my visits, it was stressed at each university that the educational emphasis was on quality and on the combination of theory with practice. It was also explained that university students are trained for research. In the first years they are divided into groups for simple research, but later on they begin to do independent research. Every student must write a thesis before graduation. I was told at Nanking University that, in science, "the principal purpose is to train students to be in a position to master the latest science." One foreign language is compulsory for all students, and a second one optional.

The teaching science laboratories at universities I visited were well equipped, and the fourth- and fifth-year physics laboratories at Fu Tan University and Sun Yat-sen University were particularly good, as were the chemistry laboratories at Nanking and Fu Tan.

There was only a little postgraduate research being carried out in the universities, much of it on instrument design. It was noticeable that much of the advanced equipment for fourth- and fifth-year experiments had been built at the universities, mostly within the past five years.

China needs more trained researchers, and it seems likely that graduate work in universities will increase. It was reported that in 1963 there were 10,000 applicants for 800 graduate places, and the number of places was expected to double in 1964.

It is difficult to assess the overall quality of higher education in China. Some clues to the comprehensive universities can be obtained from those graduates who have gone on to read for the B.Sc. (Special) examination at the University of Hong Kong. Of the thirteen students from China who have so far been admitted to this course in chemistry, all have passed, and two obtained first-class honors. The sample is small, but it does indicate that students trained in Chinese universities can fit satisfactorily into advanced degree courses at a university with British standards.

Other students who have been to polytechnical universities in China and later to British universities tell me that the engineering courses in China are a little more specialized, and have a greater practical bent than those in Britain.

Politics

As in all other phases of education, politics plays a big role in the life of the university student. In the first place, it is an important consideration in his selection for entry. Although all students must sit for a state examination for university selection, it seems to be increasingly difficult for children of ex-capitalist families to gain entry to the universities and correspondingly easier for children of workers and peasants. At Sun Yat-sen University I was told that the number of children from worker and peasant families had increased from 17 per cent in 1953 to 64 per cent in 1963.

Once the student is at a university, education in politics and current affairs continues with formal lectures, reports, and discussion groups. The aim is to teach patriotism, internationalism, and communist ethics. I was told that about 10 per cent of a natural science student's study time is taken up with political studies, and 20 per cent of the time of a social science student.

Also, all students and junior staff are required to take part in "productive labor" for about four weeks each year. The purpose is primarily ideological—to help break down the barrier

291

between the intellectuals and the workers. The work may either be manual work in the countryside, mainly at harvest time, or it can be practical work concerned with the student's academic speciality.

Quantity and Quality of Teaching Staffs

The great expansion in higher education has meant a problem with the quality of teachers. Chou Pei-yuan, the vice rector of Peking University, noted in a recent publication that the number of teachers in institutes of higher education increased nine-fold between 1949 and 1962, but that more than 60 per cent of the present teaching force are only junior assistants. At the College of Geology in Peking, of 800 teaching staff only 37 are professors or assistant professors and 140 are lecturers. At Wuhan University there were 80 professors and assistant professors out of 700 teaching staff.

A big effort is being made to improve teaching quality, but I got the impression that the shortage of experienced instructors is a constraint on the further rapid expansion of China's higher education.

Material Conditions at the Universities

Statistics on improvement in material conditions were impressive at all the universities I visited. Almost 11,870,000 square meters of buildings for higher education were constructed between 1950 and 1958. In 1962, 100 million yuan ($40 million) was spent to improve teaching and research facilities. Most students live in hostels, and more than 50 per cent receive scholarships to supplement living expenses. Tuition and medical treatment are free. About one-quarter of the students are women.

Housing is also provided for the teaching staff at a rental of 3 per cent of their salary. University professors and senior research workers are among the most highly paid workers in China. A professor, for example, can earn up to 350 yuan a

292

month, three times the salary of the manager of a large Shanghai textile factory.

Meeting the Goals

Sixteen years have passed since the establishment of the People's Republic of China. The students now graduating from the universities have received all their education under a communist government. To what extent have the educational objectives of the state been met?

The Chinese leaders and educators themselves seem to be disappointed with the progress made towards achieving their first goal—that of converting the traditional attitudes of the past to the communist attitudes of the future. At nearly all the schools and universities I was told that some of the children were still imbued with ideas from the old society. The director of a middle school in Shanghai said, "Some students think that to study only is good, they look down on manual labor and prefer to stay in Shanghai rather than go into the countryside." At Soochow a headmistress said, "Bourgeois thought still influences the students and causes difficulties for the teachers," and at a Peking middle school I was told that some of the teachers still had wrong attitudes. At Sun Yat-sen University in Canton an official said that a major problem was that some of the students wanted to choose their own jobs after graduating and did not want to be assigned by the state.

But the main evidence of disappointment comes from the intensive campaign, in full swing when I was in China, to remind the children of the bad old days. Veteran soldiers lecture to school children on the revolutionary struggles. At the October Commune near Nanking I heard an old peasant telling a group of city children about the "cruel days" before Liberation. At a new housing estate in Shanghai I was shown a slum house which had been left standing "so the children will not forget what it was like in the old days."

Everywhere there were exhibitions of photographs showing

293

the atrocities and appalling conditions of Old China. Everywhere posters and slogans urge the children "to be determined successors of the revolution."

Most impressive reminder of all was the utterly fantastic production—(with 3,000 performers and 1,000-voice choir)—of "The East Is Red," which I saw performed in Peking in the Great Hall of the People. This was a cavalcade of the history of the Communist Party in China and must have stirred the hearts of all Chinese who saw it.

That it is considered necessary to wage such an intensive campaign is good evidence that the Chinese leaders are worried about the lack of revolutionary fervor in the youth. There also seems to be surprisingly poor comprehension of politics among many students.

It would be quite wrong, however, to conclude that Chinese youth is largely unenthusiastic. On the contrary, those who have had contact with Chinese students are impressed with their enthusiasm, alert attitude, and insatiable desire for knowledge. There is also a much better civic attitude than ever existed before, and, if some students are reluctant to do manual work there are many who seem to enjoy it, and others I talked with in Hong Kong frankly admitted its beneficial effects. But this enthusiasm seems to be fired much more by national pride in a resurgent China than by any great ideological motivation.

The second objective of Chinese education is to provide appropriate training to meet the needs of the state. Here, there is more reason for the educators to feel satisfied. Major efforts have been made both to bring education to the masses and to train a highly specialized corps of experts.

An unprecedented thirst for education has been generated and a variety of experiments have been made to find the most effective ways of providing appropriate education. This willingness to experiment has meant some difficulties, but has also created opportunities for exciting innovations. The emphasis on science, on the combination of theory with practice, the insistence that each student spend some time doing manual work, and the emphasis on civic responsibilities, are all new

294

concepts in Chinese education, and all are extremely important.

Educational experiments on such a large scale are bound to include some failures and mistakes, some of which the Chinese educators recognize, others which they would strongly deny were errors. In the first place, it has not always been possible to balance manpower supply with demand, and there have been cases of students assigned to jobs not related to their training. Second, during the Great Leap Forward emphasis was put on quantity and political education, at the expense of quality. It is not necessarily wrong to emphasize quantity over quality in education at certain stages in a country's development. However, it seems that at times the effect of the accompanying political education was to denigrate the expert. In 1961, this was admitted to be a mistake. Since that time quality has been emphasized, and the expert has come back into his own. Recent evidence suggests that politics is again of foremost importance, although this time the expert has not been denigrated.

One criticism of Chinese education, which I made repeatedly to Chinese educators, concerns education in the social sciences. Visits to schools and universities in China showed that in languages, history, geography, and other social sciences, the students are presented with a totally one-sided communist viewpoint. A large body of knowledge is prejudged as being divided into right and wrong, black and white. It is impossible for a Chinese student to look rationally at this knowledge and to arrive at independent conclusions.

This is most apparent to the visitor in the unmitigated anti-American campaigns. Granted that a common enemy is a powerful unifying factor in a heterogeneous area such as China, it is still a shock to visit school after school and see wall boards devoted exclusively to the bad side of American life. And to be told, as I was, by a sweet twelve-year-old girl that she hoped "the children of your country will join with the Chinese children to fight that greatest evil in the world—American imperialism." It is true that a distinction is always made between American people and the imperialist actions of their government, but one wonders if seven-year-olds can distinguish between the two. All societies indoctrinate their children with their own particular ideology, but surely none to the same extent as the Chinese.

This prejudgment of what is right and what is wrong is bound in the long run to be detrimental to the development of China's social sciences.

The opinions expressed here are based on the extremely limited evidence available. Much study, both in China and on Chinese documents, is required before more definitive opinions can be expressed. That such studies should be pursued is vital, not only for a better understanding of China, but because of the possible relevance of some of the Chinese experiments in education to other countries.

CHART 1.[1]

Distribution of Graduates from Institutions of Higher Learning in Communist China, by Field, 1948–49 to 1962–63 (Cumulative Total)

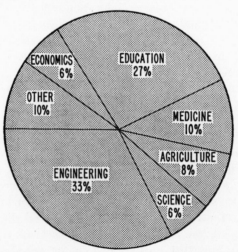

[1] Tables and Charts I and II from Chu-yuan Cheng, *Scientific and Engineering Education in Communist China,* National Science Foundation, Washington, D.C., 1965.

TABLE I.

Enrollments of Full-time Students and Graduates,
Institutions of Higher Learning, 1949–50 to 1962–63

Academic year	Enrollment (thousands)	(Index number 1949–50 = 100)	Graduates (thousands)
Pre-1949 peak year (1947–48)	155	(132)	—
1948–49	—	—	21
1949–50	117	(100)	18
1950–51	137	(117)	19
1951–52	153	(131)	32
1952–53	191	(163)	48
1953–54	212	(181)	47
1954–55	253	(216)	55
1955–56	288	(246)	63
1956–57	403	(344)	56
1957–58	441	(377)	72
1958–59	660	(564)	70
1959–60	810	(692)	135
1960–61	955	(816)	162
1961–62	819	(700)	178
1962–63	820	(700)	200

SCIENCE IN CHINA

One of the important developments of the past decade has been the widespread recognition—particularly on the part of governments—given to the role of science in society. It is now accepted that science plays an important part in such diverse fields as defense, economic growth, social development, and foreign affairs. It is no longer possible to leave this complex interaction to chance *ad hoc* measures; governments must make rational choices from among many alternatives.

This means that a science policy is required, and many

CHART 2.

Distribution of Scientists and Engineers with College
Diplomas in Communist China, by Age, 1962

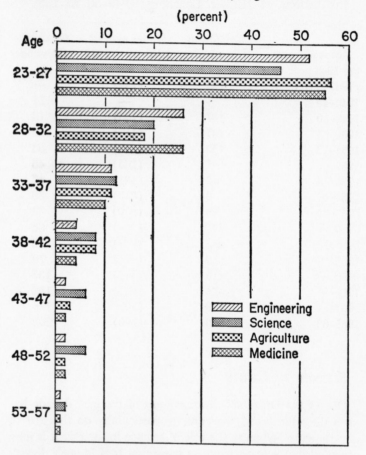

countries are still experimenting to find the best ways in which
to formulate and then implement such policies.

The role of science in China is particularly fascinating and
complex. China is a poor, economically underdeveloped coun-

TABLE II.

Educational Background of 700 Prominent Scientists and Engineers in Communist China, by Highest Degree and Place of Training, 1962

Highest degree	Total	United States	Great Britain	Germany	France	Other European countries	USSR	Japan	China
Total	700	373	112	46	37	12	15	20	85
Bachelor's	93	5						3	84
Master's	68	63	2	1	1		1[1]	3	1
Ph.D. or Sc.D.	442	269	88	38	31	10	3	3	
Degree unidentified	97	36	22	7	5	2	11	14	

[1] Candidate degree.

try committed ideologically to the use of science for practical ends, and committed politically to developing her own indigenous science in order to help her become a major world power in the shortest possible time. China's problems of scientific choice are in many ways even more crucial and difficult than those of the richer countries.

A number of recent publications in Western languages have done much to illuminate some of these problems. The extent of our knowledge, however, on most of them is still very meager. The subject is enormous and complex. I shall limit my discussion to four of the many possible types which could be included under the rubric "Science in China."

Brief Introduction to the Organization and Development of Chinese Science

China has a rich tradition of scientific and technological development, the extent of which has only recently been revealed by Joseph Needham of Cambridge University and his collaborators. Although modern science never really developed in China until the twentieth century, technological innovations have a long history of practical application. The significance of this history and tradition for contemporary China is a subject which requires further study.

The current successes of Chinese science are, in some ways, a measure of the efficacy of the science education established in China early in this century. It is the men who received their education in China and abroad, long before the communist victory, who are in many instances so brilliantly leading China's scientific and technological renaissance, although only under the present government was it possible to provide the material resources with which they could use their skill.

The early years of Communist rule brought a transformation from a science and education system modeled on essentially American lines to one modeled on Soviet lines. The Soviets also provided much help in drawing up the twelve-year science plan in 1956. More recently, the emphasis has been on finding a purely Chinese solution to organizational problems.

Throughout these sixteen years it seems to have been a problem for the Chinese leaders to determine the proper role for the Communist Party in the organization of science. At the present time it is in strong control at all levels, and this has led to some major difficulties, probably because few Chinese political leaders have scientific or technological training, and there is much they do not understand about the organization and nature of science. Although this is not a problem unique to China, it perhaps has more serious consequences there. In China, a directive from the central government can quickly be implemented throughout the country. If the directive is good, the country quickly benefits; similarly, mistakes can be very costly.

Things came to a head during the Great Leap Forward when, in science as in education, quantity and politics seem to have been emphasized at the cost of quality. Since 1961 more rational policies have been implemented, and although the Communist Party is still in tight control, many of its members have shown a willingness to learn from their mistakes. Western visitors, well qualified to judge, comment on the sensible approach to science now prevailing.

At the top of the science pyramid is the State Science and Technological Commission. This group is responsible for the planning of science and supervising the implementation of these plans. The Chairman and Vice-Chairman of the Commission are all members of the Communist Party. There are branches of the Commission in the provinces.

Under the Commission is the foremost scientific body in China—the Academia Sinica. This organization operates 112 research institutes, which concentrate mainly on oriented basic research, i.e. basic research with specific economic objectives in mind. It is usual for each Academy institute to have a scientist as director, and a member of the Communist Party, often a nonscientist, as vice-director or secretary. The Academy also has branch institutes in each province.

301

In addition to the Academia Sinica, two other academies, one for agriculture and the other for medicine, operate research institutes. Altogether, in 1963, there were 315 research institutes attached to the three academies.

Applied research is mainly carried on by institutes attached to various ministries, and by the end of 1963 the government was operating 345 research institutes.

There are about 800 research institutes in China, of which 305 are in life sciences, 205 in physical sciences, and 271 in engineering. Since the Great Leap Forward the greatest increase in effort, as judged by new institutes established, has been in the life sciences, presumably as a result of the current economic emphasis on agriculture.

In 1960, when the last statistics were published, China spent 1,081 million yuan ($441 million) on science. This represented 1.54 per cent of the national budget. In 1952, only .07 per cent of the national budget was spent on science.

In 1962, there were 40 scientific societies of national status with a membership of more than 100,000, and 53 scientific journals with nationwide coverage were published. In addition, there are more than 170 fortnightly and monthly journals which provide abstracts in Chinese of foreign scientific papers.

Observations on Scientific Research in Certain Institutes of the Academia Sinica

Over the past few years an increasing number of British, French, Canadian, and other Western scientists visited research institutes of the three Chinese academies. From their reports it is possible to piece together the following summary of impressions about some of the research institutes of the Academia Sinica.

1. The library facilities are generally excellent, with up-to-date collections of journals from throughout the world.

2. The equipment and instrumentation are variable in quality, although mostly good. At some institutes it was first class,

302

and one Fellow of the Royal Society commented on the fact that when it was sufficiently important, the Chinese appeared to have selected and purchased the best piece of equipment available in the world, America excepted. Visitors noted a growing tendency for the Chinese to develop their own equipment, and most institutes had good workshops for instrument repair and manufacture.

3. Chinese research in the physical sciences is generally more advanced than that in the life sciences.

4. Most visitors noted the relative scarcity of senior scientists, although many were impressed by the high caliber of the few there were. Also scarce are project leaders—men with more than ten years of research experience who should form the backbone of any country's research effort. By contrast, the large number of young scientists is especially noticeable. It is the consensus of the visiting scientists that the majority of these young scientists were bright and eager, and showed an excellent grasp of their research problems.

As would be expected under these circumstances, the research effort is usually concentrated on relatively few problems, which, although in basic research, have a definite relation to practical needs. In a few branches of the physical sciences the Chinese work is probably on a par with the best in the world. In the majority of their work, however, the Chinese are still laying the foundations, but they appear to be doing this in a systematic and sensible way.

5. Each institute has its own objectives and is expected to work within these limits. The funds allocated to each institute seem to be determined by the relative importance of the subject area to state development plans, although details about the allocation of research funds are not known. The individual scientists at the institutes help to determine the research program, which is submitted to the Academy for approval.

6. Political cadres were always present at my interviews and visits, and although the scientists would usually give the introductory talk and answer scientific questions, any question with a political bias was given to the cadre to answer. Also, during

303

the introductory talks mention would always be made of the importance of politics in scientific work. I found it completely impossible, however, to assess the impact of ideology on the quality of scientific work. The Pedology Institute in Nanking was both the most political—in the content of the introductory speech and the fact that many scientists had copies of Mao Tse-tung's books on their desks—and at the same time one of the most impressive research institutes I have visited in Asia.

7. One visitor commented on the fact that the Chinese did not argue when he presented one side of a scientifically controversial issue, which would have immediately provoked an intense debate in both the West and the Soviet Union. He knew that the Chinese were familiar with the literature on the subject, and therefore must have been aware of the controversy. He believed that the explanation may have been traditional Chinese politeness to a foreign guest. If this is so, it is an interesting insight into scientific life in contemporary China.

China and International Scientific Relations

China will not adhere to any international organization—scientific or other—of which Taiwan is a member. This has meant that China has effectively cut herself off from most international scientific intercourse. For example, China is not a member of the International Council of Scientific Unions, although she does belong to the International Union of the History and Philosophy of Science.

However, China is a member of the World Federation of Scientific Workers and, in August 1964, under the partial sponsorship of this organization, held a scientific symposium in Peking. Delegates came from forty-three nations, and a good deal of genuine science was discussed. The meeting also had its political objectives: only delegates from Africa, Asia, Latin America, and Oceania were invited. A continuing committee was set up and other symposia are to be arranged.

It was claimed in the Chinese press that the symposium

304

demonstrated that the monopoly of modern science by scientists from the developed world had once and for all been shattered. There seems little doubt from the available evidence that this was part of the Chinese effort to set up international organizations with membership limited to the "emerging countries" which would rival the more truly international organizations which already exist.

Bilaterally, China has had scientific exchange agreements with a number of countries. Closest ties were those once maintained with Soviet scientists. In fact, as already noted, much of the organizational framework of Chinese science is modeled after the pattern of science in the Soviet Union. The Soviet Union also provided many experts (perhaps as many as 11,000) in both science and engineering, but, as is well known, these were all withdrawn in 1960.

Despite the fact that one of the most common slogans on the walls of China today is "Rely on our own effort," the Chinese always freely admit that they have much to learn from the advanced countries of the world. English has now become the most popular foreign language and scientific exchanges are being increasingly developed with Western countries.

For example, a delegation from the Royal Society visited China in October 1964. They discussed with representatives of the Academia Sinica the exchange of British and Chinese scientists. It was proposed that both groups would continue the *ad hoc* exchanges of senior scientists, either individually or as delegations, for short visits. At a senior-to-medium level, there would be exchanges of longer duration. The Academia Sinica representatives suggested that the fields of most immediate interest for Chinese scientists to study in Britain, were meteorology, geology (especially radioactive dating), and biophysics. Second in priority were high-energy physics, molecular biology, and heart and cardiovascular surgery. Senior-to-medium level British scientists would visit China for a period of a few months to give lectures, with priority given to the fields of paleomagnetism and biophysics. At the junior scientist level, China would send a number of postgraduate research

305

workers to Britain, beginning in 1965, while junior British scientists might begin visiting China in 1966 or later, probably to work in mathematics and physiology.

Scientific exchanges are also beginning between China and France. A recent cultural exchange agreement between these two countries made provision for more than 150 Chinese students to study in France on Chinese fellowships and 30 more on French fellowships. In addition, 10 Chinese will come to France for research purposes. At the same time, 30 French students and ten research workers will go to China.

Popularization of Science and Technology in China

Popularization of science in China serves a double purpose. First, it helps to increase agricultural and industrial production. Second, it is helping to transform an old traditional society into a modern one.

This process of social change is little understood, and the role of science in the transformation is not clear. But there is evidence to suggest that science may be an important catalyst in this change. The Chinese clearly believe this is the case and are making a great effort to replace the superstitions of Old China with science and rational thought.

The comment of a commune director in Peking was symbolic. He said, "Fifteen years ago the people in this commune believed the Dragon King controlled the rain—now we understand the scientific reasons." Elsewhere, I was told that in the old days the peasants regarded a diseased crop as a visitation from the gods and did nothing about it. Now, every production team in the commune I was visiting had its own member trained to recognize the most common insect pests and types of plant disease, and to know what remedial steps to take if he found them.

Everywhere in China the people are being taught not only that the laws of nature can be understood by man, but that man can often use this knowledge for his own ends. The significance of this realization on a mass scale may yet prove to be

306

one of the most important accomplishments of the Chinese Communists.

Popularization and Use of Science in the Communes

At least six of the eight communes I visited had experimental fields where work with new seeds, new techniques of planting, and new types of fertilizer was in progress. Some of the communes which encompassed different natural regions and soil types had several experimental fields in different parts of the commune. There was no question of a single technique or seed being given universal application over the whole commune. Two of the communes had their own research institutes. These were very crude, and the experiments very simple. But the important point is that the peasants were beginning to realize that by doing scientific experiments, they could improve production. In fact, science has quite literally become one of the three revolutionary movements in China. One of the most common slogans is: "Support the three great revolutionary movements—the class struggle, the struggle for production, and scientific experiment."

This rational experimental approach has not always been the vogue in Communist China. On the contrary, many observers note that it was the wholesale application of technical innovations quite unsuited to local conditions, such as deep ploughing and close planting, that led to failures in the Great Leap Forward. These actions dictated by the central government apparently even led to an "anti-science" attitude on the part of some peasants. Also, one must be careful not to conclude that because experimental fields exist in six communes, they are necessarily general in the rest of the 74,000 communes in China. All that can be said is that these six probably represent what the Chinese are striving for.

Another interesting, and often misunderstood, aspect of the introduction of scientific innovations in the countryside has been the use of peasant scientists. These are men with little or no formal education, but with a demonstrated ability to

307

experiment, and find ways empirically to increase production. One such case was Chen Yung-kang, a peasant who was working at the Kiangsi headquarters of the Agricultural Academy of Science, which I visited in Nanking. He had been provided with a plot of land at the institute and invited to grow rice according to his own technique, which had consistently produced double the yield of his neighbors. A team of experts from the Agricultural Academy in Peking and the Soil Science Research Institute in Nanking had studied the technique to understand the reasons for his success. They made some modifications, and Chen was provided with a large demonstration field near Soochow and asked to grow rice according to his technique. In 1963, 90,000 peasants were brought in to see the demonstration.

What is particularly significant about this example is the way the peasant scientist was used as an intermediary between the professional scientists and the peasants. He was given all the credit and publicity. The peasants would be much more likely to adopt a new technique which was accredited to a fellow peasant than one promulgated by a government scientist. Also, other peasants might be encouraged to experiment as a result of the prestige and honor of being called a "peasant scientist."

There are similarities between this use of peasant scientists to popularize agricultural innovations in China, and the County Agent system, adopted by the US Department of Agriculture in the early 1900s to popularize agricultural innovations in the United States.

Again, it should be noted that not all peasant scientists have been used so sensibly. Instances of irrational use of peasant scientists were quite common during the Great Leap Forward.

Science and Technological Innovation in Industry at the Level of the Worker

I tried very hard in China to get to see an industrial research institute. I never succeeded. Instead, I was always told

308

that the workers were responsible for the technical innovations in this or that particular factory. Judging by the Heath Robinson (I think in America it's Rube Goldberg) appearance of some of the equipment, I could believe it! The workers were all supposed to have accomplished these feats of innovation by reading the works of Chairman Mao.

Other visitors tell the same story. A *London Times* correspondent reports that at one factory 2,000 suggestions for innovation had been received from the workers in one year, and 800 had been put into operation. And all are ascribed to Mao. In fact, it is impossible to visit China without coming away with a collection of "Maoisms." All begin, "After reading the works of Chairman Mao I found how to" and go on to such statements as, "increase the speed of rotation of my cotton-spinning machine from 9,000 revolutions per minute to 13,000 revolutions per minute," or "cure the children at our school of short-sightedness," or "become world table tennis champion." It became a favorite ploy of mine, when told such stories, to ask for chapter and verse and to be taken step by step from Mao's political statement to the specific technical innovation.

But in fact, this use of political indoctrination to stimulate innovation cannot be summarily dismissed as nonsense, as I had been prone to do before visiting China. The explanation of the factory manager at the No. 17 textile factory in Shanghai is revealing. I had asked him how Chairman Mao had helped increase the speed of rotation of the spinning machines. He said:

> It's like this. At the time of Liberation we were an old factory, the equipment was old, and the workers relatively old. In fact, we called ourselves "the three olds." In China's condition it was imperative to change the factory and equipment, but the big problem was the attitude of the workers. . . . It never occurred to them that the machine or process could be improved—let alone that they themselves could do it.
>
> It would have taken too long to give them a full technical education. . . . Political indoctrination was the answer.

309

The workers studied the works of Chairman Mao and gradually their political awareness improved. They said, "We must build a new country."

Before, they did not think it was possible to improve their lot. . . . Chairman Mao has liberated their thoughts. With this new spirit they look to see how they can improve their work and knowledge. Their thirst for knowledge is met by the spare-time schools and universities—so bit by bit their technical competence also improves. Once they believed it was possible to innovate, they found many places in the factory where simple innovations improved quality and productivity. One worker studied the problem of the spinning machines and found a way to increase the speed from 9,000 to 13,000 revolutions per minute.

At this level, politics obviously can help to generate enthusiasm. If this enthusiasm is directed into scientific and technical channels, and opportunities and incentives are provided—and they are—then useful innovations are possible.

Problems occur when the spirit of research and the craze for technological change go too far without the appropriate technological training to back them up. It would seem likely that when this first flush of worker-initiated innovations has passed, Chinese industry will have to turn to more science-based innovations for continued growth.

Science and Society—Present and Future

Our knowledge of Chinese science and its interrelation with the rest of society is extremely limited. About all that can be said at the moment is that a solid foundation has been laid for future development of advanced science and that a sincere effort is being made to bring the fruits of science to the people. The present emphasis of research is in agriculture, but judging by the successful detonation of two atomic bombs, national defense research is also stressed.

The Chinese are the first to admit that they are a long way behind advanced world levels in many branches of

310

science. What is impressive to the foreign visitor is the fantastic determination to catch up, primarily by their own efforts. It will be a pity, however, if in these efforts the Chinese stress "fashionable" areas of scientific research which have little relevance to the economic needs of their own country.

It is a favorite guessing game to try and estimate when the Chinese will catch up on a broad front. My own guess is about twenty years. The first reason for thinking this is that in 1960 China spent 1.54 per cent of her national budget on science, but this was still only the equivalent of about $450 million. It is difficult to make direct comparisons with other countries, but we may note that the Soviet Union spent almost ten times this amount on her science budget in 1961. Scientific research work cannot expand too rapidly, largely because of the long time it takes to train research workers. For this reason it is likely to be some time before the money spent on scientific research can be significantly and, at the same time, effectively increased.

The problem of the numbers of research workers, and highly trained experts generally, seems to be the biggest constraint on China's rapid scientific growth. There are only 12 students at higher education institutes per 10,000 of the population, compared with 72 in Japan and 1,866 in the United States. The number of research scientists with the equivalent of masters' or doctors' degrees is probably not more than 15,000 or 16,000, and relatively few of these have the necessary experience to direct projects. It will not be until the younger scientists reach scientific maturity that China will herself be able to make many significant contributions to basic science.

There is another unpredictable factor which can affect the rate of growth of Chinese science. The Communist Party may decide to de-emphasize the effort to catch up with the advanced countries in basic science and instead concentrate its scientific resources on economic and social goals.

311

Chinese Development—and World Peace

I subscribe to the view that the sooner the living standards of China's millions are improved, the better will be the prospects for world peace. I further believe that science and technology can play a big part in improving this standard of living. For this reason, I welcome the cooperative science agreements between the Academia Sinica and the Royal Society, and between China and France. Such exchanges not only promote mutual understanding and are of benefit for science, but also contribute to China's development. They should be encouraged and expanded. The State Department's relaxation of travel restrictions to China for American scientists is a step in the right direction.

Not everyone will agree with this attitude. American Congressmen have already criticized the Royal Society exchange, suggesting that this will help China's capability to wage war. To a certain limited extent they are correct, but I believe that the long-term dangers of war are lessened by such exchanges. Also, when talking of war it becomes very important to be quite clear about Chinese objectives.

It is true that the Chinese leaders are committed to communism and believe in the inevitability of a communist world. But I think it wrong to view all of China's apparent belligerence in terms of power politics and a quest for world domination. The Chinese leaders believe that two-thirds of the world's population live in societies where the majority exist in abject poverty and the few in great riches. They believe this situation is socially unjust and should be changed. Here, they are right. The majority of people do live under deplorable conditions, and this should be changed. The question is how? The Chinese argue that such a condition can be changed only by armed revolution, and have shown their willingness to support such revolutions wherever they occur in the world.

The implications for the rest of the world are clear. We must show the Chinese and the millions of undernourished,

312

sick, and illiterate people of the world that there is a way to better their condition other than by armed revolution, a way which is both more peaceful and quicker. To bring about this change will mean both technological and social upheavals; we are woefully ignorant of how best to proceed. Some of us believe that each developing country will have to experience its own scientific revolution, developing an indigenous science which will help to bring about the required technological and social changes. How to create such scientific revolutions is not clear. This is why it is so important to learn the lessons of China's scientific revolution. It is why the problem of science and the developing countries is one of the greatest challenges facing both governments and the scientific community today.

APPENDIX

Observations on Certain Institutes of the Academia Sinica

Visits by foreign scientists to the research institutes of the Academia Sinica follow a set pattern. The visitor is usually met by the principal officers of the institute, taken into a reception room, served tea, and, after an official welcome, given a historical and factual introduction to the institute. This is followed by a question-and-answer period, during which I personally found questions were answered very frankly. Visitors are then shown around a selection of the laboratories, the library, and the workshop facilities.

The following account summarizes the actual information about a number of the Academia Sinica research institutes together with the opinions of several recent British visitors. I am grateful to these scientists, many of whom are Fellows of the Royal Society, for permission to quote their impressions.

Peking

Institute of Physics (Visited by Dr. N. Kurti of the Clarendon Laboratory, Oxford, in 1964.)

313

Dr. Kurti's impression was that this was a competent institute on a par with similar Western laboratories, but on a much more restricted scale. The instruments and apparatus, many of which were Chinese made, seemed to be good. He was impressed by the keenness and eagerness of all the scientists that he met, and mentioned that in the discussions after his lectures there were always quite a few searching questions. He found Chinese physicists quite up-to-date in Western scientific literature.

Institute of Zoology (Visited by Professor C. H. Waddington, Professor of Genetics, University of Edinburgh, in 1962.)

In 1962 work was in progress on endocrinology, especially histological work on innovation of various organs, particularly aortic body. Professor Waddington's impression of the institute was that good sound work was being done, with quite high-class research standards, but not of any profound originality. However, he felt that it was a good solid basis for further development and the laboratory as a whole was clearly active.

Institute of Geology (Visited by H. W. B. Harland, geology department of Cambridge University in 1965.)

The institute has the following departments: isotope geology, geochemistry of endogenic mineral deposits, geochemistry of exogenic mineral deposits, crystal physics and mineralogy, chemical mineralogy, petrology, stratigraphy, structural geology, quarternary geology, hydrogeology and engineering geology.

Altogether there is a total of 600 to 700 scientists, of whom 400 are geologists. Several of these also lecture at other institutions. Mr. Harland found that many departments had already achieved impressive results, though perhaps the main emphasis was on developing instrumentation and methods for future work. His impression was that a sound and ambitious foundation was being made for future research, and believed that in a few years time China would be making fundamental contributions to geological science.

Institute of Geophysics and Meteorology (I myself visited

314

this institute in May 1965.) There were 500 staff members working in the institute, which is divided into four departments: meteorology and atmospheric physics (100 research workers), earthquake seismology (100 research workers), physics of the earth's interior (50 research workers), and geomagnetism (30 research workers). There is also a workshop associated with the institute for instrument repair and construction (50 staff members).

I met none of the geophysicists of international reputation who I knew worked at the institute; however, it was only a few days before the second Chinese atomic bomb explosion and it would be reasonable to expect that they were on an expedition in connection with this explosion. The scientists I met all seemed young.

Four research scientists each gave a twenty-minute summary of the work going on in the different departments. These summaries had been prepared ahead of time, and gave a good survey of the problems the institute had tackled. After the discussion, I was shown several of the seismic and meteorological laboratories, and the library. The latter was excellent and had one of the most complete collections of current journals related to geophysics that I have seen in any country. The librarian said there were 640 foreign and 140 Chinese journals.

The instrumentation at this institute was not, on the whole, very advanced. For example, some of the seismic recorders still made use of smoked-paper techniques. Despite these handicaps, the Chinese geophysicists seemed to be getting a maximum of information from the data they had collected.

Much of the work was on the application of known techniques to Chinese problems, and there was little that I saw which was fundamentally new and exciting.

Shanghai

Institute of Organic Chemistry (Visited by Professor Thompson in 1962.)

This institute was established in its present form in 1960.

315

After describing the projects being tackled, Professor Thompson wrote: "My overall impression was that in this institute they were attempting to cover a rather large field with limited resources so that some of the work seemed superficial."

Institute of Metallurgy (Visited by Professor Thompson in 1962.)

This institute, which was established in 1928, has 200 employees of whom 15 are project leaders. The institute is doing research into steel, cast iron, age hardening, thermodynamics of slags, physical chemistry of molten slag and creep, order and disorder phenomena in solids, and thermodynamics of molten metals. Professor Thompson thought that although the research workers had a clear idea of their problems, the work was only in the early stages of development.

Institute of Biology

This institute is made up of three separate institutes:

1. *Institute of Biochemistry* (Visited by Professors Thompson and Waddington in 1962.) There are about 80 research workers at this institute, 20 of whom are senior men. About half of the latter were trained in the United States, Britain, or Europe. Professor Thompson wrote, "Most of the work is conventional, and gave the impression of an active group who knew how to use the equipment available, but who were still only building foundations."

Professor Waddington noted that work was going on along good standard lines in studies of crystallizing proteins and investigating active sites of enzymes by use of inhibitors. He thought the work was sound, but pointed out that there was no work in genetic molecular biology, although some finger printing of proteins and electrophoresis had started.

2. *Institute of Physiology* (Visited by Professor Waddington in 1962.) Waddington found that there was good work going on at this institute mainly following European and American lines. Some of the scientists were clearly first class.

3. *Institute of Experimental Biology* (Visited by Professor

316

Waddington in 1962.) According to Waddington, the institute was doing good sound work on tissue culture, and histochemistry and immunology of the cell surface. Interesting but standard work was also being done on the nature of the amphibian evocator. He found the institute to be a lively go-ahead place of normal scientific character in which it was easy to feel at home. There was no work of outstanding originality, although there was a large amount of good quality work which he felt was sufficient to provide a firm basis for further development. The instrumentation and standard of equipment were good.

Nanking

Institute of Pedology (I visited this institute in October 1964.) There are more than 300 university graduates working in the institute, which is divided into six divisions: soil geography, soil agrochemistry, soil physical chemistry, soil biochemistry, soil biology, and soil physics. There was an excellent library containing 60,000 volumes, and more than 300 current journals.

The equipment seemed to be excellent, with major instruments from Britain, Czechoslovakia, the Soviet Union, Japan, East Germany, and Holland, as well as much that had been built by the Chinese themselves.

Although I was unable to assess the scientific merits of the research work, there was a sense of purpose and enthusiasm which marked this as a first-rate institution.

Appendix

‖ SELECTED BIBLIOGRAPHY

The selected bibliography that follows was prepared by Art Gundersheim, of the Center for Social Organization Studies, Graduate Student in the Department of Sociology, University of Chicago. Books marked with an asterisk are available in a paperback edition.

Barnett, A. Doak. *China on the Eve of Communist Takeover.* New York: Praeger, 1964.* Report of the disintegration just prior to the Communists achieving power.

Brandt, C., Schwartz, B., and Fairbank, J. K. *A Documentary History of Chinese Communism.* New York: Atheneum, 1966.* An authoritative documentary study of the Chinese Communist movement; covers only pre-1949.

Chassin, Lionel Max. *The Communist Conquest of China.* Translated by T. Osato and L. Gelas. Cambridge: Harvard University Press, 1965. A first-rate history of the 1945–49 civil war.

Clubb, O. Edmund. *Twentieth Century China.* New York: Columbia University Press, 1963.* A history of modern China by a former American diplomat.

Fairbank, John King. *The United States and China,* revised edition. New York: Compass, 1962.* Covers Chinese history;

culture; society; and politics, both ancient and modern; with comprehensiveness, perception, and contemporary relevance.

Fitzgerald, Charles. *The Birth of Communist China*. Baltimore: Penguin, 1966.* Interesting thesis about why the Communists triumphed in the revolution.

Johnson, Chalmers A. *Peasant Nationalism and Communist Power*. Stanford: Stanford University Press, 1962. A concentrated study of the period 1937–45 during which the Communists became a strong military power.

Loh, Pichon P. Y. (editor). *Kuomintang Debacle of 1949*. Boston: Heath, 1965.* A collection of excerpts on why the Nationalists lost and the Communists gained power.

North, Robert. *Chinese Communism*. New York: McGraw-Hill, 1965;* *Kuomintang and Chinese Communist Elites*. Stanford: Stanford University Press, 1952. Comparison of the men who led the Kuomintang and the Communist Party, and the social forces they represented.

Schwartz, Benjamin. *Chinese Communism and the Rise of Mao*. Cambridge: Harvard University Press, 1952. The classic study of the early years of the Chinese Communist movement.

FOREIGN AFFAIRS AND INTERNATIONAL RELATIONS

General Surveys

Ambekar, G. V. and Divekar, V. D. *Documents on China's Relations with South and Southeast Asia, 1949–1962*. Bombay: Allied Publishers Private Ltd., 1964. Comprehensive sourcebook as its title indicates; no analysis presented.

Barnett, A. Doak. *Communist China and Asia*. New York: Vintage, 1960.* Concentrates on China's foreign policy aims and the means used to pursue them; *Communist China in Perspective*. New York: Praeger, 1962.

Boyd, R. G. *Communist China's Foreign Policy*. New York: Praeger, 1962.* Largely an explanation rather than a description of China's foreign policy, questionable in places.

Dutt, Vidya Prakash. *China's Foreign Policy*. Bombay: Asia Publishing House, 1964. Covers 1958–62 only.

Halperin, Morton. *Is China Turning In?* Occasional Papers in International Affairs, *12*. Cambridge: Harvard University

Press for the Center for International Affairs, 1965. Argues that because of recent setbacks in foreign affairs, China will now concentrate on domestic affairs.

Halpern, A. M. (editor). *Policies toward China: Views from Six Continents.* New York: McGraw-Hill for the Council on Foreign Relations, 1966.* Summarizes the policies of the major noncommunist countries toward China.

Hinton, Harold. *Communist China in World Politics.* Boston: Houghton Mifflin, 1966. Comprehensive and valuable survey.

Lindsay, John. *China and the Cold War.* Melbourne: Melbourne University Press, 1955. An analysis of Chinese Communist policy and Western analysis of that policy.

War, Peace, and Military Strategy

Buchan, Alastair. *China and the Peace of Asia.* London: Chatto and Windus for the Institute for Strategic Studies, 1965. Collection of articles on China's role in the war or peace of Asia, as seen from various countries, particularly military strategy, security, and international relations.

China Quarterly, 21, January–March, 1965. Three articles on China and nuclear strategy by Morton Halperin, William Harris, and Hungdah Chiu.

Halperin, Morton. *China and the Bomb.* New York: Praeger, 1965;* and Perkins, Dwight. *China and Arms Control.* New York: Praeger, 1965.* Studies of China's nuclear strategy and what it means for international arms control.

Hsieh, Alice Langley. *Communist China's Strategy in the Nuclear Era.* Englewood Cliffs, N.J.: Prentice-Hall, 1962. A history of China's thinking on war in the nuclear age. Though written before China exploded her first bomb, most of it is still relevant today.

Joffe, Ellis. *Party and Army: Professionalism and Political Control in the Chinese Officer Corps, 1949–1964.* East Asian Monograph No. 19. Cambridge: Harvard University Press, 1964.* An excellent study of the Party-army relations, especially the clash between the demands of an emerging military professionalism and the need for political control.

Lin Piao. "Long Live the Victory of the People's War!" *Peking Review,* VIII, No. 36, September 3, 1965, pp. 9–30. The

323

widely publicized statement by China's Minister of Defense on revolutions and China's view of change.

Mao Tse-tung. *On Guerrilla Warfare.* Translated by Samuel Griffith. New York: Praeger, 1961; *Selected Military Writings.* Peking: Foreign Languages Press, 1963.

American-Chinese Relations

Greene, Felix, *A Curtain of Ignorance.* Garden City, N.Y.: Doubleday, 1964. An outspoken critique of the misinformation the American public receives from the mass media; the chapter on the Chinese-Indian border war is especially notable.

New China Policy: Some Quaker Proposals. American Friends Service Committee Report. New Haven: Yale University Press, 1965.* Considered proposals for the improvement of US-Chinese relations.

Newman, Robert. *Recognition of Communist China?* New York: Macmillan, 1961.* Presents the various arguments revolving about this problem.

Rusk, Dean. "United States Policy Toward Communist China," testimony at the hearings of the House Foreign Affairs Subcommittee on the Far East, March 16, 1966. (Released April 16, 1966; excerpts in *The New York Times,* April 17, 1966.)

Steele, A. T. *The American People and China.* New York: McGraw-Hill for the Council on Foreign Relations, 1966. A thorough study of American public opinion toward China and our China policy at both the mass and the elite levels.

Tsou, Tang. *America's Failure in China, 1941–50.* Chicago: University of Chicago Press, 1963. Excellent historical study.

US House of Representatives, Committee on Foreign Affairs Subcommittee on the Far East and the Pacific. *Hearings On United States Policy Toward Asia.* January 25–February 3, 1966.

The Sino-Soviet Split

Bromke, Adam (editor). *Communist States at the Crossroads: Between Moscow and Peking.* New York: Praeger, 1965.* A series of papers on the impact of Sino-Soviet schism upon

324

the communist world and the resultant spread of "polycentrism."

Chiang Kai-shek. *Soviet Russia in China.* New York: Noonday, 1958.*

Crankshaw, Edward. *The New Cold War: Moscow vs. Peking.* Baltimore: Penguin Books, 1963.* Short introduction to and summary of the split.

"Communist China and the Soviet Bloc." *The Annals of the American Academy of Political and Social Science,* CCC-XLIX, September 1963. Articles by experts in three general areas of the split: its history; cooperation and conflict; implications for third countries.

Floyd, David. *Mao Against Khrushchev: A Short History of the Sino-Soviet Conflict.* New York: Praeger, 1964.* Gives the economic, military, diplomatic, organizational realities of that abstraction "ideological conflict."

Griffith, William. *The Sino-Soviet Rift.* Cambridge: MIT Press, 1964.*

Hudson, G. F., Lowenthal, Richard, and MacFarquhar, Roderick. *The Sino-Soviet Dispute.* New York: Praeger, 1963.* Largely documents of the 1950–60 period with introductory essays.

London, Kurt (editor). *Unity and Contradiction: Major Aspects of Sino-Soviet Relations.* New York: Praeger, 1962. Papers from an international symposium in September, 1960.

Mehnert, Klaus. *Peking and Moscow.* New York: Mentor, 1964.* Concentrates on the history and culture of the two countries as they underlie the conflict.

North, Robert. *Moscow and Chinese Communism.* Stanford: Stanford University Press, 1963.* Largely the history of Chinese Communist-Soviet relations from 1921 to 1950.

US House of Representatives, Committee on Foreign Affairs Subcommittee on the Far East and the Pacific. *Report on Sino-Soviet Conflict and Its Implications.* Hearings of March 10–31, 1965.

Zagoria, Donald S. *The Sino-Soviet Conflict, 1956–1961.* New York: Atheneum, 1962.* The scholarly, authoritative study of the split.

China-India-Tibet

Ginsburg, George and Mathos, Michael. *Communist China and Tibet: The First Dozen Years.* The Hague: Martinus Nijhoff, 1964. China's policy in Tibet from 1950 to 1962.

Lamb, Alistair. *The China-India Border.* London: Oxford University Press, 1964.* Documentation on key disputed points.

Van Ekelen, W. F. *Indian Foreign Policy and the Border Dispute with China.* The Hague: Martinus Nijhoff, 1964. An informative, comprehensive study of the conflict; the author favors the Indian side.

THE POLITICAL SYSTEM AND GOVERNMENT

General

Gourlay, W. E. *Chinese Communist Cadre: Key to Political Power.* Cambridge: Harvard University Press, 1952.

Hinton, Harold. "China." In George McT. Kahin (editor), *Major Governments of Asia.* Ithaca: Cornell University Press, 1963, pp. 3–149. College political science course introduction to China's government; *Leaders of Communist China.* Santa Monica, Calif: Rand Corporation, 1956.

Lewis, John Wilson. *Leadership in Communist China.* Ithaca: Cornell University Press, 1963. One of the best descriptions and analyses of the Chinese Communist political system; *Major Doctrines of Communist China.* New York: Norton, 1964.* The content of the system described in Lewis's other books; excellent.

Schurmann, F. H. *Ideology and Organization in Communist China.* Berkeley: University of California Press, 1966. Concentrates on the organizational aspects of the Party, government, industry, and rural villages.

On or by Mao Tse-tung

Boorman, Howard. "Mao Tse-tung: The Lacquered Image." *China Quarterly,* XVI, December, 1963, pp. 1–55. A short, up-to-date biography.

Chen, Jerome. *Mao and the Chinese Revolution.* London: Oxford University Press, 1965.* The best biography currently available, but stops at 1949. Includes 37 of Mao's poems.

Cohen, Arthur. *The Communism of Mao Tse-tung.* Chicago: University of Chicago Press, 1964.* Cohen finds Mao lacking originality as a philosopher but a first-class guerrilla leader and revolutionary.

Holubnychy, Vsevolod. "Mao Tse-tung's Materialistic Dialectics." *China Quarterly,* XIX, July-September, 1964, pp. 3–37. A concise summary of Mao's philosophy.

Mao Tse-tung. *An Anthology of His Writings.* Anne Fremantle (editor). New York: Mentor, 1962*; *The Political Thought of Mao Tse-tung.* Stuart Schram (editor). New York: Praeger, 1963.* An excellent study of Mao's ideology; *Maoism: A Sourcebook.* H. Arthur Steiner (editor). Los Angeles: University of California Press, 1952*; *Selected Works.* 5 vols. New York: International Publishers, 1954–63. Some of the pieces have had minor changes made since their original appearance.

The Social and Cultural Life

Barnett, A. Doak. *Communist China: The Early Years, 1949–1955.* New York: Praeger, 1964.

Chao, K. C. *Mass Organizations in Communist China.* Cambridge: Center for International Studies, MIT Press, 1953.

Chen, Theodore. *Thought Reform of the Chinese Intellectuals.* Hong Kong: Hong Kong University Press, 1960.

Clark, Gerald. *Impatient Giant: Red China Today.* New York: David McKay, 1959. A good account by a journalist.

Geddes, W. R. *Peasant Life in Communist China.* Ithaca: Society for Applied Anthropology, Cornell University, 1963.* A study of village life in Communist China that has the advantage of being a restudy of the village that was the basis of one of the best studies of precommunist days, Fei Hsiao-tung's *Peasant Life in China.*

Gelder, Stuart and Roma, *The Timely Rain; Travels in New Tibet.* New York: Monthly Review Press, 1965. Visit to Tibet in 1962, stresses the material improvements that have taken place and everyday life, but includes nothing on Tibetan reaction to Communist control and changes.

Gould, Sidney, *Sciences in Communist China.* Washington, D.C.: American Association for the Advancement of Science, 1961.

Greene, Felix. *China* (original title: *Awakened China*). New York: Ballantine Books, 1961.* A good report by a journalist; especially conveys the flavor of life in China.

Ho, Ping Ti. *Studies on the Population of China, 1368–1953.* Cambridge: Harvard University Press, 1959.

Holler, Joanne. "China," in *Population Trends and Economic Development in the Far East.* Washington, D.C.: Population Research Project, George Washington University, 1965, pp. 10–17.* Information on China's population, birth control programs, and food intake per person.

Houn, Franklin. *To Change a Nation: Propaganda and Indoctrination in China.* East Lansing, Mich.: Michigan State University and Free Press, 1961.

Klatt, Werner (editor). *The Chinese Model: A Political, Economic, and Social Survey.* New York: Oxford University Press, 1965.

Klochko, Mikhail. *Soviet Scientist in Red China.* New York: Praeger, 1964. Condemns the interference of politics in science, makes some interesting comparisons between China and Russia—in many areas China will do much better than Russia—and includes an "on the scene" account of the withdrawal of Soviet experts from China.

Lifton, Robert Jay. *Thought Reform and the Psychology of Totalism.* New York: Norton, 1963.* One of the few studies on "brainwashing" in China.

MacFarquhar, Roderick. *The Hundred Flowers.* London: Stevens & Sons, 1960. Selected documents; gives the feeling of what happened during this dynamic period; *The Hundred Flowers Campaign and the Chinese Intellectuals.* New York: Praeger, 1961. The resultant reform of the intellectuals after their "blooming and contending."

Mu Fu-sheng. *The Wilting of the Hundred Flowers.* New York: Praeger, 1963.* Ranges over much more than its title indicates—history, culture, communism in China, etc. Mu is a Chinese scholar in the West opposed to the communist means of persuasion.

Myrdal, Jan. *Report from a Chinese Village.* Translated by Maurice Michael. New York: Pantheon Books, 1965. A village as seen in late summer 1962 near Yenan by this Swedish writer.

Selected Bibliography

Schwartz, Benjamin. "The Intelligentsia in Communist China."
Daedalus, LXXXIX, No. 3, Summer, 1960, pp. 604–21.

Snow, Edgar. *The Other Side of the River: Red China Today.*
New York: Random House, 1962. Massive but easy reading;
an informative book on life in Communist China today.

Some Aspects of Contemporary Chinese Society. Staff and
Associates of the Human Relations Area Files. New York:
Taplinger.* Brief, interesting excerpts on Chinese culture,
society, family, values, and patterns of living.

Tang, Peter. *Communist China Today: Domestic and Foreign
Policies.* New York: Praeger, 1957–58. Anticommunist bias.

Townsend, Peter. *China Phoenix.* London: Jonathan Cape,
1955. Good journalistic account.

US Department of Commerce, Bureau of the Census. *International Population Reports.* A series that includes studies
on the population of China.

Walker, Richard. *China Under Communism; The First Five
Years.* New Haven: Yale University Press, 1955.* Empha-
sizes the negative aspects of the Communist regime.

Yang, C. K. *Chinese Communist Society: The Family and the
Village* (Previously two separate books: *A Chinese Family
in the Communist Revolution* and *A Chinese Village in Early
Communist Transition*). Cambridge: MIT Press, 1965.* Excellent accounts of the changes in family and village life during the early years of the Communist regime by a social
scientist.

Yu, Frederick T. C. *Mass Persuasion in Communist China.*
London and Duninow: Pall Mall, 1964. Describes the various
mass media and their ideological content.

THE ECONOMY

Adler, Solomon. *The Chinese Economy.* New York: Monthly
Review Press, 1957. Good on the early years of the Communist regime, especially in conveying the enthusiasm that went
into the reconstruction. His predictions have turned out to
be overoptimistic.

Buck, John Lossing, Dawson, Owen L., and Wu Yuan-li. *Food
and Agriculture in Communist China.* New York: Praeger
329

for the Hoover Institution on War, Revolution, and Peace, 1966.

Chao Kuo-chun. *Agrarian Policy of the Chinese Communist Party, 1921–1959.* New Delhi: Asia Publishing House, 1960. A detailed and good history of the Communist rural policy.

Cheng Chu-yuan. *Communist China's Economy: 1949–1962, Structural Changes and Crises.* South Orange, N.J.: Seton Hall University, 1963. An adequate short description of the Chinese economy.

Eckstein, Alexander. *Communist China's Economic Growth and Foreign Trade.* New York: McGraw-Hill for the Council on Foreign Relations, 1966. A comprehensive book on China's economy; the best book in the field thus far for the nonspecialist.

Far Eastern Economic Review (and Yearbook) (Hong Kong). Excellent short reviews of the economic year on the mainland, a good source for up-to-date information.

Hughes, T. J. and Luard, D. E. T. *The Economic Development of Communist China.* New York: Oxford University Press, 1959.* Many statistics and little analysis.

Perkins, Dwight. *Market Control and Planning in Communist China.* Cambridge: Harvard University Press, 1966. Technical, but demonstrates that at times the Chinese Communists use market controls to a much greater degree than most presume.

Walker, Kenneth. *Planning in Chinese Agriculture: Socialism and the Private Sector, 1956–1962.* Chicago: Aldine, 1965. This short book gives an excellent analysis of the part that the private plot of land plays in Chinese collectivized agriculture.

BASIC SOURCEBOOKS ON CHINA

History

Fitzgerald, C. P. *China: A Short Cultural History,* rev. ed. New York: Praeger, 1954.

Eberhard, Wolfram. *A History of China.* Berkeley: University of California Press, 1950.

Goodrich, L. Carrington. *A Short History of the Chinese People.* New York: Harper, 1959.

Selected Bibliography

Latourette, Kenneth Scott. *The Chinese: Their History and Culture*, 4th rev. ed. New York: Macmillan, 1964.

Herrmann, Albert. *Historical Atlas of China*, rev. ed. Chicago: Aldine, 1966.

Geography

Cressey, George. *Land of 500 Million: A Geography of China*. New York: McGraw-Hill, 1955.

Tregear, T. R. *The Geography of China*. Chicago: Aldine, 1965.

Society

Hu Chang-tu. *China: Its People, Its Society, Its Culture*. New Haven: Human Relations Area Files, 1960.

Thought

de Bary, W. T., Chan, W. T., and Watson, B. *Sources of Chinese Tradition*. New York: Columbia University Press, 1960.

Creel, H. G. *Chinese Thought from Confucius to Mao Tsetung*. New York: Mentor, 1960.*

Fung Yu-lan. *A History of Chinese Philosophy*. Princeton University Press, 1952 and 1953.

PERIODICALS

Asian Survey (Berkeley), *China Quarterly* (London), *Contemporary China* (Hong Kong), *Journal of Asian Studies* (Ann Arbor), *Pacific Affairs* (Vancouver, Canada). All contain articles on contemporary China; the first two almost exclusively. To list all the important articles would have made this bibliography unnecessarily long.

World Politics frequently contains articles on China, especially in the area of foreign affairs.

"Contemporary China and the Chinese." *The Annals of the American Academy of Political and Social Science*, CCCXXI, January, 1959. "Special Number on Communist China." *Political Quarterly* (London), xxxv, July-September, 1964. Both are good symposia by recognized scholars on diverse topics.

Peking Review (Peking) is the official view of the world from China, often contains interesting and important articles.

‖ ABOUT THE AUTHORS

ROBERT F. DERNBERGER is Assistant Professor of Economics and a member of the Committee on Far Eastern Civilizations, University of Chicago. Professor Dernberger is also a former editor of *Economic Development and Cultural Change* (1963–65).

AUDREY DONNITHORNE is a lecturer in Chinese economic studies at University College, London. She was born in Szechuan Province of China, and educated at the West China Union University and at Oxford. Dr. Donnithorne is currently engaged in a study of the economic organization of China, to be published by Allen & Unwin and entitled *China's Economic System*. Her article here is based upon that study.

JAMES S. DUNCAN was previously President and Chairman of Massey-Ferguson (Canada), and Chairman of the Hydroelectric Power Commission of Ontario, he is now retired. He is the author of *Russian Bid for World Supremacy* (1955), *A Businessman Looks at Red China* (1965), *In the Shadow of* the Red Star (1962), *Russia Revisited* (1960), *The Great Leap Forward* (1959).

C. P. FITZGERALD is Professor of Far Eastern History at the Australian National University, Canberra. He lived in China from 1923 to 1939, working during the latter part of that period at Tali, in Yunnan Province, under a fellowship for anthropological research; and again from 1946 to 1950, as a representative of the British Council in North China. He has subsequently visited China twice, in 1956 and 1958. He is the author of *China: A Short Cultural History* (1935, 1961; paperback 1965), *The Third China* (1965), and *The Chinese View of their Place in the World* (1964–66).

JACK GRAY is Lecturer in Far Eastern history at the University of Glasgow. From 1953 to 1965 he lectured at Hong Kong University; in 1966 he visited the People's Republic of China. He is the author of articles on modern Chinese history and Chinese Communist political organizations, and of a forthcoming work, *Revolution and Consolidation in the Chinese Countryside, 1947–56*.

A. M. HALPERN is a research fellow at the Council on Foreign Relations, and was formerly head of the Research Group on Far Eastern Policies at the RAND Corporation. He is the editor of *Policies toward China: Views from Six Continents*, published by McGraw-Hill in 1966.

THEODORE HSI-EN CHEN is Professor of Asian studies and Director of the East Asian Studies Center at the University of Southern California. He was formerly Dean and President of Fukien Christian University in China. He is the author of *Chinese Communism and the Proletarian-Socialist Revolution* (1955), *Thought Reform of the Chinese Intellectuals* (1960), and *Teacher Training in Communist China* (1960).

JOSEF KOLMAŠ is a fellow of the Oriental Institute in Prague, and a member of the Institute of State and Law of the Czech-

334

oslovakian Academy of Sciences. His special field is Tibetan culture and history. At present he is serving as Visiting Lecturer in Chinese at the Australian National University, Canberra.

JAN MYRDAL, of Mariefred, Sweden, is a writer, and columnist for the Aftonbladet of Stockholm. His books in English include *Report from a Chinese Village* (1965) and *Chinese Journey* (1965). His publications in other languages include novels, essays, and books on Afghanistan and Turkestan.

C. H. G. OLDHAM is a fellow of the Institute of Current World Affairs, and served as a consultant to the scientific directorate of the Organization for Economic Cooperation and Development in Paris; he was previously associated as a senior research geophysicist with the Standard Oil Company of California. Dr. Oldham spent four years based in Hong Kong, and traveled widely in Asia studying the problems of science and development. He has visited China twice, in 1964 and again in May 1965, when he traveled with his wife and four children by train from Hong Kong to Paris. He is presently on the staff of the Unit for the Study of Science Policy, at the University of Sussex, England.

LEO A. ORLEANS is Associate Studies Director in the Office of Economic and Manpower Studies of the National Science Foundation; he was previously a senior research analyst at the Library of Congress. He is the author of *Professional Manpower and Education in Communist China* (1961), and of numerous articles on China's population and manpower. Mr. Orleans spent the first fifteen years of his life in China.

JOAN ROBINSON is Professor of Economics at Cambridge University, England. She is the author of *Economic Philosophy* (1962), *Essays in the Theory of Economic Growth* (1962), *The Accumulation of Capital* (1956), *Collected Economic*

335

Papers (1951), *An Essay on Marxian Economics* (1942), and *The Economics of Imperfect Competition* (1933).

HAN SUYIN, also known as Elizabeth Kuanghu Chou, is a physician and writer. Miss Suyin was born in Peking (her father was Chinese; her mother, Belgian), and educated at the universities of Yenching, Brussels, and London. She is the author of nine novels, including *A Many-Splendored Thing* (1952) and *This Crippled Tree* (1965). Miss Suyin lives in Hong Kong.

G. LESLIE WILLOX is a physician and clinical professor of surgery at the University of Alberta, Canada.

DICK WILSON is an author, and a free-lance journalist and broadcaster on Asian affairs. From 1958 to 1964, he lived in Hong Kong, where he was editor of the *Far Eastern Economic Review*. He visited the People's Republic of China in 1964. He is the author of *The Colombo Plan Story* (1960) and *A Quarter of Mankind, An Anatomy of China Today* (1966).